941.08323(ADE)

VICTORIAN RADICALISM (THE MIDDLE - CLASS
EXPERIENCE)

PAUL ADELMAN   LONGMAN   1984

18537

STUDIES IN MODERN HISTORY

General editors: *John Morrill and David Cannadine*

Titles already published

FRANCE IN THE AGE OF HENRI IV
M. Greengrass
VICTORIAN RADICALISM
Paul Adelman

VICTORIAN RADICALISM

The middle-class experience, 1830–1914

Paul Adelman

LONGMAN
London and New York

LONGMAN GROUP LIMITED
Longman House, Burnt Mill, Harlow
Essex CM20 2JE, England
Associated companies throughout the world

*Published in the United States of America
by Longman Inc., New York*

First published 1984

BRITISH LIBRARY CATALOGUING IN PUBLICATION DATA
Adelman, Paul
  Victorian radicalism.
  1. Middle classes – England – Political activity –
  History – 19th century   2. Middle classes –
  England – Political activity – History – 20th century
  3. Radicalism – History – 19th century
  4. Radicalism – History – 20th century
  I. Title
  323.3′2   HD8391

  ISBN 0-582-49197-5

LIBRARY OF CONGRESS CATALOGING IN PUBLICATION DATA
Adelman, Paul.
  Victorian radicalism.

  (Studies in modern history)
  Bibliography: p.
  Includes index.
  1. Radicalism – Great Britain – History – 19th century.
  2. Great Britain – Politics and government – 19th century.
  3. Middle classes – Great Britain – Political activity.
  I. Title. II. Series: Studies in modern history (Longman)
  HN400.R3A3 1984   322.4′4′0941   83–17545
  ISBN 0–582–49197–5

Set in 10/11pt Linotron 202 Times
**Printed in Hong Kong by
Wilture Printing Co Ltd**

CONTENTS

PREFACE

Most recent writing on Victorian Radicalism has been concerned with the working classes, while Maccoby's older standard history of the subject covers any and every reform movement during the long period from the later eighteenth century to the 1920s (Maccoby, 5 vols, 1935–61).

My approach is a much narrower one. This is a book about middle-class Radicalism. Much is gained, I believe, in clarity and historical understanding by limiting Radicalism in this way, and distinguishing it from that tradition of popular radicalism which embraces, for example, Chartism, secularism and the later Victorian labour movement. This is not to deny that there are important interactions between middle- and working-class Radicalism, particularly in the age of the Charter and the Anti-Corn Law League in the 1840s; in the struggle for parliamentary reform in the later 1860s; and, as Edward Royle has shown, within the secularist movement throughout the nineteenth century (Royle, 1974, 1980b). In a general way of course, both middle- and working-class Radicals denounced 'privilege' and demanded 'reform'. Nevertheless, the distinction between the two traditions remains a crucial one, particularly when we try to comprehend the weaknesses and failures of middle-class Radicalism at the end of the nineteenth century.

This short study arose primarily out of the practical needs of teaching Victorian history rather than the demands of original scholarship, and is aimed more at the student than the professional historian. I am grateful, therefore, to my students and colleagues at Kingston Polytechnic who in various ways have contributed to the ideas in this book; and, above all, to David Cannadine for his helpful criticisms and courtesy as joint editor of the series in which this study appears.

PAUL ADELMAN

Kingston Polytechnic
February 1983

INTRODUCTION

For the men of the early nineteenth century, one of the most remarkable social phenomena of the age appeared to be 'the rise of the middle classes'. 'The public feeling in favour of parliamentary reform', commented one Whig observer in 1818, 'seems to me to result from the diffusion of knowledge and wealth among the middle classes. . . .' At the height of the Reform Crisis in 1831, Earl Grey, the Whig Prime Minister, concurred: concessions were needed 'to the middle classes, who have made such wonderful advances in property and intelligence' (Cannon 1973: 166, 251). No one agreed more heartily than the self-appointed spokesmen of the middle classes themselves. The denomination and canonisation of 'the middle classes' had already begun in the later eighteenth century (Briggs 1960); it reached its apotheosis perhaps in the famous panegyric at the end of James Mill's *Essay on Government* of 1820, and was reaffirmed by the members of the Manchester School with their emphasis on the virtues of work and progress. 'If you talk of your aristocracy and your traditions', proclaimed Cobden, 'and compel me to talk of the middle and industrious classes, I say it is to them that the glory of this country is owing.' (Reader 1966: 1)

The names of James Mill and Richard Cobden personify the two main centres of middle-class Radicalism in the early Victorian age. First, a section of the professional classes, and the growth of great new professions outside the traditional triumvirate of law, medicine and the Church, is one of the most important aspects of middle-class development during this period (Reader 1966). Particularly significant here are the new breed of civil servants cum men of letters, like the Mills, father and son, who through their promulgation of the Utilitarian philosophy acted as ideologues to the professional classes. It was a tradition which was carried on by the Radical dons and journalists of the next generation associated with the *Fortnightly Review*, and *Essays in Reform* of 1867. The second important group were the manufacturers, men like Bright, Henry Ashworth and Samuel

1

Morley. 'The most remarkable circumstance in our social progress', wrote the contemporary historian of the middle classes, 'has been the rapid increase and ascendancy of manufacturing wealth and population. This is the distinguishing feature of society.' (Wade 1833: iii–iv)

What were the aims of the Radicals? The one great attribute that links together these and later Victorian middle-class Radicals, and marks them off from the rank-and-file members of the Whig and Liberal parties, is their detestation of 'the aristocratic ideal' and all that it implied in terms of social, political and religious domination based on rank or prescription. The 'laying the axe to the root of corruption and aristocratical tyranny' (in the famous phrase of John Wilkes) is an aspiration which unites them all. But it is one which is best conceived not as the expression of an idealized Radical 'tradition' based on abstract political principles (Maccoby 1966), but rather in terms of specific demands – the abolition of the Corn Laws, for example, the extension of the franchise or the reform of the land laws. Despite the extravagance and indeed eccentricity of some of its practitioners, middle-class Radicalism is essentially a practical reforming creed, a characteristic which marks it off (it has been suggested) from its more apocalyptic working-class counterpart (Parkin 1968). 'Above all things', wrote a leading Radical journalist in the 1880s, 'Radicalism is a body of practical doctrines ready for immediate expression in legislation, seeking first and foremost earnestly the reforms which are nearest to hand and easiest to conclude. It is not the creed of mere theorists, but is practical alike in its objects and its methods.' (Escott 1883) It is important, therefore, to be aware of the specific historical context in which Radical men and movements actually operate, and the power of the different interests they serve.

In the later 1830s and 1840s, the Radicals attempted to attack the aristocracy on two fronts – political and economic. They hoped, in the first place, to continue the work of parliamentary reform which had been only partially fulfilled through the Great Reform Bill of 1832, by forcing the Whig governments of Grey and Melbourne to introduce further 'organic' reform. The main instrument here was the small group of 'Philosophic Radicals' in the House of Commons, spurred on by their mentor, John Stuart Mill. But by the end of the 1830s their attempt had ended in failure, and the group itself was in a state of disintegration. There were a number of reasons for this. After the great achievement of 1832 both government and public relapsed into a state of apathy; in the House of Commons too the Radicals lacked both effective organization and leadership. As Mill complained bitterly, 'an attempt was made to breathe a living soul into the Radical party – but in vain – there was no making these bones live' (Mineka 1963: 426).

The assault on the aristocracy by the Anti-Corn Law League was ultimately more successful, at least as far as its economic arguments were concerned. The Corn Laws were repealed, even though the timing of the final Act owed more perhaps to Peel's political prescience than pressure from the League; free trade was quickly accepted by the public at large; and 'the entrepreneurial ideal' ultimately carried all before it. Even in foreign policy, though they were execrated during the Crimean War, the ideals of Cobden and Bright in favour of peace, non-intervention and disarmament were eventually accepted by British statesmen in the age of Gladstone, and also became part of the established Radical critique of British foreign policy (Taylor 1969). Hence in a lapidary comment, Engels wrote: 'Free Trade meant the readjustment of the whole home and foreign, commercial and financial policy of England in accordance with the interests of the manufacturing capitalists – the class which now represented the nation.' (Marx and Engels 1962: 25) It is a view which can easily be justified out of the mouths of the free traders themselves – 'most of us entered upon this struggle', said Cobden, 'with the belief that we had some distinct class interest in the question' – and one that in a general way many Victorian critics like Matthew Arnold accepted.

But if the economic triumph of the manufacturers was swift and sure, their transformation of the social and political structure was slow and uneven. 'The party of Cobden and Bright', wrote one reformer to the Yorkshire landowner, Sir Charles Wood in 1852, 'are striving for power. Their object is to form a middle class administration in contradiction to the aristocratic element which has hitherto predominated in the country.' (Fraser 1976: 241) This was a delusion. The middle classes lacked both the power and the will to undermine effectively the political domination of the traditional ruling class. They were neither as united, as class-conscious, nor as belligerent and radical, as has often been made out. The great pre-industrial commercial–financial interest was conservative in outlook; the new professional men – concerned with status and advancement – were largely unsympathetic to Radicalism; even the northern manufacturing classes – and especially the cottonocracy – the mainstay of the Anti-Corn Law League in the 1840s, proved to be weak-kneed reformers once their economic grievances had been settled, as Cobden and Bright discovered to their cost in the aftermath of Repeal. 'It is not our aim to overthrow the aristocracy', a Lancashire industrialist then affirmed, 'we are ready to have the government and high office in their hands. For we believe, we men of the middle class, that the conduct of the national business calls for special men, men born and bred to the work for generations, and who enjoy an independent and commanding situation.' (Best 1971: 242)

This platonic ideal implied no fundamental quarrel with the political status quo – as the strongly belligerent and pro-Palmerstonian sentiments of the commercial and manufacturing classes during the Crimean War revealed; so too did the ignominious rout of the anti-war Radicals in the general election of 1857. Hence the decline of Radicalism in the 1850s and the pessimism of its leaders. 'Perhaps we are wrong', wrote Cobden to Bright in 1859, 'in aiming at producing too large results within a given time. . . . I do every year . . . feel less sanguine in my hope of seeing any material change in my own day and generation. . . . The Church and Aristocracy are great realities, which will last for your life and your sons.' (Morley 1903: 13–14) The Radicals represented, therefore, not 'the nation', not 'the middle classes' *tout court*, but simply the 'vanguard of the bourgeoisie'.

It was the 1860s that saw the real revival of Radicalism with the re-emergence of the movement for parliamentary reform. This was particularly linked with events abroad – the Italian War of Liberation in 1859, the Polish Revolt of 1863 and above all, the American Civil War of 1861–65 – all of which helped to stimulate the political consciousness of the British labour movement and gave fresh opportunities to the middle-class Radicals. This culminated in the formation of the working-class Reform League in 1865 which demanded manhood suffrage and the (secret) ballot. Yet the political revival of these years was largely dominated by John Bright as *de facto* leader of the middle-class Radicals who had organized their own Reform Union in 1864, committed not to manhood but to household suffrage. It was John Bright who had initiated a new phase of the Reform movement with his campaign of 1858–59 – even though it proved to be premature; it was Bright too who emerged as the leading campaigner on behalf of the American North during the Civil War, as all sections of British society recognized. It was then, after 1863, that he successfully evolved the political strategy that he had always hankered after: that union of middle-class leadership and working-class numbers directed against aristocratic power, that formed the basis of the national extra-parliamentary Reform campaign of 1865–67 which lasted until the passage of the Conservatives' Reform Bill in the summer of 1867.

The middle-class Radicals, however, lacked a wide and generous conception of working-class representation. Why indeed should they gratuitously support the working-class vote? Bright admitted he was no democrat. 'I do not pretend myself to be a democrat. . . . I never accepted the title. . . . What I am in favour of is such freedom as will give security to people, but I am not in favour of that freedom that will destroy it.' (Briggs 1965: 209) Hence his hostility to the 'residuum' at the bottom of the working-class scale, his emphasis on the vote as a 'trust' rather than a 'right', his antipathy to trade unions and state interference in industry and commerce, and his profound belief in the role of the middle classes as the custodians of the political and economic interests of the masses. The emphasis by the middle-class reformers on *household* suffrage implied the enfranchisement of an élite of skilled workers largely committed to the moral and social ideals of the middle classes, and therefore prepared to do their bidding. George Holyoake, the great popular radical and secularist, averred that Bright's only interest in the franchise was to secure 'the creation of a popular force for the maintenance of free trade, international peace and public economy' (Holyoake 1892, vol. 2: 271–2). This was unfair: but as Bagehot noted, Bright's mental outlook remained immutable, formed by Quaker history, the platitudes of Samuel Smiles and the great struggles of the 1840s and 1850s (Bagehot 1876).

The Second Reform Act of 1867, by introducing household suffrage in the boroughs, conceded the central principle of the middle-class reformers, though other aspects of the Act – the limited redistribution of seats, especially – were much less favourable to their claims. On the wider political front, their victories were even greater. The First Liberal government of Gladstone which followed hard upon the heels of the Reform Act (and which contained Bright as an ineffective member) passed a mass of legislation which seemed to embody the ethos of middle-class Radicalism. Moreover, as its exponents had foreseen – the dons' *Essays in Reform* of 1867 spelled it out in detail – the great upsurge of working-class militancy that the opponents of reform had expected to follow the onset of democracy, failed to occur. Labour independence was easily contained. At the general election of 1868, the leaders of the Reform League still accepted the patronage of the middle class; they subordinated their own class interests to the needs of the Liberal Party, though in the end not one of the four labour candidates who stood was returned to Parliament. On the one hand, therefore, the mid-Victorian middle classes were able to obtain from a still aristocratically dominated Parliament much of what they wanted by way of social and administrative reform as the corollary of their earlier economic triumphs; on the other hand, they largely succeeded in imposing their own conception of class collaboration upon a newly enfranchised working class – as the rise of the labour aristocracy and Lib/Labism shows. In this way England moved cautiously into 'a viable class society' (Perkin 1969: Ch. IX).

But if the middle classes had gained so much from the triumph of free trade, what then was the *raison d'être* – the inspiration – of Radicalism in the later Victorian period? The answer surely lies (as Matthew Arnold perceived) in some consideration of the religious dimension of Victorian life. Its political and social implications were profound. As Clarke suggests, it was religion more than any other factor that moulded Victorian political consciousness: in determining electoral allegiance, 'status' was more important than 'class' (Clarke 1972). 'I fancy a good deal of our radicalism gets into our sermons' wrote one Congregationalist minister. 'In any case my own opinion is that religious and political Liberalism play into each other's hands, and that whatever promotes one advances the other also.' (Koss 1970: 17) It was in fact Nonconformity – the Dissidence of Dissent – that provided the powerful sense of injustice and grievance, the moral energy, enthusiasm and devotion, that sustained Radicalism during this period. It gave passion to the campaign over church rates, education, disestablishment – and to the 'classic crusade' against Balfour's Education Act of 1902 (Bebbington 1982). The evangelical fervour of militant Dissent spilled over into such quasi-religious movements as temperance reform and the 'Bulgarian Agitation'; and it appears also as a distinct strain in the 'civic gospel' at Birmingham and other provincial cities and in the work of the National Liberal Federation (NLF). Not all the reforms demanded by the Radicals in the age of Bright and Chamberlain were cast in the Nonconformist mould, but nearly all of them bore in some way its imprint. Seventy per cent of Radical MPs in the Parliaments of 1874–80 and 1880–85 were Nonconformists: it was this allegiance more than anything else that divided them from their fellow Liberals.

How were the Nonconformist aims to be achieved? The 'pressure group' was the classic device invented by nineteenth-century middle-class Radicals to achieve their specific demands. It was to be used, firstly, to create and organize a national opinion 'by those means', as Cobden indicated, 'by which the middle class usually carries on its movements' – meetings, petitions, the distribution of literature, etc. (Morley 1903: 249). It would then move into the political field, and through electoral pressure and blackmail at constituency level, impose its views upon prospective parliamentary candidates and Liberal MPs. Finally, by working with and through the Liberal Party organization itself, the Nonconformists would create a Radical bloc of MPs in the House of Commons who, allied with 'pressure from without', would force the Liberal leadership to accept their demands and eventually pass appropriate legislation.

Yet, as Brain Harrison has argued, these methods – 'inflexible, unrealistic and often irresponsible' – were not necessarily well adapted to the end in view (Harrison 1971: 35). The all-or-nothing approach of the great pressure groups inhibited support from potential sympathisers, and – as the early dogmatic attitude of the United Kingdom Alliance showed – helped to destroy the possibility of moderate temperance reform. The Alliance's major spokesman in the House of Commons, Sir Wilfred Lawson, pronounced defiantly; 'I am a fanatic, a faddist and an "extreme man", opposed to the peerage, the beerage and war.' (Emy 1973: 48) Similarly, the sectarianism of the supporters of the National Education League led them to concentrate on the glories of the distant educational prospect, and prevented them seeing the real Radical gains contained in the hated Education Act of 1870. The practical reforms the Nonconformists did obtain, in the field of religious equality especially, were achieved by working with rather than against the grain of the Gladstonian Liberal Party. Nor were the pressure groups as representative or as powerful as they made out. Their methods probably antagonized almost as many people as they won over. The abysmal failure of the Nonconformists to understand the true nature of their position in the country and within the Liberal Party, left them bruised and bewildered after the Conservative victory at the general election of 1874.

It was out of this world of provincial Nonconformity and pressure-group politics that Joseph Chamberlain, the most formidable Radical of the later 1870s and 1880s, emerged. After he entered the House of Commons in 1876 his major ambition was not to encourage but to overcome the limited vision and diverse causes of middle-class Radicalism, and then create a 'concentrated' Radical movement which could be used to reconstruct the Liberal Party. This was the purpose of the NLF of 1877. It purported to be a democratic organization representing Liberal opinion in the nation at large, and therefore opposed to the élitism of the Parliamentary Party and (after the retirement of Gladstone in 1875) its supine leadership. In fact the Federation was neither as democratic nor as representative as it made out, and in many ways it became the instrument of Chamberlain's personal ambition. It enabled him to secure his 'forced entry' into Gladstone's Liberal Cabinet of 1880, where he remained rather unhappily as President of the Board of Trade, while the enthusiasm of his Radical supporters in the country drained away as a result of the government's controversial policies in Ireland and overseas, until his resignation in the spring of 1885. A few months later, freed from office and confident that the electoral legislation of 1883–85 would favour his cause, he launched his 'Radical Programme' – the basis of his campaign in the general election of November 1885. What was its purpose?

Chamberlain's clear powerful speeches certainly lend substance to the comment that 'he pursued one idea, the extension of democracy and the betterment of the working classes' (Fraser 1966: xii). It is not self-evident (as Cooke and Vincent intimate in their more sceptical view of Chamberlain the social reformer) that his political style or practical policies encouraged those goals (Cooke and Vincent 1974: 11–12). Indeed, what recent scholars have emphasized in the record of Chamberlain's Radical career after 1876, is not his devotion to democracy and reform in any simple sense, but his authoritarian leadership, his energy and ambition, his insularity of mind and purpose, his manipulation of the processes of mass politics and his commitment to a rationalized society based on the ethics of enlightened capitalism. What stands out is his lack of positive and permanent achievement. Chamberlain's work as Mayor of Birmingham was almost his sole practical success on the domestic front. He held no major ministerial office and was associated with no great reform: his career was surrounded 'by an aura of failure – a sense of grand plans and ambitions stridently promoted, and subsequently abandoned or brought to nothing' (Jay 1981: 321).

This is true of the campaign with which Chamberlain is particularly associated through his notorious 'Ransom' speeches and the 'Unauthorized Programme' of 1885 – that against the landowning class. Chamberlain did not initiate such polemics, nor was he the last to use them. The 'land question' was one of the *idées fixes* of middle-class Radicalism from Cobden to Lloyd George (Offer 1981). The attack on the landlord class in later Victorian England was partly political – to build up electoral support for the Radicals among the newly enfranchised masses, and partly diversionary – to create the image of the landlord rather than the capitalist as the scapegoat for the ills of society, as Henry George did so effectively in *Progress and Poverty* (1881). It was also an attempt to provide – as the Anti-Corn Law League had done earlier – an emotional focus for Radical aspirations and energies at a time when other questions – parliamentary reform, religious equality, for example – were being resolved by the impulse of Gladstonian Liberalism. 'The tendency of legislation in the future must be to suppress landlords', wrote Henry Labouchere in 1885. Yet the irrelevance, even timidity, of the reforms proposed by the Radicals – free trade in land, smallholdings, tax reforms – stood in stark contrast to the enormity in Radical demonology of the evil attacked, and helped to underline perhaps the real nature of the Radical land campaigns. As F. M. L. Thompson suggests, it was 'the potency of the symbols' invoked against the landlords rather than the practicality of the remedies suggested, that was of importance in the Radical conception of the land question (Thompson 1965: 24).

The anti-landlord campaign of the 1880s failed on two counts. It had no real appeal to the urban masses, as the results of the general election of 1885 in London and other cities revealed; and it only served to scare sections of the middle classes into rallying to the defence of 'the rights of property', and thus helped to push them increasingly into the arms of the Unionist Party (Perkin 1973). Yet despite the weaknesses of the Victorian land campaigns, the image of 'the landlord' – idle, rapacious, reactionary – remained firmly entrenched in the Radical consciousness. It was to be invoked once again by Lloyd George, a generation later, in another and greater attack on 'the land monopoly'.

After the general election of November 1885 all roads led to Home Rule. The desertion of Joseph Chamberlain to the Unionists over that issue was a heavy blow to the Radical cause; but, paradoxically, the fact that the majority of Radicals supported Gladstone's Home Rule Bill in 1886, meant that after its defeat and the Unionist triumph at the following general election, the Liberal Party became more rather than less Radical. This was symbolized by the 'Newcastle Programme' of 1891, a long list of Radical demands – Irish Home Rule, Welsh disestablishment, land, tax and local government reforms, reduction of the Lords' powers – which were passed by the NLF that year and, apparently, endorsed by the party leadership. Yet little was done to implement them during Gladstone's last ministry of 1892–94. The government was dependent on Irish votes and faced by the wrecking tactics of the House of Lords; and much time and labour was spent on a futile effort to pass a Second Home Rule Bill. The resignation of Gladstone in March 1894 and the succession of Lord Rosebery as Liberal leader, was followed by the electoral smash of 1895 – a real turning point in the history of the modern Liberal Party. During the next few years a period of recrimination and disillusionment followed, though this was also a time when the meaning of Liberalism itself was being reexamined – as the rise of 'New Liberalism' revealed.

The electoral rout of 1895 was in a way a verdict on traditional Radicalism. Its well-worn policies – disestablishment, temperance reform, Irish Home Rule, especially – aroused little enthusiasm in England, and it failed to come to grips with the growing social and industrial problems of the age. The NLF made no determined effort to attract working men into its organizations or overcome the suspicions of their leaders. 'The borough caucuses', said one such leader, 'would work admirably as traps in which to shut up the workingmen of the country, allowing them only political actions as their masters and managers permit.' (Pelling 1956: 46) In the last years of Victorian England, therefore, traditional Radicalism was ground between a powerful revivified Conservative Party, on the one hand, appealing more and more to a property-minded middle class, and on the other, a burgeoning labour movement committed, implicitly, to political independence and social reform.

Yet once the Liberal revival got under way in the early years of the new century, partly as a result of the mistakes of the Unionists, the aspirations of traditional Radicalism were not forgotten. This was not only because of the old-fashioned outlook of Campbell-Bannerman, the party leader – his immediate successors too were affected by the long shadow of Gladstone and Cobden. The Edwardian Liberal Party was tied irrevocably to its Victorian past. It could not wipe the slate clean, even if it had wished to, without destroying the very identity of Liberalism. Hence, though the most significant legislation passed by the Liberal Party during the Edwardian period lay in the field of social reform, an enormous amount of time and effort was devoted – not unsuccessfully – to the resolution of older, less vibrant, Radical causes. It is true that some of them – opposition to rate-aid for church schools, temperance reform – received only perfunctory support from hard-pressed Liberal ministers. But the absolute power of the House of Lords was destroyed; a Welsh Disestablishment and Irish Home Rule Act were passed; the 'idle rich' were more heavily taxed; and a real attempt was made by Lloyd George to tackle 'the land question'. This was a considerable achievement. The Edwardian Radicals did attempt to pay their debts to their predecessors, though there were of course other motives at work in their reform programme. But their very success helped to bring to a close the Victorian Radical tradition. As Lloyd George commented during the First World War: 'The old hide-bound Liberalism was played out, the Newcastle programme had been realized.' (Wilson 1970: 257)

Chapter one

RADICALISM AND THE ANTI-CORN LAW LEAGUE

The middle-class Radicals of the later 1830s lived out their political lives in the shadow of the Great Reform Bill, for it was that Act and the political system it helped to fashion that largely determined their power and prospects. If Chartists denounced the Reform Bill as 'a delusive, time-serving, specious and partial measure', and fulminated against the great Whig 'betrayal', the sentiments of many middle-class Radicals were equally sour. 'I had thought', protested one such Radical in 1832, 'that we had obtained a reform of parliament and that henceforth members were to be instruments of the electors for the purpose of making laws.' (Gash 1953: 32) Yet the Bill itself, in origins at least, was a response to what the Whig leaders saw as 'the wonderful advances in property and intelligence' of the middle classes during the previous half-century, and therefore an acceptance of their claim for some significant political recognition of that progress. Unless concessions were made to 'the rational public', the alliance of middle-class grievances and popular discontent 'will lead rapidly', as Earl Grey argued on the eve of the Reform Crisis, 'to republicanism and the destruction of established institutions' (Cannon 1973: 250–1). What the Whig leaders wanted, therefore, in 1831–32 was 'a permanent settlement' that would dispose of the Reform question once and for all by buying off the middle-classes with 'effectual' political favours, and to achieve this they were prepared to go far. Hence the 'radicalism' of the Reform Bill that so astonished the House of Commons when it was first introduced: the extension of the vote to the £10 householders in the boroughs, the destruction of a host of rotten boroughs, and the granting of representation to great commercial and manufacturing centres. Even the younger Mill was enthusiastic and looked forward to a time when 'the whole of the existing institutions of society are levelled with the ground' (Brock 1973: 315). But the Whig aim was to strengthen rather than weaken aristocratic power by buttressing it with middle-class support, and, since the vote was still linked with 'property and intelligence', isolating the working classes and leaving them politically impotent. 'From the multitude therefore', observed Lord Durham, 'we take the body from whence they derived their leaders. . . . To property and good order we attach numbers.' (Cannon 1973: 252)

The terms of the Reform Act fell far short of the hopes of the Radicals, and its ultimate purpose – the defence of aristocratic government – was anathema to men of the stamp of Place and James Mill, let alone Cobbett and Hunt. 'The Reform Bills are in themselves of little value', wrote Place, 'but as a commencement of the breaking up of the old rotten system they are invaluable.' (Wallas 1898: 326) Out of the ferment of debate and discussion since at least the days of Wilkes and Paine, the English Radicals had hammered out a political programme anchored on four major political demands: universal suffrage; the Ballot; annual parliaments; and election pledges, by which the people's representatives could be more effectively controlled. The ultimate purpose of this programme was to produce a more democratic and just society by undermining the political power of the aristocracy, and then proceeding to the business of fundamental reform in government and administration. As James Mill argued in his persuasive and influential tract *On Government*, it was the ignorance and selfishness of the aristocratic minority, especially when compared with the talents of 'the middle rank', that rendered them unfit to govern (James Mill 1820). It was a Radical argument put succinctly by his son, writing of his own political outlook in 1830. 'I was as much as ever a Radical and Democrat. . . . I thought the predominance of the aristocratic classes, the noble and the rich, in the English constitution, an evil worth any struggle to get rid of . . . as the great demoralising agency in the country.' (Mill 1924: 145)

How were these Radical aims now to be realised? On the morrow of the Great Reform Bill, the political agitation 'out of doors' which had lasted on and off since 1830, had petered out. The only hope for the Radicals lay, therefore, through parliament, and the pressure they could generate there to push the Whig government and party – revelling in the triumphant majority obtained at the general election of 1833 – further in the direction of organic reform. The motto of the Whig leaders may have been 'finality'; but the Radicals believed, with J. A. Roebuck, MP for Bath and a leading Philosophic Radical, that the Bill was to be taken 'as an instalment of justice – as . . . a stepping stone to further great improvements' (Hamburger 1977: 23). As the new Parliament assembled in 1833 that prospect did not seem altogether remote.

Out of the enormous majority of some 500 'reformers' who sat in the House of Commons in that year, the Radicals – including the Irish 'tail' led by O'Connell – formed a section of about 100–120

MPs, regarded by the official Whigs as a separate and hostile bloc. The English group of some sixty to seventy were perhaps the most heterogeneous that has ever sat in the House of Commons. Though they all belonged to the Radical persuasion they differed widely in temperament, background and ideas, and formed 'a motley, confused, jarring miscellany of irreconcilable theorists' (Bulwer-Lytton 1833, vol. 2: 287). Sir Francis Burdett and Joseph Hume were there – heroes of an earlier age; Cobbett personified popular radicalism; Attwood, the currency reformer, represented the distinctive Radicalism of Birmingham. The most important representatives of middle-class Radicalism were the score or so 'Philosophic Radicals, whose leading members were George Grote, banker and historian of Greece, J. A. Roebuck, who was educated in Canada and regarded himself as a fiery denunciator of all English shams, and Sir William Molesworth, country gentleman and later Hobbes' editor. The greatest of the Philosophic Radicals was, of course, John Stuart Mill himself, who had invented the term; but since his work at the East India Company debarred him from Parliament, his Radical energies went into the editorship of the *London and Westminster Review* which he used, *inter alia*, to instruct, admonish and cajole his *confrères* in the House of Commons into greater enthusiasm and political activity. Mill hoped, above all, for the emergence of a leader among the parliamentary Radicals who would weld 'the whole body of radical opinion . . . into a union' which could become a powerful force in politics. He was continually disappointed. 'The lamentable truth is', he wrote as early as July 1833, 'that our *Gironde* . . . are a rope of sand . . . there are no leaders, and without leaders there can never be organisation. There is no man or men of commanding talents among the Radicals in public life.' (Mineka 1963, vol. 1: 380, 165)

Partly because of these weaknesses, even the nuisance value of the English Radicals was limited and their influence steadily declined down to the general election of 1835. That election was precipitated by the resignation in 1834 of Earl Grey, tired of the wrangles and intrigues within the Cabinet, especially over Irish reform, and the self-imposed dismissal by the King of his successor, Lord Melbourne. Sir Robert Peel then became Prime Minister – and appealed to the country for support. Though the election results showed a clear Conservative recovery, Peel still failed to obtain a majority in the Commons; only the disunity of the opposition kept him in office. The number of official Whigs had slumped, but both the Irish and Radicals had increased their numbers; if all three groups combined together, the Conservative administration must collapse and Melbourne be returned to power. That is exactly what did happen as a result of the Lichfield House Compact of March 1835, 'one of the most decisive events in British political history between 1832 and

1847' (Macintyre 1965: 144). By this agreement O'Connell, for purely opportunist reasons, was prepared to prop up the Whig government in return for Irish reforms; as a result Melbourne returned to office and the Whigs were able to limp along for another six years, dependent on Irish support and, increasingly, the forbearance of Peel. The real losers were the English parliamentary Radicals. They were forced to acquiesce in an unpalatable Whig government, since the only and worse alternative were the Conservatives under Peel. By doing so they lost their capacity to act as a separate 'party' or to impose terms upon the Whig leadership – O'Connell had already pre-empted that role.

It also meant that organic reform was ruled out, a point that was driven home by Russell's 'finality' speech on parliamentary reform in 1837. In other ways, however, the Whig leaders adopted a more liberal position on a number of current issues, thus responding, despite their aristocratic pretensions, to the inexorable pressures of middle-class and Dissenting interests in the country at large. A new Poor Law Act had already been carried through in 1834 – a major source of division among the Radicals, and also some measure of Irish Church reform. The great Municipal Corporations Act followed in 1835, based on ratepayers' suffrage, and the Dissenters received certain minor concessions over registration of births and marriages in the following year. The key topics of the ballot and Corn Law repeal were shortly made open questions; in May 1840 a Select Committee on Import Duties was set up under Joseph Hume. By that date time was running out for the Whigs, and even more so for the parliamentary Radicals. At the general election of 1837 the number of Radicals returned was down to about fifty, and many of them soon drifted into mainstream Whiggism. The Conservative reaction swept away Hume at Middlesex and Roebuck at Bath; Attwood retired two years later; and in 1841 Grote gave up his seat at the City of London and was succeeded, ironically, by Lord John Russell; Molesworth soon followed. This marked the effective end of this phase of parliamentary Radicalism. As Mrs Grote, a politician *manqué*, commented: 'Political affairs have died out and left us stranded.' (Thomas 1979: 426) Thus the parliamentary Radicals failed. No leader emerged to create a united Liberal Party and thus fulfil the dreams of Mill; no organic reforms were passed to continue the work of 1832; the political mongering of the Whig patriciate continued much as before.

Why did they fail? Mill, in a famous passage of the *Autobiography*, (1924: 165–6) wrote of the parliamentary Radicals:

> And now, on a calm retrospect, I can perceive that the men were less in fault than we supposed and that we had expected too much from them. They were in unfavourable circumstances. Their lot was cast in the ten years of inevitable reaction, when the Reform excitement being over, and the few legislative improvements which the public really

called for having been rapidly affected, power gravitated back to its natural direction, to those who were for keeping things as they were.

This is clearly true, though it is not the whole truth. Grote and his friends underestimated the strength of the Conservative reaction. They also underestimated the force of the Whigs' commitment to the Reform Act as it stood, and the complacency of the 'shopocracy' in the boroughs enfranchised in 1832; hence the lack of enthusiasm that their support for the ballot aroused either inside or outside the House of Commons. But they also suffered from faults of character and temperament. Their obsessive individuality and pride, their distaste for the practical chores of political life, made it difficult for them to act together to impose their 'weight' on the House of Commons or make a practical bid for leadership, as Mill noted despairingly (Mill 1839). This was because they were, as William Thomas suggests, 'amateurs in politics', as the later literary careers of both Grote and Molesworth demonstrate. As 'amateurs' too they had no real roots in the country. No group or interest in the nation at large looked to them for leadership or sustained them as they played out their parliamentary roles. 'The Radicals in parliament have, at this time', as one of their number admitted in 1840, 'no public out of doors of sufficient influence to fall back upon. . . .' (Thomas 1979: 427) Few of them sat for popular constituencies; they had no real knowledge of, or links with, the people for whom they claimed to speak; they were metropolitan gentlemen ignorant of the provinces and cut off from Nonconformity. Hence they were too fastidious to throw in their lot unequivocally with the great movements 'out of doors' that were just beginning to develop at the end of the 1830s, Chartism and the Anti-Corn Law League. It was with the League, however, that the future of middle-class Radicalism lay.

In September 1838 the Manchester Anti-Corn Law Association was formed by a group of local Radicals and businessmen. Among those who were prominent at the inaugural meeting or who joined shortly afterwards were J. B. Smith, Henry Ashworth, George Wilson, Archibald Prentice, Radical editor of the *Manchester Times* and later the historian of the League, John Bright and Richard Cobden, fresh from his successful campaign for the incorporation of Manchester. The aim of the Association was 'total and immediate abolition' of the Corn Laws, a demand which cut them off from the Whigs almost as much as the Tories. The members immediately organised lecture tours in the north of England to win converts to their cause, especially among businessmen, and encouraged the formation of similar local associations. In December, mainly as a result of the efforts of Cobden – rapidly emerging as the outstanding leader in the Association – the Manchester Chamber of Commerce was won over, and in the following month the Manchester Anti-Corn

Law League was formally constituted. Links were then established with the London free traders, and a delegate meeting to represent all the anti-Corn Law associations was held in the capital on 4 February 1839, the same day as the Chartists presented their first petition to the House of Commons. The London meeting was not very successful. Few delegates attended; the metropolitan Radicals resented the domination of the Manchester men and – as Francis Place admitted – were far less committed to free trade than they were. The delegates were also hotly opposed by the London Chartists who regarded the anti-Corn Law agitation as a middle-class ploy to divert working-class attention away from the Charter. The attitude of the capital merely confirmed Cobden in his belief that the primacy in the anti-Corn Law movement must lie with Manchester. '*My hopes of agitation are anchored on Manchester*', he wrote to Smith. 'We can do more there with a sovereign than a mixed committee in London would with two. We have money and also business habits . . . let all our funds and our energies be expended in working the question from Manchester as a centre.' (McCord 1958: 44).

So it turned out. When the House of Commons decisively rejected both the Association's petitions and the motion of C. P. Villiers against the Corn Laws, the delegates proceeded in March 1839 to set up the Anti-Corn Law League as a national organisation. Its headquarters were to be at Manchester and arrangements were made to raise money to cover expenses. Control was to be vested in a council of the largest shareholders, though the League was in effect run by the triumvirate of Smith, Wilson and Cobden. The policy of 'Manchester first' meant that the League might lapse into provincial obscurity. In the first year or so of its existence, when the spotlight was turned on Chartism and the anti-Poor Law agitation and the new organisation suffered from financial and administrative problems, it was indeed a small struggling society. Moreover, its influence was limited not only by the indifferences of London but by the diversion of middle-class Radical energies once again into a demand for organic reform through the Leeds Suffrage Union, a tactic which Cobden bitterly opposed. The work of the League was also hampered by the Chartists, ideologically and physically. Nevertheless, its growing mastery of the arts of propaganda was exploited to the full. Lecturers were employed, both voluntary and paid, on a large scale throughout the country; subscriptions soon flowed in, from businessmen particularly; electors and MPs were canvassed; books, pamphlets and circulars poured forth from Manchester on a massive scale, and, after 1840, their circulation was aided by the Penny Post. This propaganda effort marks the first 'didactic' phase of the League's work – the attempt to convert the public to the case against the Corn Laws (Jephson 1892, vol. 2: 304).

Why did a national anti-Corn Law movement emerge during these years? The background to the rise of the League of 1839 is – as with Chartism – the impact of profound economic depression during the period between 1838 and 1842, after the relatively prosperous years of the earlier 1830s. Wheat prices rose from an average of 35s. 4d. a quarter in 1835 to 73s. in 1838, and remained over 60s. a quarter until 1842. High food prices for the working classes were accompanied by declining prices and profits and heavy unemployment in the cotton industry particularly – ever the index of British industrial progress. It is no coincidence, therefore, that Manchester, the centre of the cotton industry, also became the headquarters of the Anti-Corn Law League; or that the Manchester Chamber of Commerce, after its 'seven years' sleep' over the question, came out at the end of 1838 in support of Cobden's demand for 'total and immediate' repeal of the Corn Laws. For, to the Manchester men, the cause of the depression in their industry was the decline of the export trade – and cotton normally provided about half the total of British exports – due to the limited markets available abroad and the inability of foreigners to pay with grain and raw materials for the import of British manufactured goods. This, they believed, was a direct consequence of the Corn Laws, which also, for similar reasons, stimulated foreign industrial competition. Lancashire merchants and industrialists supported the League, therefore, because 'they genuinely believed the prevailing political and fiscal arrangements to be slowly throttling the economy' (Hobsbawm 1969: 77).

Clearly, the Anti-Corn Law League *was* the creature of northern business interests. Cobden confessed, in a famous remark, 'that most of us entered upon this struggle with the belief that we had some distinct class interest in the question' (Morley 1903: 140–1). But it was something more. It has been argued, notably by Professor McCord, that the rise of the Anti-Corn Law League also marks the beginning of a new and successful phase in the history of British Radicalism. 'The League', he writes, 'was essentially an offshoot of the Radical party, and its success was in great measure due to the fact that an attack on the Corn Laws was found an acceptable focus for Radical energies at a time when the Radicals were sadly in need of such a rallying point.' (McCord 1958: 16) From this point of view, therefore, the League was an attempt to fill the vacuum created by the decline of the parliamentary Radicalism of the 1830s, and provide a realistic alternative to the dead-end of the Chartist Six Points.

This was roughly how Richard Cobden saw the problem. What was needed, he believed, was a movement that avoided the weaknesses of both the parliamentary and the popular radicals: one that could unite the middle and the working classes on the basis of a clear practicable objective that yet possessed intense emotional power.

Writing to his brother in October 1838 at the time of the Chartist disturbances in Lancashire, he said (Morley 1903: 126):

> As respects general politics, I see nothing in the present radical outbreak to cause alarm, or make one dread the fate of liberalism. On the contrary, it is preferable to the apathy of the three years when prosperity (or seemingly so) made Tories of all. Nor do I feel at all inclined to give up politics in disgust, as you seem to do, because of the blunders of the Radicals. . . . I think the scattered elements may yet be rallied round the question of the corn laws. It appears to me that a moral and even a religious spirit may be infused into that topic, and if, agitated in the same manner that the question of slavery has been, it will be irresistible.

For Cobden and his friends then, the Anti-Corn Law League was to be just such a movement. The enthusiasm generated by the attack on the Corn Laws could rally all the liberal forces, all those who saw in the Corn Laws the symbol of aristocratic domination and privilege. The simplicity of the League's aim thus concealed a wider radical purpose: after the disappointments of the Reform Bill it was to be the new battering-ram to break down the pillars of aristocratic power.

The League was thus an economic pressure group, but also an outstanding Radical organisation which 'served as a focus for several different motives and interests' (McCord 1958: 15). What arguments did the League adduce in its support and what interests did it serve? The free traders opposed the Corn Laws (even the modified ones of 1828 and 1842) because they argued that they raised the price of bread artificially by keeping out of the country supplies of cheap foreign grain. The working classes thus suffered from 'the infamous injustice of the bread-tax'. This was the simple humanitarian argument. But the economic depredations of the Corn Laws were even more profound. What they did was to undermine the very foundations of British industrial and commercial supremacy by thwarting the fundamental principle upon which it ultimately depended. As the petition of the Manchester Chamber of Commerce to the House of Commons put it in 1838: 'Holding one of these eternal principles to be – the inalienable right of every man freely to exchange the results of his labour for the productions of other people . . . your petitioners earnestly implore your honourable house to repeal all laws relating to the importation of foreign corn . . . and to carry out to the fullest extent . . . the true and peaceful principles of free trade.' (Prentice 1968, vol. 1: 87)

The thrust of the free-trade argument was given additional weight by the supreme authority of Adam Smith's *Wealth of Nations*, and the support of the doyen of contemporary economists, David Ricardo, who argued in his *Principles of Political Economy* (1817), implicitly at least, that the landlord was a member of an unproductive and parasitic class since he added no additional wealth to the nation's stock. Furthermore, Cobden suggested that the so-called 'special burdens' on the land, produced as a defence of the Corn Laws, were largely mythical. 'The Corn Law', he asserted, 'is the great tree of Monopoly, under whose baleful shadow every other restriction exists. Cut it down by the roots, and it will destroy the others in its fall. The sole object of the League is to put an end to and extinguish at once and for ever, the principle of maintaining taxes for the benefit of particular classes.' (Bright and Rogers 1870, vol. 1: 77–8) The Corn Law monopoly benefited one section, the landed interest, only by thwarting the expansion of manufacturing industry which benefited all. Implicit in all these arguments is an exaltation of the Victorian gospel of work: of 'honest toil', of 'the *industrious* classes', as compared with those who (in Mill's words) 'grow richer . . . in their sleep, without working, risking or economising' (Perkin 1969: 227).

The injurious effects of the Corn Laws were seen, the free traders believed, in the record of the years of depression between 1838 and 1842, as described above – the first crisis of British industrial capitalism, according to Hobsbawm (Hobsbawm 1969: 77). Remove the Corn Laws and the channels of commerce would again flow freely. New markets would be opened up; our exports would increase in return for grain and raw materials from abroad; manufacture and employment would thrive; prosperity would abound. Some of these arguments have been treated with considerable respect by economic historians (Clapham 1945–46; Fairlie 1965). Nevertheless, they were tendentious and self-interested. Many employers believed, on the basis of the contemporary myth that wheat prices and wage rates rose and fell together, that Repeal would enable them to reduce their costs by cutting wages and competing more effectively. If it was 'a belly question' for the worker, as Henry Ashworth put it, it was 'a pocket question' for the manufacturer (Boyson 1970: 203). It was against this 'low wage' argument, which branded the League supporters as both callous and class-ridden, that Cobden passionately remonstrated. Free trade would mean increased demand for British goods, therefore more demand for labour and higher wages – which in turn would stimulate production. Wages were determined not by the price of wheat but by the laws of supply and demand, 'as unerring . . . as any other operation of nature'. Cobden believed it was, therefore, as much in the interests of the working classes as of the manufacturers to support the campaign of the Anti-Corn Law League.

This was of course as much a political as an economic argument. The League needed the workers to show that their cause was a 'national' rather than a 'sectional' one, and to add the weight of numbers to their campaign. Their support was also necessary for the creation of the united Radical Party that Cobden and his friends aspired to. 'My great object in getting them (the working classes) to speak out', wrote Villiers to Smith, 'is that I am convinced that until they do, the Aristocracy will never yield – I grieve to say that the *brickbat argument* is the only one that our nobles heed.' (Brown 1965: 348) The industrial working class, at least as expressed through the views of the Chartist leaders, was unimpressed by either argument. Most of them remained suspicious of the motives of the League, and sceptical of the views on wages expressed by men like Cobden and Ashworth – employers, opponents of the Ten-hour Day and supporters of the new Poor Law. 'Every reduction in the price of produce', commented the *Northern Star* in 1842, 'has been accompanied by a more than corresponding reduction in the wages of labour.' (Kitson Clark 1953) Such a fate was inevitable, whatever the general merits of the free trade argument, unless the position of the worker was first safeguarded by the Charter. It was an attitude reinforced by class hatred. The Sheffield Chartists called upon the workers to resist their seduction by those who 'are endeavouring to persuade you to sacrifice your principles on the altar of expediency, by leaving the people to join a party comprised of avaricious, grasping money-mongers, great capitalists, and rich manufacturers . . . let them fight their own battle without our assistance' (Royle 1980a: 107). The League leaders had to accept by 1842 at least that they had largely failed to win the support of the industrial workers; though Cobden was convinced that they were deluded by their leaders, particularly O'Connor with his obsessive hatred of industrialisation.

Yet it is not altogether fanciful to suggest that in some respects the long-term aims of the Chartists and the League did overlap (Hollis and Harrison 1967). 'The aristocracy', said Bright to the workers, 'regard the Anti-Corn Law League as their greatest enemy. That which is the greatest enemy of the remorseless aristocracy of Britain must almost of necessity be your firmest friend.' (Prentice 1968, vol.: 378) For the League represented not just the economic but the social and political interests of the commercial middle classes, and indeed all those who wished to humble the power of the aristocracy and the landed interest. The Corn Laws were the potent symbol of that power. 'They are', wrote the radical *Nottingham Review*, 'the outwork of the citadel of corruption, and if we can bombard this outwork until we gain admission we shall then plant the banner of rational liberty upon the ruins of the despotism of the aristocracy.' (Fraser 1976: 242) This anti-aristocratic rhetoric – an attempt as it were to shout louder than the popular radicals – was an important part of the ethos and mythology of the Anti-Corn Law League. It led many contemporaries to consider the Corn Law controversy in terms of the clash of opposing 'interests' and social classes. 'Questions of prices of corn and rates of wages', proclaimed the arch-Tory, J. W. Croker, 'are mere *accidents*; the *substance* is the existence of a landed gentry, which has made England what she has been and is. . . .' (Kemp 1961–62) 'I believe this to be a movement of the commercial and industrial classes against the lords and great proprietors of the soil', exulted Bright on the eve of Repeal (Read 1967: 95). For the League, therefore, the struggle against the Corn Laws was also a crusade against the social and political power of the landed interest, 'the bread-taxing oligarchy, unprincipled, unfeeling, rapacious and plundering'.

However successful the propaganda of the League was in influencing middle-class opinion, it had little direct affect in achieving its one great aim – the repeal of the Corn Laws. As Cobden saw more clearly and sooner than any other free-trade leader, that could only be achieved through electoral activity with the ultimate aim of forcing the House of Commons to yield. 'You will perhaps smile at my venturing thus summarily to set aside all your present formidable demonstrations as useless', he wrote to J. B. Smith in 1839, 'but I found my conviction in the present construction of the House of Commons, which forbids us hoping for success. *That House must be changed before we can get justice.*' (McCord 1958: 82) This conviction inaugurated the second phase of the League's activity. The new policy was tried out at the Walsall by-election in 1841 when Smith stood as the free-trade candidate; the Whig withdrew and the Tory just scraped in. This at least showed the potentiality of the League as a third force in politics, and this strategy was applied in a number of favourable constituencies in the key election of 1841. At that election League candidates were victorious at a handful of industrial seats in the North and Midlands. Cobden himself won at Stockport, though he was disgusted at having been passed over by Manchester in favour of Milner Gibson, a landowner, who was elected. 'What wonder that we are scorned by the landed aristocracy, when we take such pains to show our contempt of ourselves', he wrote to Place (Read 1967: 46). The Whigs had come out at the election in favour of a modification of the Corn Laws – thus moving nearer to the League's position. But the outstanding fact about the 1841 contest was the decisive victory of Peel and the Conservative Party.

That election was certainly a personal success for Cobden, who now through sheer force of character and conviction displaced Villiers and emerged as the real leader of the anti-Corn Law forces in the Commons. But the victory of the protectionist party at this juncture was disquieting. It meant, in the first place, a public rebuff to the arguments of the League, though as the free-trade tenor of Peel's budgets soon showed, that was more apparent than real. It also led, secondly, to a revival of the demand by some middle-class Radicals for organic reform in association with the Chartists, as an accompaniment or even prelude to Corn Law repeal. This was the aim of Joseph Sturge's Complete Suffrage Union, which even John Bright supported. Cobden made sympathetic noises about the Union, 'I am not sorry to see Sturge taking up this question. It will be something in our rear to frighten the aristocracy', he told Smith (Read 1967: 30). But he was determined to maintain the independence of the League and the primacy of its one great aim. 'I have been thinking of our future plans', he told Bright, 'and am more and more convinced of the necessity of keeping ourselves free of all other questions.' (Morley 1903: 229) Since O'Connor's attitude *vis-à-vis* the Six Points was just as absolute, Sturge's attempt to find a programme that could embrace both the Charter and free trade and reunite middle- and working-class Radicals, was doomed to failure (Wilson 1974). By the middle of 1842 the Complete Suffrage Union had collapsed.

That did little to resolve the League's dilemmas. 'I am told on all sides that, unless we do something . . . we shall lose public confidence', lamented Cobden. *'What can we do?'* (McCord 1958: 111) Sturge's experiment in class collaboration had already shown the divisions within the free-trade camp. The bitter years of 1841–42 with depression, unemployment, hunger and unrest widespread in the North, were also years of crisis for the Anti-Corn Law League. Their disquiet at the government's failure to act decisively over the Corn Laws and thus, as they believed, help restore industrial prosperity and employment, led to wild talk among the Lancashire Radicals of forcing Peel's hand by closing factories or refusing to pay taxes. Such desperate talk gave some credence to the claim of the League's enemies that they were involved in the Plug Plots of 1842 – though in the end they drew back from that precipice. 'I consider the present disturbances', wrote R. H. Greg to Wilson, 'to be properly styled a *Chartist Insurrection*; and if the Anti-Corn Law League were to join it would end in a Revolution. . . .' (McCord 1958: 126) The Chartists *were* involved, and it was their association with disorder and industrial sabotage that gave the government the excuse for widespread arrests and imprisonments and thus helped the movement's decline.

The League learnt its lesson. By the end of 1842 it was back on course and emerged stronger and more confident than before. Cobden wrote (McCord 1958: 136):

> We have at the end of four years agitation got a pretty strong hold of public opinion, and at the present moment the Free Trade party is gaining ground more rapidly than at any former period. The Whig aristocracy will be compelled to come over to us, for Peel will occupy Lord John's position, and unless the latter moves on to our principle, he will be tripped up by his rival. There is no earthly doubt now of the ultimate triumph of our cause. It is merely a question of *time*.

The great free trader was perhaps being a bit over-optimistic. Nevertheless, as *The Times* said, simply, in a famous editorial in November 1843: the League is 'a great fact.'

After 1842–43 the League aimed at widening and deepening its influence on public opinion, using its well-tried methods. Its organisation was overhauled and improved. A £50,000 fund was established, and was soon well on the way to fulfilment. A great lecture campaign was launched by Cobden, and Bright who had been returned in 1843 as member for Durham City, aimed particularly at the metropolis; their efforts were rewarded by the capture of the vacant seat of the City of London. The use of the press became even more important: the foundation of the *Economist* as a free-trade journal was a notable event. But the League's main work was centred on electoral activity in order to influence Parliament where, it was now accepted, the battle would eventually be fought and won. 'The people should be told that the country's salvation must be worked out at the hustings and the polling booth', Cobden had written earlier (Hollis 1974: 10). Attempts were therefore made to win over the tenant farmers to the free-trade cause, regarding them as the key to the control of county seats, and relying perhaps on their latent antagonism to the landlords in a period of uncertainty for agriculture. 'They are the people *really* who have the government of this country in their hands – they surrender it at present to the landlords but if they had sense and courage enough they would act independently ... ' wrote Villiers to Cobden at this time (McCord 1958: 143). But even if they had acted independently – and many of them did – it is doubtful whether their verdict of opposition to Repeal would have been any different. As Kitson Clark has shown, it was often the tenant farmers who influenced the landlords into adopting a protectionist stance, rather than the other way round (Kitson Clark 1951b).

Since direct assault on the shires largely failed, indirect methods were employed using all the 'tricks of the trade' that the contemporary political system allowed. In the counties the League organised the practice of postal objection to hostile votes on an extensive scale; and, more importantly, began to create new free-trade votes by buying up freeholds in key constituencies. They achieved some striking success, notably in South Lancashire, and the West Riding where in February 1846 Lord Morpeth was returned unopposed as a free trader (Thompson 1959). Free traders also intervened as third candidates in occasional by-elections, continuing the policy begun at Walsall in 1841, much to the annoyance of the Whigs; but they were badly defeated in a string of seats in 1844 (Prest 1977: 79). By the summer of 1846 only a small number of seats had been made safe for free trade in this way. The organisation of these policies may make Cobden 'one of the nineteenth century's greatest electoral strategists' (Hamer 1977: 62); but their overall results were extremely limited. It seems unlikely, therefore, that the policy of creating freehold votes scared Peel into repealing the Corn Laws in order to avoid an anti-Tory landslide in the counties, as one historian argues (Prest

Victorian Radicalism

1977). McCord believes it is doubtful whether 'the free traders would have emerged victorious from a general election in 1846, had such a trial of strength proved necessary' (McCord 1958: 208). Perhaps the cutting edge of League propaganda was blunted as a result of the revival of trade in the mid-1840s linked, ironically, with Peel's free-trade budgets and lower food prices.

The League's electoral policies looked forward to a general election in 1848. As is well known, however, the resolution of the Corn Law question occurred not through argument and conflict at the hustings, but inside Cabinet and Parliament, as a result of the impact of the Irish Potato Famine in the autumn of 1845. This meant that in the final crisis of 1845–46 the League, despite its years of strenuous commitment to Repeal, was pushed off the centre of the stage by Peel and the Commons, and forced to watch, impotent and angry, from the wings. It is true that the conversion of the Whig leader, Lord John Russell, to total repeal in his 'Edinburgh letter' of November 1845 may be attributed to League pressure. It is doubtful whether the same may be said of Peel, even though he had become convinced that the Corn Laws could no longer be defended well before the impact of the Irish Famine. His conclusion was the same as the League's; but the reasons for it were much more subtle and complex. In economic terms, he seems in the last resort to have been pushed over the brink into acceptance of Repeal by his fears for the sources of British wheat supply abroad and the need to encourage home wheat production in an age of rising population (Fairlie 1965; Moore 1965). Peel's political thinking was even more important. The Corn Laws were a divisive element in British society. Repeal was vital, therefore, in order 'to terminate a conflict which, according to our belief, would soon place in hostile collision great and powerful forces in this country' (Briggs 1959: 325), a conflict which the aristocracy might lose. Retreat was necessary for the defenders of the Corn Laws. But it was to be an orderly retreat, controlled, step by step, by the Prime Minister *within* Parliament, and not as the result of an electoral contest or Radical 'pressure from without'. In this way the forces of the landed interest could regroup in good order again.

This, it has been suggested, is how the repeal of the Corn Laws *was* affected by the Commons in May 1846, despite the split in the Conservative Party (Kemp 1961–62). The following month, under the influence of the Duke of Wellington, it passed through the Lords. The Repeal Act did not in fact allow for 'total and immediate' repeal; that was not to come until 1849, and in the meantime a small duty was to remain. But it was near enough to the League's aim to be acceptable: and in July 1846 after a final poignant meeting at Manchester the League was wound up.

What then was the significance of the Anti-Corn Law League in the development of Victorian Radicalism? It is a commonplace of

24

economic history to point out that the immediate results of Repeal did little to justify the worst fears of either protectionists or free traders. If the economic consequences of the work of the League have been cut down to size, it may be argued that its political consequences have similarly been exaggerated. On the eve of Repeal the *Manchester Examiner* rejoiced over its native city's 'victorious conflict with the spirit of feudalism . . . the men who made the country, and keep it have effectually vindicated their right to rule it' (Read 1967: 95). That is exactly what did not happen. The personal prestige of Cobden in the aftermath of Repeal, as typified by Peel's remarkable tribute in the House of Commons, was extraordinarily high, and the gospel of free trade soon became part of the mental furniture of every educated Englishman. By 1852 protection was 'not only dead but damned'. It is true also that the triumph of Repeal meant an increasing recognition of the aims and interests of the urban middle classes in terms of legislation – a process, however, that was already well under way in the 1830s. What is more to the point is that aristocratic government easily survived the crisis of 1846. The Age of Russell and Palmerston which followed in the mid-Victorian period was even more aristocratic than the preceding years, when Peel (in Cobden's famous phrase) represented 'the Idea of the Age'. A few concessions were made to the middle classes over government; Cobden refused office, but Gibson and Villiers were given minor posts in Russell's administration of 1846. The realities of political power, however, were still retained by the old ruling caste. No organic reforms, neither the ballot nor the extension of the suffrage were passed until after 1865.

This was not unexpected. It was not only that the bias of the contemporary political system was strongly tipped in favour of landed property and the rural areas – a factor soon to be strengthened by rising rent rolls and farming profits. The timing and manner of Repeal was, as we have seen, deliberately chosen by Peel in order to insulate the question within Parliament and thwart the Radical pressure from the League outside. This meant that the landed interest in the House of Commons, despite its own internal divisions on the issue, in the end passed the final Repeal Act independently and advisedly as a considered measure of parliamentary statesmanship. By doing so its members maintained their own unity and right to govern. Indeed, by ending the Corn Law question once and for all and with it the *raison d'être* of the Anti-Corn Law League, they helped to restore the waning power of the traditional party leaders and their own pre-eminence. In that sense repeal of the Corn Laws was not a defeat for the landed interest, as has often been supposed. Nor, for Peel, was it intended to be. For him, 'Repeal was a strategic retreat, the sacrifice of the bastion of the Corn Laws in order to keep intact the main stronghold of aristocratic power.' (Chambers and Mingay 1966: 157) That, he believed, he had secured. 'It is my firm persuasion', he told his Tamworth constituents in July 1847, that 'our commercial and financial policy . . . has tended to fortify the established institutions of the country . . . to maintain the just authority of an hereditary nobility, and to discourage the desire for democratic change in the constitution of the House of Commons' (Kemp 1961–62). It was a reasonable verdict.

The resilience of the aristocracy and the self-confidence of Peel even in the hour of defeat, is a measure of the real political weakness of the Anti-Corn Law League and the middle classes during the 1840s. Peel's cool reaction to Cobden's famous letter of 1846 written just after Repeal, urging him to 'rule through the middle classes', is a reflection of this, just as the letter itself is a striking illustration of Cobden's profound misunderstanding of Peel's motives for Repeal (Morley 1903: 390–7). Nor could the League really claim to be the spokesman for 'the middle classes' *tout court*. It received strong support from the Lancashire cottonocracy and many other northern businessmen. But not all members even of the business community were prepared to give unlimited allegiance to the League, as in Leeds and Birmingham; protectionist groups existed in other cities – Bristol and Liverpool, for example. Moreover, the powerful financial and commercial élite of London – outstripping the manufacturers in wealth and prestige – were uncommitted if not actively hostile to the aims and ethos of the free-trade movement. Hence the middle classes were no more a united, coherent and self-conscious group than the working classes; and far less so than the landed interest whom they opposed (Rubinstein 1977a & b).

The League was not only less powerful, it was also less Radical than it appeared. Its anti-aristocratic rhetoric was intended to spur on the faithful by personalising a somewhat abstract issue, and widening the basis of its support by appealing to groups like the Nonconformists in whose hearts and minds such sentiments struck a powerful chord. It also aimed perhaps to prove to the Chartists that the free traders' Radical credentials were as good as theirs. It was not intended to nor could it be part of a serious plan of campaign aimed at superseding aristocratic government, despite the dire warnings of Tory pessimists such as J. W. Croker and the more blood-curdling parts of League propaganda. The conflict of middle and upper classes which some contemporaries, and modern historians, see as typical of the period is something of a myth (Aydelotte 1967). Many members of the urban bourgeoisie were, socially and politically, timorous and conservative. Their ambitions were often centred on local rather than national affairs; on their businesses, on the council chamber and the mayoralty and the penumbra of municipal activities that surrounded them, rather than on the House of Commons. Indeed, the proportion of businessmen in the House of Commons hardly changed between the First and Second Reform Acts (Garrard 1978; Fraser 1976).

This parochialism of the business classes was reinforced after 1846 by the growing acceptance of free trade and the 'entrepreneurial ideal', which gave them the excuse to abandon politics and return to their natural avocations, and the re-emergence of Chartism in 1848. The disbandment of the League, whose organisation survived only in Manchester under George Wilson, made it very difficult to provide any focus for the formation of a new united Radical Party, even if agreement could be reached on what its programme should be. Hopes for financial or administrative reform soon collapsed. Radicals were divided over religion and education, and, as the Don Pacifico Incident of 1850 showed, over foreign policy too. Enthusiasm for organic reform was at a low ebb. 'A large portion of the middle classes will oppose you steadily and to the last', wrote W. R. Greg to Cobden in 1848, 'on questions involving any radical remodelling of our representative system.' (Fraser 1976: 250) Cobden, unhappily, agreed.

All this meant that Cobden and Bright became increasingly isolated from their erstwhile middle-class supporters; and, as far as the substance of real power was concerned, impotent. They and their followers of the Manchester School formed a small and dwindling band in the House of Commons, one small section of the mixed bag of fifty or so Radicals giving general support to the Whig government of Lord John Russell. The real weakness of their position was seen in their electoral fortunes. Cobden had been elected MP for the West Riding in 1847 (while he was absent abroad) mainly as a result of the strong support of the urban liberals. But he was conscious of how vulnerable the representation of the constituency was 'by one', as he wrote later 'unconnected with it by birth, property or residence' (McCord 1967: 97). Bright's position at Manchester was even more difficult. He had set his heart on representing the city; but his brashness and outspokenness over the iniquities of the Establishment upset many of the respectable businessmen of this supposedly Radical city. He *was* eventually accepted as candidate and returned at the general election of 1847, and both he and Cobden were re-elected five years later. But their opposition to the Crimean War revealed only too clearly their isolation even within the Radical Camp.

The position of the Radicals in the aftermath of the Repeal campaign was thus a difficult one. In terms of its economic objectives the League had been enormously successful. Moreover, its methods of organisation and propaganda were far in advance of anything that had previously existed, and were to become the model for similar Radical pressure groups in the later nineteenth century (Hamer

1977). But politically the middle-class Radicals seemed to have gained very little. Now, like their predecessors of the 1830s, they were weak, disunited and largely leaderless. Above all, they were still faced with the problem which had concerned them for so many years. What should be their relationship with the working-class radical movement?

Chapter 2

THE AGE OF BRIGHT

For the men of the Manchester School free trade was a more exalted doctrine than a simple creed of economic liberalism. The removal of trade barriers throughout the world and the economic progress and prosperity that must surely follow, would also serve to undermine the more deep-rooted impediments – social, religious and psychological – to peace and amity between nations. 'I see in the Free-trade principle', said Cobden, 'that which shall act on the moral world as the principle of gravitation in the universe – drawing men together, thrusting aside the antagonisms of race, and creed and language, and uniting us in the bonds of eternal peace'. (Bright and Rogers 1870 vol. 1: 363) The victory of free trade in Britain, however, seemed merely to confirm Cobden's habitual conviction of the bellicosity of John Bull. Already in 1850, the remarkable triumph of Lord Palmerston in the Don Pacifico debate against the combined moral eloquence of Cobden, Peel and Gladstone, presaged a new, more belligerent strain in British foreign policy and national attitudes. Even the commercial middle classes supported Palmerston, another factor which added to the growing mutual irritation between Bright and his constituents. 'My recent vote against the f.p. of the government has been much condemned in Manchester', he recorded in his diary, 'by men who ought to know better . . . I cannot and will not be in Parliament a mere joint of the Whig tail'. (Walling 1930: 112–13) A year or so later the country was obsessed with the danger from France that followed the *coup d'état* of Louis Napoleon, and Cobden published his *1793 and 1853* to try and assuage this Gallomania. The public mood became even more frenetic in 1853 – 54 at the time of the outbreak of the Crimean War. That conflict revealed dramatically the deep divisions within the Radical camp, and in particular, the isolation of the Manchester School.

It was John Bright who emerged as the leader of the tiny anti-war minority in the House of Commons, partly because Cobden, always more pessimistic, felt strongly the futility of swimming against the tide. The arguments he put forward, in some of his greatest parliamentary speeches, owed much to Cobden's writings of the 1830s, *England, Ireland and America* (1835) and *Russia* (1836). Bright opposed the war not only because he believed that Russia had had a good case in the diplomatic preambles that preceded the conflict, but because he was opposed to the basic assumptions of British foreign policy: the pursuit of national interests, mounting arms expenditure, meddling abroad and the maintenance of that 'mischievous delusion' – the balance of power. Since these phenomena were inextricably linked with the power and fortunes of the English upper classes, they provided – in Bright's later magnificent phrase – 'a gigantic system of outdoor relief for the aristocracy of Great Britain' (Rogers 1883: 470).

Turkey, he believed, could not really be independent nor saved from disintegration, Russia could not really be crushed. 'It is a delusion to suppose that you can dismember Russia – that you can blot her from the map of Europe . . . Russia will be always there – always powerful, always watchful, and actuated by the same motives of ambition'. To support Turkey against Russia would mean supporting 'the most universal and filthy of all despotisms' in a conflict which could produce only misery and economic ruin for Great Britain (Rogers 1883: 235, 275). How then, he asked, were the interests of England involved in the question? The negative answer he gave was not based on pacifist premisses, for later he strongly supported the struggle of the North during the Civil War and steered clear of the peace and arbitration societies with which Cobden was strongly associated. He argued on practical grounds that the best policy for Great Britain was non-intervention and sticking to her true interests, those eternal verities which Cobden had proclaimed during the Don Pacifico debate – 'the maintenance of peace, the spread of commerce and the diffusion of education' (Taylor 1969: 49).

In all this the men of the Manchester School were out of touch with some of the deeper currents of feeling, chauvinist but also idealistic, that moved the English people in the 1850s, and which Tennyson expressed so fervently in *Maud*.

> And many a darkness into the light shall leap,
> And shine in the sudden making of splendid names,
> And noble thought be freer under the sun,
> And the heart of a people beat with one desire;
> For the peace that I deem'd no peace is over and done.

'If war begins', Bright had observed to Cobden, 'then 9/10ths of the men on our side will back the Govt. and shout even more vociferously than the Tories.'[1] So it turned out. Most Radicals in the House of Commons strongly supported the declaration of war against Russia in March 1854. Sir William Molesworth stood by the Aberdeen government, of which he was the only Radical member; so did leading Radical back-benchers such as Edward Baines, 'Tear-em' Roebuck, Henry Layard, the fanatically anti-Russian David Urquhart and the veteran Joseph Hume, who voted for the government's military estimates in 1854 for the first time in thirty years. On the other hand, Edward Miall, editor of the *Nonconformist* and elected MP for Rochdale in 1852, belonged to the anti-war camp, though many of his Nonconformist brethren outside the House of Commons, such as James Martineau and R. W. Dale, supported the war. These pro-war middle-class Radicals were moved by a variety of motives. Some were affected by a simple blind patriotism; others believed profoundly that they were fighting a 'just war' which could lead to a moral and political regeneration at home and abroad; some saw the war as a war of liberation against the 'gendarme of Europe' – Russia.

Nor were the working classes unaffected by such ideas. A generation of education by Polish exiles had convinced them that Russia was the prop and symbol of Continental despotism, and the patient work of the Poles was reinforced by the eloquence and prestige of Kossuth after he came to England in 1851 (Brock 1953). The crackbrained anti-Russian propaganda of David Urquhart(who believed that Palmerston was a spy in Russian pay) also had its effect (Shannon 1974). Thus the Crimean War could be regarded as in some sense a Radical triumph. 'Rather a costly war than dishonour', William Newton of the Engineers Trade Union had demanded in October 1853 in the name of the London working men; and George Harney, the Chartist, summed up their aims succinctly: 'policy, alliance with the oppressed nations; object, the annihilation of Russian supremacy' (Taylor 1969: 54). His fellow Chartist, Ernest Jones, denounced the peace moves of the Manchester School in 1853 as 'Russian propaganda' and his passionately anti-Russian views received the blessing of Marx and Engels (Saville 1952: 55–6).

By the summer of 1854 the mood of Bright and most of the anti-war group was one of pessimism. 'Miserable session', he recorded in his journal, 'much labour and no result; politics gloomy; Europe overrun by war or despotism, and England no wiser than in the last generation.' (Walling 1930: 176) The reports of the sufferings of the army at Sebastopol drove home some of the lessons which Bright and his supporters had been proclaiming for nearly a year. Even *The Times* commented on 'the incompetency, lethargy, aristocratic hauteur, official indifference, favour, routine, perverseness, and stupidity which revel and riot in the camp before Sebastopol' (Martin 1963: 242). That indictment was underlined, though in a more muted form, by the Reports of the Select Committee on the Conduct of the War, set up – in defiance of the government – as a result of Roebuck's famous resolution of January 1855. Within a month of that vote

Aberdeen's government had collapsed, and Lord Palmerston – the only man who now commanded the confidence of the Commons, and the hero of the pro-war Radicals – became Prime Minister. 'Palmerston Prime Minister', commented Bright, 'what a hoax! The aged charlatan has at length attained the great object of his long and unscrupulous ambition.' (Walling 1930: 184)

For all the Radicals the conclusions to be drawn from the Crimean débâcle were crystal clear. A Radical meeting at Finsbury resolved: 'That the disasters of the Crimean expeditions are mainly attributable to the incompetence of HM Ministers, the corruption of the House of Commons and the general inefficiency of the public service – the results of the undue influence of the aristocracy in the councils of the sovereign. (Maccoby 1938: 43) Cobden wrote similarly to Bright at the beginning of 1855 (Morley 1903: 630):

> The break-down of our aristocratic rulers, when their energies are put to the stress of a great emergency, is about the most consolatory incident of the war. I am not sure that it will so far raise the middle class in their own esteem as to induce them to venture on the task of self government. They must be ruled by Lords. But the discredit and slaughter to which our politicians, civil and military, have been excused, will go far to make real war unpopular with that influential class for another generation to come.

It has been argued that one result of the war was in fact to increase the self-confidence of the middle classes by revealing the superiority of their ideals of efficiency and expertise to the amateurism and nepotism of the aristocracy (Anderson 1967). This was linked with the foundation in May 1855 of the Administrative Reform Association, supported by some forty Radical MPs and many London commercial and professional men (Anderson 1974a). Its watchwords were 'efficient government' and, with wider Radical implications, the 'career open to the talents'. This led Sir James Graham to write indignantly to Gladstone that the Association was inspired by 'the hope of wresting from the Aristocracy and the Crown the remnant of their sway by means of the clamour for Administrative Reform and by the insolence and Predominance of the Press' (Anderson 1967: 121). His fears were premature. The Association collapsed before the year was out. It had only limited support in the House of Commons – which refused at first even to consider the moderate recommendations on Civil Service reform of the Northcote–Trevelyan Report of the same year – and very little outside London. It was dogged, as so often, by the not unreasonable suspicions of the working-class radicals that the Association was merely part of a plan for middle-class self-advancement. More importantly, the Association was overtaken by events on the wider fronts of war and politics. In the autumn of 1855, after considerable improvements in the Allied war effort, Sebastopol was at least captured and, despite the clamour of the 'patriotic' Radicals for a continuation of the war, peace negotiations were begun with Russia. In March 1856, the 'disgraceful peace' of Paris, as *Reynolds News* the pro-working-class newspaper termed it, was finally signed.

These events, aided immeasurably by the skill and self-confidence of the Prime Minister, checkmated the growing swell of protest against the political and military Establishment and did much to restore its prestige. The Crimean War was followed not by an Age of Reform, as so many had expected, but by the Age of Palmerston. At the general election of 1857, called by the Prime Minister as a riposte to his defeat in the House of Commons over the government's Chinese policy, Palmerston was triumphantly vindicated. The anti-war group were soundly beaten: Miall, Cobden, Gibson, Bright all lost their seats. Ironically though, in the field of foreign policy, the especial preserve of the aristocracy, the Manchester School won an almost total victory. The disasters of the Crimean War 'made Bright and Cobden the masters of British foreign policy', and convinced one Cabinet after another, Liberal and Conservative alike, of the wisdom of non-intervention (Taylor 1969: 57). Their long-term victory was even more profound. Opposition to national armaments and the 'Balance of Power', suspicion of 'secret diplomacy', contempt for national interests, support for non-intervention; these were some of the ideas of Cobden and Bright that bit deep into the Radical consciousness and reappeared time and time again in the later nine-teenth and twentieth centuries.

The 1850s was thus a depressing period for the fortunes of Radi-calism. 'I have been looking out for signs and omens of the political future', lamented Cobden to Bright at the beginning of the decade, 'but cannot say I see any indication of a breeze in the direction of Reform ... (Morley 1903: 557) The period of general prosperity which began in the later 1840s and lasted till at least the commercial depression of 1857, blunted the edge of political discontent and encouraged both employers and workers to opt for immediate social and economic gains within the established system of class and power. Moreover, the long period of political confusion, weakness and inst-ability which followed the break-up of the Conservative Party in 1846 and lasted until the formation of Palmerston's Liberal ministry in 1859, inhibited any great reforming impulse in the House of Commons. The foundering of Russell's two Reform Bills of 1852 and 1854 bore witness to this. The increasing concern with foreign affairs during the same period, often used deliberately to divert attention from domestic issues Cobden believed, worked to the same end. By ranging themselves behind the banner of Lord Palmerston the pro-war Radicals helped to undermine their own independence and cred-ibility, and encouraged that deference – at once corrupting and emollient – that sustained the authority of the old ruling class. Cobden was therefore being no more than just when he wrote at the end of the war (McCord 1967: 113–14):

> During my experience the Higher classes never stood so high in relative social and political rank, as compared with the other classes, as at present. The middle class has been content with the very crumbs from their table. The more contempt a man like Palmerston . . . heaped upon them the more they cheered him. The Radicals have turned more warlike than the Tories – what have they to promise the country in the way of practical benefits as a result of Parliamentary Reform? Not 'peace, retrenchment and reform' . . . but the very reverse. No, depend upon it, the Radicals have cut their throats before Sebastopol. We don't stand now where we did 8 years ago. The aristocracy have gained immensely since the people took to soldiering.

Something of a new phase in the history of the Reform movement began in 1858 following Bright's re-election to the House of Commons. In August 1857 Bright was returned unopposed for Birmingham, and this change from the great capitalist constituency of Manchester to the more open egalitarian one in the Midlands, symbolised his own development. 'It was', says A. J. P. Taylor, 'the Crimean War which helped to set Bright on the democratic path'. (Taylor 1976: 84) It made him an even more furious opponent of the English aristocracy, and determined therefore to obtain a union of the middle classes – still denied political influence, as he insisted – and the working classes in a campaign against their common enemy, with household suffrage as the engine of reform. In 1858 Bright thus returned to his *métier* as a Radical agitator and became leader of an extra-parliamentary campaign aimed at forcing the House of Commons – where a minority Conservative government under Derby and Disraeli was now in power – to grant a large measure of parliamentary reform. He preached a Radical crusade against the upper classes who, he argued, in language that infuriated his opponents and even worried Cobden, had misgoverned and despoiled the English people for centuries. He proclaimed at Birmingham (Smith 1881, vol. 1: 485):

> There is no actuary in existence who can calculate how much of the wealth, of the strength, of the supremacy of the territorial families of England has been derived from an unhappy participation in the fruits of the industry of the people, which have been wrested from them by every device of taxation, and squandered in every conceivable crime of which a Government could possibly be guilty.

As far as the franchise was concerned, Bright was not prepared to go beyond household suffrage in the boroughs and, in the counties, the enfranchisement of the £10 householders. A policy of manhood suffrage was too frightening to be practicable; and he justified himself in a letter to Joseph Sturge. 'I am not working for failure, but for success, and for a real gain, and I must go the way to get it. I am sure putting manhood suffrage in the Bill is not the way. This has been done by the Chartists, and by the Complete Suffragists, but what has become of their Bills?' (Trevelyan 1913: 270) He was less and less convinced in any case that the franchise issue was the key one; it was redistribution that was 'the very soul of the question of reform'. 'The franchise itself offers no real power, unless accompanied by the right on the part of all the possessors of it to elect something like an equal number of representatives.' The corollary of radical redistribution, he argued, was the ballot: 'it is not so much a principle as a convenience. It does not bestow the franchise, it guarantees that which the law has already conferred.'(Leech 1895: 78, 80) Bright's Bill, based on these principles, was never discussed in the Commons as the Conservatives at the beginning of 1859 were preparing to introduce their own measure of parliamentary reform. But the Conservative Bill, which eschewed any lowering of the borough franchise and was designed to increase Tory influence in the counties, was attacked mercilessly by Whigs, Peelites and Radicals in the House of Commons. Their opposition to this 'country gentlemen's bill' (as Bright called it) and the government's lukewarm policy towards Italian unity, helped to stimulate further agitation in the country and pushed the 'liberal' forces in the House closer together. As a result, Derby's government was quickly defeated, and the Liberals emerged with a clear majority at the general election of April 1859.

How successful was Bright's reform campaign of 1858–59? Trevelyan suggests that the winter campaign had a considerable impact (Trevelyan 1913: 276). Asa Briggs is more sceptical. 'The campaign', he writes, 'had a very limited success outside the great cities', and the working classes, he believes, remained uninspired by Bright's association of the benefits of parliamentary reform with financial improvement and economy (Briggs 1965: 229). It is true that important middle-class Reform Unions sprang up at this time in the Midlands and north of England; and leading parliamentary Radicals, like Bright's old Crimean War opponent, J. A. Roebuck, supported him vigorously. But the middle classes generally remained apathetic. 'The more Mr. Bright talked of reform, the less the country seemed to desire it', commented *The Times*. He frightened and disgusted the upper classes without conciliating the lower.' (Gillespie 1927: 157) This was a fair verdict. George Wilson, now President of the Lancashire Reform Union, insisted that 'there was no fear of the old game being played . . . the working classes were thoroughly prepared to accept the leadership of Mr. Bright' (Tholfsen 1961). It seems difficult to believe that this was so in 1858–59, years which mark the beginning of what the historian of British labour during this period calls 'a new phase of the labour question,' with the beginning of the builders' nine-hour movement and the major trade union developments that flowed from it (Gillespie 1927: 136). Frederic Harrison, just beginning his long association with the trade union movement, wrote to his friend Edward Beesly: 'I went to another man who goes a great deal among the workingmen's associations. . . . He says the workingmen of London care very little about Bright's bill. They would not stir for it. They want manhood suffrage and they dislike and fear Bright and his class. They have never forgiven him for the 10 hours bill opposition . . . .'[2]

This was the attitude of other popular radicals. In the aftermath of the Crimean War Ernest Jones had come to support the idea of a union between the middle and working classes in favour of organic reform, and pinned his hopes on Bright as 'the best man of the Manchester school'. But he was an ex-Chartist, and the tenor of Bright's proposals of 1858 disgusted him. 'A partial ratepaying or property vote-extension is . . . a class step strengthening class power. It is a step that gives votes to the middle class at the cost of the working classes. We are not going to depose aristocracy, merely that the millocracy may be enthroned instead.' (Saville 1952: 64, 67, 189) Once again Bright and the middle-class Radicals were faced with the perennial problem of the terms on which active working-class collaboration could be obtained.

Bright's campaign did have one important personal effect. In June 1859 Lord Palmerston returned to power as head of a reconstituted ministry which contained both Whigs and Peelites, and two Radicals, Milner Gibson and Charles Villiers. John Bright was refused office because, as Palmerston insisted to Cobden when the latter supported his friend's claim on the grounds that he had avoided attacking personalities in his campaign, 'It is not personalities that are complained of . . . . But it is his attacks on *classes* that have given offence to powerful bodies, who can make their resentment felt.' (Morley 1903: 695–6) Having been passed over for office – for which he had no great hankering – Bright at least expected a 'good' Reform Bill in return for the support given by the Radicals to the Liberal bloc which had turned out the Tories. Russell did introduce a Reform Bill the following year, based on a £6 suffrage in the boroughs, which Bright now considered 'probably the best franchise that could be adopted for the country' (Walling 1930: 236). Even that met with little favour in the Cabinet and it was withdrawn in June 1860. As far as the government was concerned, the Reform question went into cold storage until the death of the 'aged charlatan' in October 1865. Bright was indignant at Lord John's 'betrayal'. But Russell justified himself to the Prime Minister. 'It is pretty clear that the only measure which would be likely to pass would be one of a very moderate character . . . But who wants it? . . . The apathy of the country is undeniable. Nor is it a transient humour, it seems rather a confirmed habit of mind. Four Reform Bills have been introduced of late years. For not one of them has there been the least enthusiasm.' (Walpole 1889, vol. 2: 331) This was not an unfair diagnosis. Bright wearily accepted the inevitable. 'I am tired of agitation', he wrote to Cobden, 'but would give something to lift up our population into free men and to bring down the lofty pretensions of the ruling class.' (Robbins 1979: 149) For Bright, that opportunity lay dormant until stirred into life again by the conflict in America.

It was events abroad that vitally affected the cause of Radicalism during Palmerston's second ministry. The years between 1859 and 1865 were followed in rapid succession by one great crisis after another in foreign affairs – Italy in 1859, the Polish Revolt of 1863, the American Civil War 1861–65 – each of which caused intense excitement in Great Britain, particularly among the working classes. The American Civil War, especially, stimulated working-class unity and interest in politics, even though at first a vociferous group of trade unionists led by T. J. Dunning and George Potter supported the Confederacy (Harrison 1965: Ch. 2). For most British working-class leaders Lincoln and the North appeared to be fighting *their* battle for Democracy on the other side of the Atlantic; just as the opponents of Democracy at home saw in the government of the North 'what our own might be if the most dangerous elements of our Constitution should become dominant' (Adams 1925, vol. 1: 279).

In the eyes of English Radicals, the bitter opposition shown by the English upper classes towards the 'promiscuous democracy' of the North (in the *Saturday Review's* contemptuous phrase) expressed, vicariously, their even greater hatred of democracy nearer home. It was this feeling, as much as opposition to slavery, that gave passion to the great campaign now waged throughout the country by John Bright in favour of the North. He proclaimed at Rochdale early in 1863 (Rogers 1883: 117):

> In America the workingman does not find he belongs to what is called the 'lower classes'; he is not shut out from any of the rights of citizenship; he is admitted to the full enjoyment of all political privileges . . . In America he finds the land not cursed with feudalism . . . there hope prevails everywhere, because every where there is an open career; there is no privileged class . . . there is no point in the social ladder to which he may not fairly hope to raise himself by his honest efforts.

Bright was supported by the Emancipation Society, founded in 1862, led by such middle-class Radicals as Mill, Stansfeld, Hughes, Edmund Beales – later President of the Reform League – and Professor Beesly. Lincoln's Emancipation Act in the following year was the signal for a whole series of meetings throughout England. It was now impossible to ignore the element of native political protest in the support of British workers and middle-class Radicals for the Northern democracy. For Bright, this was increasingly the major purpose of the whole campaign, as his tendentious view of the Northern cause and British reaction towards it indicates (Ellison 1972).

The American Civil War was important not only because it stimulated working-class interest in politics, but also because it affected the coming struggle for reform at the level of organisation and class alignment. Labour leaders such as George Howell and Robert Applegarth, together with their middle-class Positivist allies, Harrison and Beesly, were anxious to draw the trade unions into the wider fields of political action, if necessary – despite their profound differences over economic issues – in alliance with John Bright and his manufacturing supporters. For Bright, admired by Lincoln and in constant communication with Seward, the American Secretary of State, was now the leader of the growing movement in favour of the Federalists, and therefore of British parliamentary reform – as both his friends and his enemies recognised. 'His is a political fanaticism', commented *The Times*, 'whose master passion is the love of that great dominant Democracy'. The American Ambassador wrote to Seward about a year later, 'The very moment the war comes to an end and restoration of the Union follows, it will be the signal for a reaction that will make Mr. Bright perhaps the most formidable public man in England.' (Adams 1925, vol. 1: 296, 298)

Hence on 26 March 1863 a great trade union meeting was organised by Beesly in St James's Hall, London, in favour of the American North, chaired by John Bright, 'to be a sort of reconciliation between him and them.' [3] About 3,000 trade unionists attended the meeting; Mill, Fawcett, and Harrison among others sat on the platform, and Karl Marx and the young Henry Adams, the Ambassador's son, were present in the body of the hall. Howell, and Odger, secretary of the London Trades Council, spoke on behalf of the working men. But the most important speeches were made by Beesly and Bright, both of whom appealed directly to the working men and uninhibitedly linked domestic politics with the cause of the American North. Bright said (quoted in Rogers 1883: 125–6):

> Privilege thinks it has a great interest in this contest, and every morning with blatant voice it comes into your streets and curses the American Republic. Privilege has beheld an afflicting spectacle for many years past. It has beheld thirty millions of men, happy and prosperous, without emperor, without king, without the surrounding of a court, without nobles . . . without State bishops and State priests.

He concluded:

> America was a country which amongst all the great nations of the

globe, is that one where labour has met with the highest honour, and where it has reaped its greatest reward.

The importance of this speech for the cause of 'democracy' in Britain was emphasised by Henry Adams in an account of the meeting that his father sent to the State Department. The young Adams wrote of Bright (quoted in Glicksberg 1942):

> His presence and his speech were significant as showing that on this question of the safety of Republican institutions in America the radical class of labourers who have hitherto devoted their energies to the contest with the power of capital . . . were fairly brought to cooperate heartily with a capitalist and to ask him to act as their representative in political action. The meeting was a demonstration of democratic strength, and no concealment of this fact was made.

About a month later, in April 1863, a similar great meeting was held in London in defence of the Polish rebellion, and this marked yet another stage on the road to unity in favour of domestic political reform. In 1864 the tide now flowing strongly in favour of reform was strengthened by the famous visit of Garibaldi to England, even though the visit was cut short by the government, alarmed by the mass enthusiasm the Italian hero aroused.

By that time the middle classes had formed a new reform association. This was the National Reform Union which, drawing upon the traditions of middle-class membership and organisation established by the Anti-Corn Law League and the northern franchise reform associations founded in the 1850s, was set up in Manchester in 1864. It supported household suffrage, vote by ballot and a redistribution of seats; and though it welcomed working-class support, it was in fact predominantly a middle-class body whose hero and *de facto* leader was John Bright. It became the archetypal middle-class reform union of the 1860s. As far as the problem of the suffrage was concerned, the supporters of the Reform Union thought not in terms of the realisation of the 'class' aims of the workers through their enfranchisement and domination of the House of Commons – that was implied by manhood suffrage; but rather of using the power of an enfranchised working-class minority to secure the traditional aims of middle-class Radicalism. This meant all that was implied in Bright's vision of an attack on 'feudalism': complete free trade, land, educational and tax reform, religious equality, economy – particularly in arms expenditure – and a peaceful foreign policy. Much of this was secured by the Liberals after 1868.

The supporters of the Reform Union were certainly moved by the concept of political justice for the working classes; but it was a limited concept of 'justice', in terms of Victorian middle-class values. If the vote was no longer thought of as a species of property, it was certainly not a 'right' to which all were entitled. It was best regarded as a 'trust', fit only to be exercised by those worthy to do so, and this excluded the lower ranks of the working classes, the 'residum' (as Bright called them) 'sunk in almost hopeless poverty and dependence'. Household suffrage, therefore, meant the enfranchisement of an élite of relatively well-to-do working men, largely committed to the ideals of the middle class and therefore prepared to accept their tutelage in politics. This view was linked with the fundamental belief of Bright and the manufacturers in the common interests of capital and labour which, in the words of one Reform Union pamphlet, 'are identified with and dependent upon each other' (Brewster 1867: 7). The granting of the vote to the skilled working men would therefore help in the reconciliation of classes and their common commitment to progress and prosperity through a beneficent capitalism.

In February 1865 Edmund Beales and George Howell went ahead with their own plans for establishing a new reform association based on manhood suffrage and appealing mainly to the working classes. At the same time they took steps to sound out middle-class opinion. In the middle of March a meeting was held attended by Bright, Samuel Morley, the great hosiery manufacturer, and other middle-class Radicals, but the meeting broke up as Bright and his supporters were not prepared to go beyond household suffrage. Nevertheless, the possibility of at least 'unofficial' collaboration between the two classes in pursuit of reform, on lines already established by the experience of 1863, was not ruled out, especially as a number of Reform Union leaders gave moral support to the League, and Samuel Morley supported both bodies financially. In a letter read out at one of the workers' preliminary meetings, Bright indicated those tactics which in fact he pursued until 1867 (Gillespie 1927: 251):

> I think you are quite right to move for manhood suffrage, for that is what you must approve ... I think the people everywhere should ask for what they must, but, at the same time, I would recommend that they who ask for much should not regard as enemies and opponents those who ask for less. By a combined and friendly movement we shall get something, and that once gained is never again lost, but becomes an additional power to obtain more.

On 23 March, therefore, at St Martin's Hall, London, the Reform League was officially inaugurated. Beales was elected president, Howell, secretary; vice-presidents and a council were also elected, though Mill, Godwin Smith and even Beesly and Harrison refused to serve, thus indicating the reservations of even the most sympathetic intellectual Radical over manhood suffrage. Yet the aims of the League were not perhaps as far removed from those of the Reform Union as they seemed. The League supported manhood suffrage and the ballot; but it was *resident* and *registered* adult male suffrage, thus excluding both women and the bulk of the residuum.

Like their middle-class mentors, the aristocracy of labour saw the vote as 'a passport of approval rather than as an instrument of political power'. Beales himself said that an extension of the suffrage would 'weld all classes together by unity of interest into one harmonious whole' (Smith 1966: 14, 23), an aim which that 'Respectable Radical', George Howell, pursued as a labour official over the next ten years (Leventhal 1971).

In the general election of July 1865 something of an *entente* was created between the League and Bright, and the result of the election was not only an increase in Palmerston's majority, but also the return of a number of advanced Liberals with working-class support, notably Hughes at Lambeth, Fawcett at Brighton and Mill at Westminister. Though the election was not fought on the issue of parliamentary reform, this verdict was interpreted by the Radicals as a vindication of their views. 'I think we are very near a step in reform', wrote Bright after the election results (Trevelyan 1913: 343). Thus by the middle of 1865 at least two outstanding political organistions in favour of parliamentary reform had been created: only one political obstacle remained before they could spring into life. 'As soon as the great political trickster of the age is gone', wrote Frederic Harrison in July, 'something will have to be done'; and on 18 October 1865 Lord Palmerston died.[4] His old political opponent, Richard Cobden, had died a few months before, with his Radical ideals largely unfulfilled. The death of Palmerston meant the end of a political era. The old parties were galvanised into life; the Radicals looked forward to the realisation of their hopes.

Gladstone and Russell, the new leaders of the Liberal Party, were now committed to the principle of reform, but they believed that the new Palmerstonian House of Commons would only accept 'a safe measure'. They were prepared to use Bright, as before, as a sounding board for reform, but had no intention of inviting him to join the Cabinet 'his name would sink the government and their bill together', Gladstone commented to Russell – or slavishly submitting to his views (Cowling 1967: 86). Bright thus had no direct hand in shaping the Reform Bill that Gladstone presented to the House of Commons in March 1866. This was a very moderate measure, which aimed at enfranchising £7 householders in the boroughs and £14 occupiers in the counties; redistribution was to be dealt with later. Despite its defects, Bright believed that the Bill should be supported as the best that could be got, partly because of his personal admiration for Gladstone's strong moral commitment to reform since his 'pale of the Constitution' declaration of May 1864. 'The Franchise Bill now before Parliament is a perfectly honest Bill . . . .. It appeals to the middle and working class alike. It is a measure of enfranchisement to both of them, and they should heartily unite in an effort to make it a law.' (Leech 1895: 87–8)

It was to this end that Bright began to stir up the country in favour of the Bill, in a campaign which made him, as he confessed to his wife, 'the great terror of the squires'. The supporters of the Reform League believed that there was no alternative but to follow where Bright led. Beesly wrote to Howell on 15 March: 'The Bill is undoubtedly a poor one. But as the acknowledged leader of the liberal party Mr. Bright wishes it to be carried, I think we ought for the sake of union to give him our support, while repeating our intention not to rest until we have got manhood suffrage.'[5] This was the policy soon adopted, reluctantly, by the Reform League, and something of an unofficial alliance was now created between Bright, the Reform Union and the Reform League in favour of the Gladstone Bill, the League spurred on particularly by the offensive remarks of Robert Lowe in his speech in the House of Commons on 13 March about the venality of the working classes. But the alliance was an uneasy one. Invitations were issued to a number of middle-class supporters, including Mill, Bright and Samuel Morley, to attend a Reform League demonstration at Primrose Hill on 21 May, but – a revealing comment on the limits of middle-class support for mass demonstrations – none appeared, though Mill and Bright wrote letters in support.

On 18 June as a result of a union of Conservative and Adullamite votes in the House of Commons, the government was defeated. Bright would have liked a dissolution, believing that a general election 'for a great principle and a great cause' would sweep the Liberals back into power (Smith 1966: 16). But practical considerations prevailed, and within a fortnight the government had resigned and Derby and Disraeli were once again leaders of a minority Conservative administration. It was now that the power of the trade union movement was really thrust behind the Reform campaign. With the advent of the Conservative government, the activities of the Reform League – which had died down during the early spring of 1866 – resumed in full force with monster meetings and processions. This movement culminated in the famous Hyde Park affair on 23 July, when a League procession was refused access into the park by the police, and the mob broke down the railings and took over the park for three days. It was the League itself, with the support of Mill, that helped restore order. Bright had by now moved nearer the League's position, at least on tactics. He supported the Hyde Park meeting, even though he prudently stayed away in the north of England. Declaring that 'Lord Derby's government had declared war on the working classes',in a series of monster (indoor) meetings in the cities between August and December 1866 in association with the League, he became the spearhead of the attack on the government, bent on either destroying it or forcing it to yield over reform. There was nothing basically new in Bright's denunciation of the 'corruption' of the parliamentary system, though the note of class hatred was now more strident. What was impressive was the vigorous unity of the Reform movement (Park 1920: 111):

Then shout with all your might
God save Gladstone, Beales and Bright;
Wave your banners, let your ranks closer form,
And let your watchword be –
Old England, Liberty;
Manhood Suffrage, Vote by Ballot and Reform.

It looked as if the last aim at least would be achieved. Disraeli, despite the Hyde Park affair, remained unconvinced during the summer recess that reform had become a genuine popular demand. It was Derby who now set the pace within the government. 'I am coming reluctantly to the conclusion', he wrote to Disraeli on 16 September, only a few weeks after the opening of Bright's autumn campaign, 'that we shall have to deal with the question of Reform', and by December he was already thinking in terms of household suffrage (Buckle 1916, vol. 4: 458). Thereafter the conversion of the two Conservative leaders was fairly rapid. By January, Disraeli himself was looking for a basis for an enduring Reform Bill; and at the end of February, defying the die-hards in the Cabinet, he and Derby accepted a Reform Bill based on the principle of household suffrage plus safeguards, which they believed would still leave the working classes a minority of the electorate. This in turn was accepted by the Conservative Party in the House of Commons.

It has been suggested that the actions of the two Conservative leaders were dictated primarily by party considerations that sprang from their minority position in the House of Commons (Cowling 1967). In particular, Disraeli was determined to destroy Gladstone's leadership over a united Liberal Party by seizing the initiative in reform himself, and shaping the character of the Conservative Reform Bill for his own opportunist purposes. Yet the ebb and flow of parliamentary debate and the tergiversations of ministers must be seen, Royden Harrison has argued, within the total context of the events of 1866–67 (Harrison: Ch. 3 1965). It was no longer possible for the government to ignore the popular clamour in favour of reform, sharpened that winter by economic distress and the anger felt by trade union leaders over the calumnies arising out of the 'Sheffield Outrages', and the *Hornby* v. *Close* decision. The Reform League was a major factor in keeping the political situation fluid. There were hints by some of its members of resorting to direct action, which made Bright uneasy: 'These great meetings . . . were not meetings so much for discussion, as they were meetings for the demonstrations of opinion, and, if you like, I will add for exhibition of force. Such exhibitions, if they are despised and disregarded, may become exhibitions of another kind of force.' (Harrison 1965: 87) But the implied reproof – or threat – was unconvincing. As Marx disdainfully noted, the whole ethos of the League meant that it sought to avoid a violent confrontation with the authorities, as they in turn did with the League (Marx and Engels 1962: 541). 'The working classes themselves', Beales protested, 'are deeply interested in the preservation of law and order, of the rights of capital and property; of the honour and power and wealth of our country.' (Harrison 1965: 114) The League leaders were as opposed as the middle-class Radicals to the activities of 'the mob'. Their tactics were based on peaceful 'pressure from without' to force the government to accept the artisans' right to enter 'the pale of the constitution'. But this implied a willingness to accept something less than 'manhood suffrage'. What Beales, Howell and Co. wanted was 'social recognition' rather than the substance of political power; hence their unconcern with the problem of redistribution which so obsessed Bright. All this, together with their poor financial position and their lack of outstanding national leaders or spokesmen in the House of Commons, meant that the Reform League was impelled to go along with the Reform Union and the *de facto* leadership of John Bright. The combination of working-class numbers and middle-class leadership in 1866–67 was a powerful one. It determined that there would be a Conservative Reform Bill, outbidding the discredited Liberal Bill of 1866. It in no way decided what the contents of that Bill would finally be.

That depended on the debates that took place in the House of Commons between March and July 1867. Since these were largely concerned with the petty details of rating and rental qualifications, their significance only dimly appreciated in terms of numbers of voters, they inevitably degenerated into 'a tangle of tricky manoeuvres, of apparently senseless wrangles and misdirected votes' (Smith 1966: 1). Out of this sublime confusion the Second Reform Act eventually emerged, and 'the character of the Bill was so materially altered that for all practical purposes it became a new measure' (Hamersham Cox 1868: 281). In a way Disraeli was hoist with his own petard. By pursuing single-mindedly his policy of separating Gladstone from his party and refusing to accept any amendments that he inspired, he played into the hands of the Radicals. Their importance was enhanced, and they were given a control over the shaping of the final Act out of all proportion to their numbers, or their talents. Unlike their disorientated leader, most Radicals in the Liberal Party knew what they wanted. They believed that the basic principle of the Conservative Bill, household suffrage, was a sound one: the rest was expendable. What they aimed at, therefore, before the prospect of a dissolution loomed, was an immediate settlement that excluded 'fancy franchises' but also any possibility of 'toppling into manhood suffrage'. In this way middle-class control of the new electorate could be retained.

One by one the 'safeguards' in the Bill were destroyed and new clauses inserted by Radical and Liberal amendments, often against their own leader and in collusion with Tories. This was seen in the decision of the notorious 'Tea Room' meeting of 8 April 1867, when fifty dissident Liberals refused to support Gladstone's plan of trying to return to a £5 borough franchise. Bright was not a party to this: though he was sympathetic to the aims of the 'Tea Room' Radicals, as a loyal Gladstonian he abhorred their methods. 'The corruption of the House', he recorded in his diary, 'is something extraordinary. Men fear a dissolution and will descend to any measure to escape it. They are destroying the unity and power of the Liberal Party, and are making its leader an object of commiseration.' (Walling 1930: 301) The climax of Disraeli's process of accommodation with the Radicals came in May. He agreed to Torrens' amendment which enfranchised £10 lodgers; he accepted on the 17th, even more remarkably, Hodgkinson's amendment which abolished the distinction between compounders and personal ratepayers in the boroughs, and thus added about four times as many voters to the electoral roll as had originally been contemplated. It has been argued by Royden Harrison that Disraeli's action was directly connected with the events earlier in the month, by which the government had failed to maintain its veto on the Reform League meeting in Hyde Park planned for 6 May (Harrison 1965: Ch. 3). This seems doubtful. It may have been 'a moral triumph', as Beales described it. But all the evidence seems to point to the fact that Disraeli – a subtle parliamentarian to his fingertips – in accepting the famous amendment of 17 May was influenced much more by the momentum of debate in the House of Commons than by 'pressure from without', which he neither feared nor was particularly impressed by.

In many ways the Second Reform Act of 1867 was a political triumph for the middle-class Radicals. As a result of their successful tactics, both inside and outside Parliament, their reputation was enhanced in the Commons and the country, and this was further emphasized by the victory of the reunited Liberal Party at the general election of 1868. As a result, Bright was appointed President of the Board of Trade by Gladstone, though his Radical fire was now dying rapidly and, as an administrator, he was a failure; he retired in 1870 as a result of another attack of nervous depression. Forster, in charge of education, was the only other Radical in a government largely dominated by Whigs and Peelites. Yet this government passed a mass of legislation which exemplified the ethos of traditional middle-class Radicalism. One of the reforms was the introduction at last in 1872 of the ballot, a measure which Bright had urged upon the Reform League in August 1867 as 'the next great question for which . . . they ought to contend' (Leech 1895: 96).

The major victory for the Radicals was the achievement of household suffrage. This meant that a million new voters were added to the electoral list, mainly in the great cities where the working classes now became a majority of the electorate. Yet, as the parliamentary Radicals had rightly expected, the working classes made little attempt to exert that electoral power in an independent or 'class' way after 1867. At the general election of 1868 the Reform League continued to accept the patronage of the middle classes. It was weakened by internal squabbles and lack of money; Fawcett's vital amendment in favour of the defrayment of electoral expenses by the local authorities was overwhelmingly defeated during the Reform debates. This meant that the League's leaders, especially Howell and Cremer, were strongly committed to a Liberal victory; partly because of their instinctive Gladstonianism, partly in order to win middle-class money and goodwill. For the same reason they failed to give priority in their electoral manifesto to the urgent legal demands of the trade unions. Howell went even further. He concluded a secret electoral pact with Glyn, the Liberal Chief Whip, by which in return for financial help the resources of the League's membership were placed at the disposal of the Liberal Party, and none of the funds supplied were to be used to fight Liberals. In the end the Liberals gained a majority of more than 100, and not one of the 4 working-class candidates – including Howell and Cremer – who stood for election was returned. About a year later, in the spring of 1869, the Reform League was wound up. The year 1868 thus marks 'the real beginning of the Lib-Lab era in working class politics' (Harrison 1965: 209).

Other aspects of the Reform Act were much less favourable to middle-class Radical aspirations. For though, as all contemporary observers saw, there was really sweeping change in the large boroughs, in the counties the position was very different. There the vote was given to the £12 householders, a relatively small and deferential group. In addition, since in county areas the rural districts were strongly reinforced by boundary changes which deliberately lopped off suburban areas and added them to the boroughs, conditions there were not very much different after 1867. In the counties the old hierarchical order continued almost undisturbed, and they normally remained the chief stronghold of the Conservative Party in the later nineteenth century. Moreover, as Bright had always perceived, redistribution was 'the very soul of the question of reform', and here the traditional nature of the Act was even more evident. In England and Wales only 52 seats were redistributed in 1867: 25 went to the counties to enlarge an already Conservative franchise, and only 19 went to the urban areas. The four greatest provincial cities, Manchester, Birmingham, Leeds and Liverpool, were fobbed off with an extra member each in addition to the two they already possessed, and the 'minority clause' – which gave their electors only two votes each – was tacked on by the House of Lords to add insult to injury. After 1867 there were still more than 70 boroughs with a population of less than 10,000 voters, and the boroughs as a whole remained considerably over-represented. Hence many of the corrupt electoral habits of a previous generation were carried over into the post-Reform period; and, despite the Ballot Act, corruption, bribery and intimidation still remained important features of the new electoral system (Wright 1970: 80–1).

Thus despite the remarkable social and economic progress of the middle classes during the mid-Victorian period, and the enfranchisement of the urban artisans, the composition of the House of Commons changed comparatively slowly after 1867. A Radical writer had cynically suggested in 1866 that a stranger viewing the House of Commons in that year 'would naturally infer that we were an aristocratic, a warlike, and a litigious people' (Wilson 1866). This was almost as true in the 1880 Parliament when there were still 155 MPs related to the peerage, compared with 165 in the 1866 Commons, and only 112 members represented the manufacturing interest compared with 90 in 1866 (Seymour 1915: 311–12). There were the same number of army and naval officers and lawyers in both Parliaments. What was true of the House of Commons was just as true of government as the personnel of both Liberal and Conservative Cabinets shows.

Despite their successes in the Age of Gladstone in limiting the area of privilege, middle-class Radicals still felt themselves confronted in politics by the power of their old enemy – the 'remorseless Aristocracy of Britain'. This was due not only to the subtle and complex processes of English political life, but, ironically, to the very economic changes that Bright and his friends had helped to bring about. It was, argues Professor Hanham, mid-Victorian prosperity that maintained the old order. 'Its influence was twofold: it created the atmosphere of optimism and confidence which made possible the great reforms of the late sixties and early seventies, and it sustained and invigorated the old hierarchical society which in the forties had seemed doomed to decay.' (Hanham 1959: xiv)

NOTES

1. Bright to Cobden, 27 Dec. 1853, Bright Papers.
2. N.d., 1858, Frederic Harrison Papers, Box 1.
3. Frederic Harrison to Mrs Hadwen, 24 Mar. 1863, Frederic Harrison Papers, Box 1.
4. *The Bee-Hive*, 1 July 1865.
5. Howell Collection.

Chapter 3

INTELLECTUAL RADICALS AND DEMOCRACY

John Stuart Mill was of course the greatest intellectual Radical of the mid-Victorian period, and as heir to the Utilitarian tradition he believed profoundly that his political ideas could have a direct bearing on practical affairs. The problem of democrary which had been debated with such brilliance in the Parliament of 1866 and to which he had made a notable contribution, had been at the centre of his political thinking since the Great Reform Bill. At that time Mill had regarded himself as an orthodox Radical, albeit a philosophic one, accepting the traditional Radical demands of universal suffrage, the ballot, payment of MPs and shorter Parliaments. These were practical demands which, to Mill, seemed to follow from the theory of Bentham and his father that 'good government' rested upon an identification of the interests of the governors and the governed – ultimately a recognition of the will of the numerical majority.

But as a result of his disillusionment with the Parliamentary Radicals of the later 1830s, and the impact on his mind of the writings of De Tocqueville and Coleridge, Mill began to question both the presuppositions of the Utilitarian theory of government and the political remedies they generated. He accepted, as in his essay of 1830, *Civilization*, that the social forces of contemporary society tended towards democracy. But in his review of *Democracy in America* (published in 1840) he was impressed by De Tocqueville's arguments that democracy – which the French writer largely identified with equality – could lead to a regime of mediocrity, instability and above all, uniformity of opinion. Granted that public opinion must in the end prevail in government, 'in order to the formation of the best public opinion, there should exist somewhere a great social support for opinions and sentiments different from those of the mass' (Williams 1976: 244). 'Now, as ever, the great problem in government is to prevent the strongest from becoming the only power; and repress the natural tendency of the instincts and passions of the ruling body to sweep away all barriers which are

capable of resisting, even for a moment, their own tendencies.'
(Williams 1976: 247) At that time Mill believed that the greatest
danger came from the domination of 'the commercial classes'; but,
more optimistic than De Tocqueville, he believed that in England at
any rate the possibility of 'a countervailing power' did exist, in the
form of 'an agricultural class' – ever an element of stability and
traditional values in society – and 'a leisured and learned class'
(Williams 1976: 246).

In the light of these views it was natural that Mill, in his famous
essay on *Coleridge* (1840), should sympathise with the poet's conception of 'the clerisy' – 'the principle of an endowed class, for the
cultivation of learning, and for diffusing its results among the
community' (Mill 1859: 364). Indeed he praised Coleridge's philosophic and reflective conservatism, which stressed the value of those
elements in society – tradition, community, religion, nationality –
ignored by Bentham and the Utilitarians. His reflections on the
French Revolution of 1848 also led Mill to criticise a Constitution
which gave too much power to the legislature as against the executive, and rested upon an extravagant extension of the suffrage. By
the end of the 1840s, therefore, Mill had begun to raise a number of
searching questions concerning the character of popular government
which led him a few years later either to abandon or modify many of
his cherished Radical beliefs. What were the true functions of a
representative assembly? How could representative government be
coupled with efficient government? How to obtain the rule of 'the
wisest and the best'? Above all, how could the rights of minorities
be safeguarded against 'the tyranny of the majority'? (Burns 1969)

An answer to some of these problems was adumbrated in the essay
Thoughts on Parliamentary Reform, published in 1859 but probably
written in response to the Reform Bill of 1852. Here Mill accepted
that everyone should have a voice in government. But he denied that
everyone should have an equal voice; for since the exercise of the
vote implied power over others, he refused to admit that that meant
that 'all persons have an equal claim to power over others' (Mill
1859: 323). 'I see no tenable ground', he wrote to Chadwick, 'for
resisting the democracy of mere numbers, but by directly and openly
asserting two broad principles – that everyone is entitled to *some*
voice in the representation, and that every *intelligent* person is entitled to a *more potential* voice.' He was now prepared to argue in
favour of giving more votes to the educated (conceived in a wide
sense) and more representation to minorities through a system of
cumulative voting. He also definitely abandoned support for the
ballot, arguing that with the decline of influence and intimidation at
elections, the individual voter had an obligation 'to avow and justify
whatever he does affecting the interests of others' publicly. Similarly,
he now opposed payment of MPs, for he believed that this would

tend to produce a class of professional politicians on the American model (Mineka and Lindley 1972: 558, 588).

What Mill had not yet devised was any detailed practicable plan by which minorities could be represented. But within a month of the publication of the 'Thoughts on Parliamentary Reform', he read Thomas Hare's pamphlet on proportional representation, and it came to him like a revelation from heaven. 'The more I think of your plan', he wrote to him, 'the more it appears to me to be *the* great discovery in representative government'. This conviction remained with him until the end of his life, spurred on by a sense of desperate urgency. As he wrote to his friend and disciple, Henry Fawcett, commending Hare's plan, 'in my deliberate belief [it] contains the true solution of the political difficulties of the future. It is an uphill race, and a race against time, for if the American form of democracy overtakes us first, the majority will no more relax their despotism than a single despot would.' (Mineka and Lindley 1972: 653, 672)

The essay on *Representative Government* of 1861, the most elaborate exposition of Mill's views on democracy, was thus not an original treatise but a summary of ideas (as Mill indicated in the Preface) 'which I have been working up during the greater part of my life'. In it Mill saw clearly and expounded powerfully one fundamental argument in favour of democracy: that the rights and interests of the governed can only be secured when they themselves elect the governors (Mill 1910: 209):

> In the absence of its natural defenders, the interest of the excluded is always in danger of being overlooked; and, when looked at, is seen with very different eyes, from those of the persons whom it directly concerns. In this country, for example, what are called the working classes may be excluded from all direct participation in the government . . . does Parliament . . . ever for an instant look at any question with the eyes of a working man?

Moreover, only representative government promoted what in some respects Mill regarded as an even more important prin- ciple – since upon it the very existence of a 'participatory' system depended – the active moral and intellectual qualities of the indi- vidual. Though Mill believed that democracy was superior to any other form of government in the two essential respects of 'its actions upon men, and by its actions upon things; by what it makes of the citizens, and what it does with them' (Mill 1910: 195), he did not believe that a representative assembly was fit to legislate. It was too large, too clumsy and its members too ignorant; the details of lawmaking were better left to a legislative Commission. The primary purpose of an assembly was to deliberate, to act as 'a watch dog over government' and 'to be at once the nation's Committee of Griev- ances, and its Congress of Opinions' (Mill 1910: 239). It was vital, therefore, that a representative assembly should be as truly *representative* as possible.

Mill's discussion on the proper function of a representative assembly linked up with the fears he expressed on 'the tyranny of the majority'. For if all holders of power acted in their own interests, why should a democratic majority be immune? 'One of the greatest dangers, therefore, of democracy, as of all other forms of government, lies in the sinister interest of the holders of power: it is the danger of class legislation; of government intended for (whether really effecting it or not) the immediate benefit of the dominant class.' (Mill 1910: 254) The potential dangers of democracy were compounded, moreover, by the fact that, given the current standard of education in England, it would be founded on a numerical majority of the least educated; a political system could then emerge in which an ignorant majority could rule and ride roughshod over the interests of all others. This was 'false' democracy, since it struck at the very heart of democratic doctrine – the notion of equality; 'true' democracy implied 'government of the whole people by the whole people, equally represented' (Mill 1910: 256). How was this to be secured?

In answering this question, Mill refused to renege on his theoretical commitment to universal suffrage, though he believed that the vote should be limited to those who could pass a simple educational test, who paid taxes and were not on poor relief; and he reiterated his earlier opposition to both the ballot and payment of MPs. This would still mean, however, that the less educated would form a numerical majority, and a reign of 'collective mediocrity' could result, a problem he had already discussed more philosophically in the essay *On Liberty* of 1859. Therefore, developing the ideas already touched on in his earlier pamphlet on Parliamentary Reform, Mill argued in favour of a system of plural voting based not on property but on occupation, which he believed could be roughly equated with character and intelligence so long as the needle was not allowed to swing too far in an anti-democratic direction. His main solution to the problem of the representation of minorities in a democracy, was to support the detailed scheme of Thomas Hare. This plan, by abandoning local constituencies and allowing voters to elect any candidate in any part of the country who obtained more than a fixed number of votes, aimed at ensuring that any and every minority opinion could be represented in the assembly in proportion to its strength. For Mill this would create a truly *representative* assembly which would have the additional advantage of returning able men outside the ranks of majority opinion; men like his friend, the great social reformer, Edwin Chadwick, who found it virtually impossible to get elected under the existing system. Such an assembly would also contain within itself the supreme principle of antagonism – which Mill in *On Liberty* had already seen as a necessary condition of a progressive society – by forcing the majority to confront and test its opinions against the views of minorities. Nevertheless, Mill accepted 'that in the last resort the majority must get its own way, but that it ought not to do so without a struggle' (Ryan 1974: 191).

The wheel had thus come full circle. Mill believed he had now answered satisfactorily the questions he had posed in the 1850s concerning the nature of democracy. 'The great difficulty of democratic government has hitherto seemed to be, how to provide, in a democratic society . . . a social support . . . for individual resistance to the tendencies of the ruling power; a protection, a rallying point, for opinions and interests which the ascendent public opinion views with disfavour.' (Mill 1910: 268) This problem would be solved by an acceptance of Hare's electoral scheme. Moreover, he concluded, 'by combining this principle with the otherwise just one of allowing superiority of weight to superiority of mental qualities, a political constitution would realise that kind of relative perfection which is alone compatible with the complicated nature of human affairs' (Mill 1910: 290). Nor did Mill believe, in opposition to the views of his critics, that his modifications to established Radical doctrine placed him outside the democratic pale. 'If they had really read my writings' he protested, 'they would have known that after giving full weight to all that appeared to me well grounded in the arguments against democracy, I unhesitatingly decided in its favour. . . .' (Mill 1924: 262)

Mill's singular ideas on parliamentary reform, and more especially his support for Thomas Hare's electoral proposals, received little support even in the Radical camp, except for an occasional intellectual such as Henry Fawcett and Lord Amberley. As exemplified by the attitude of Bright, his views were regarded as those of an eminent thinker remote from the realities of political life; and it is true that in his *Representative Government* and elsewhere in his writings, Mill largely ignored the role of political parties and elections in the creation of governments. Yet in the later 1860s, on many issues, Mill's views were close to those of Bright, despite his undoubted antipathy to the ethos of the manufacturing class displayed earlier in his writings and his seeming indifference to the work of the Anti-Corn Law League. Like Bright he was critical of British foreign policy, though he refused to support national disarmament; and however sympathetic he was to the claims of Italian and Polish nationalism he deprecated going to war in their favour in 1859 or 1863 (Mineka and Lindley 1972: 1033 – 34). Both men, above all, supported the cause of the American North firmly and passionately; Mill with less *parti pris* and more intellectual insight into the nature of the conflict than the Birmingham Radical, an attitude that was well displayed in his pungent pamphlet, *The Contest in America* (1862).

It was Mill's support for Lincoln and the North and, increasingly, the democratic cause in Great Britain, that led to his being invited to stand for Parliament in the popular constituency of Westminster. Mill accepted, mainly because as he indicated to his Radical sponsors, it would give him the opportunity to advance his own distinctive views before a new and influential audience. If elected to the House of Commons he would as it were symbolise in his own person the cherished principle of antagonism to conventional beliefs. Mill's candidature thus ranks as one of the most extraordinary in the annals of parliamentary elections, since he refused to canvass, spend any money, concern himself with local affairs or give any pledges on issues other than those that he designated. Nevertheless he was returned triumphantly at the general election of July 1865. As this incident reveals, Mill's stiff-necked commitment to his own idiosyncratic principles was yet coupled with considerable sympathy for working-class aspirations, and a cautious realism where practical politics were concerned. Despite his intellectual idealism, Mill rarely forgot that in the real world only 'relative perfection' applied.

All this comes out in his relations with the Reform League. He refused to join the League, or indeed any other political organisation. 'I think that I can probably do more good as an isolated thinker, forming and expressing my opinions independently', he wrote to the Manchester reformer, T. B. Potter, in March 1865, 'than by associating myself with any collective movement, which, in any case, would almost always imply putting some of my opinions in obeyance.' (Mineka and Lindley 1972: 1014) As he indicated in the same letter, it was the Reform League's commitment to manhood (rather than adult) suffrage and the ballot that he found objectionable. Nevertheless, he gave moral, and some financial, support to the League, and he supported the workers' claim to the vote not only on grounds of principle but because he felt that the upper classes had shown themselves incapable of governing effectively. 'I am hopeless of any improvement but by letting in a powerful influence from those who are the great sufferers by whatever evil is done or is left uncorrected at home.' (Mineka and Lindley 1972: 1209) Thus, despite their theoretical differences, he wrote to Howell, the League's secretary, on the eve of the 1865 election (Mineka and Lindley 1972: 2010–11):

> But I do not the less confidently expect that I shall be found acting in general cooperation with the members of the League, as my opinions on Reform, though in some respects different, are fully as radical as theirs. I think that the general promotion of the Reform cause is the main point at present, and that advanced reformers, without suppressing their opinions on the points on which they may still differ, should act together as one man in the common cause.

Yet, as with Bright, there were limits to Mill's support. He was prepared to address the occasional public meeting; but (as we have seen) he drew the line at supporting mass demonstrations, even when directed at the Conservative government in the summer of 1866. Indeed, he attempted, successfully, to act as a conciliator during the Hyde Park affair and its aftermath in late July, as he records with some self-satisfaction in a famous section of the *Autobiography* (Mill 1924: 246). He followed this up by helping to destroy a later Conservative Bill to ban public meetings in the Royal parks. Early in the New Year, though appreciating the growing working-class irritation at the lack of progress towards reform, he again urged moderation and realism upon their leaders (Mineka and Lindley 1972: 1247–8):

> My conviction is that any Reform Bill capable of being passed at present and for some time to come must be more or less of a compromise ... ultimate success can only in this country be obtained by a succession of steps ... a large portion of the middle and some portion of the higher classes ... would certainly resist a passage all at once from the present distribution of political power to one exactly the reverse. ...

Hence the futility and indeed wickedness of appeals to physical violence, which, Mill felt, were hinted at at some working-class meetings without any real overwhelming justification.

In his attitude to the Reform movement 'out of doors' and to the problems of parliamentary reform discussed within the House of Commons, Mill's political stance was thus closely akin to Bright's. He was after all a Liberal MP as well as a political philosopher, and he took his parliamentary duties seriously. Like Bright, he too fell under the spell of Gladstone. He strongly supported the Liberal Bill of 1866 in an impressive speech that has been touchingly described by his young friend and disciple, Kate Amberley, mother of his godchild, Bertrand Russell (Russell and Russell 1937, vol. 1: 483); and he was crestfallen when the government resigned rather than dissolve and go to the country. As he had earlier indicated, he had entered the House of Commons 'to promote my opinions'. In the debates on the Conservative Bill in the following year he therefore seized the opportunity to introduce amendments in favour of two of his dearest political aims – Hare's proportional representation scheme and female suffrage. The first was attacked by both sides of the House. Bright described Hare's scheme as one of 'peculiar crotchets and dreamy propositions' (Smith 1966: 213); Disraeli subjected it to his characteristic brand of mockery, and it was easily defeated. The famous amendment on female suffrage, though it had no possible chance of success, received the respectable total of seventy-three votes – including Bright's, though later he apostatised.

Yet the failure of his own pet schemes did not prevent Mill from recognising the realities of the parliamentary situation. During the debates on the Conservative Bill between March and July 1867, he

supported with his votes most of the Liberal and Radical amendments introduced (Zimmer 1976). There is much to be said therefore
for Vincent's view that Mill was 'a good party man in Parliament'
(Vincent 1966: 158). And this was true as far as the wider Liberal
programme was concerned. In 1865 when invited to stand for Westminster he had listed the reforms he supported. These included not
only the widening of the suffrage, but religious equality, land and
army reform and improvement in national education – all of which
were dealt with in Gladstone's first ministry (Mineka and Lindley
1972: 1033–4). By that time, however, Mill was no longer an MP.
He lost his Westminister seat in the general election of 1868, the
victim of that 'swing to the right' in outer London seats typical of the
later nineteenth century. He left the House of Commons without any
great regret, believing that his work in stimulating new ideas had
been more or less accomplished. 'It is doubtful', he considered,
'whether there remains anything of the first importance which I could
more effectively help forward by being in Parliament.' (Mineka and
Lindley 1972: 1535)

For the remaining few years of his life, which he spent in France
until his death in 1873, Mill's main political interests were concentrated on supporting Hare's electoral scheme, and in giving
sympathy, support and advice to the burgeoning movement for
women's rights. In 1869 he had published his essay on *The Subjection
of Women*, proclaiming the great principle of 'perfect equality'
between the sexes, 'admitting no power or privilege on the one side,
nor disability on the other' (Mill 1975: 427). Typical of his attitude,
therefore, was the fact that he became one of the leading opponents
of the Contagious Diseases Act, regarding it as an abominable
piece of sexist legislation. He also encouraged working men to stand
for Parliament, and helped them financially to do so, so 'that the
wants, the grievances and the modes of thought and feeling of . . .
the most numerous of all classes' could be heard there, and help to
produce 'wise and just' legislation – a practical example of his views
on the role of minorities in a representative assembly. To the last,
therefore, Mill remained – not a 'book in breeches' as his greatest
Victorian critic, Fitzjames Stephen, averred – but a 'public' thinker,
committed to the union of theory and practice in politics and
convinced of the contribution that the intellectual could make to 'the
improvement of mankind'.

Even apart from his age and eminence, Mill was in many ways an
unrepresentative figure among the intellectual Radicals of mid-
Victorian England. Educated at home by his father according to the
strict tenets of Utilitarian educational theory, he was ignorant of the
life of public school and university and temperamentally averse to
the masculine world of clubs and coteries with which it was linked;
he remained essentially a solitary and independent thinker. The

younger generation of Radical intellectuals, men of the stamp of Henry Fawcett, A. V. Dicey, Goldwin Smith, Leslie Stephen and James Bryce, were pre-eminently university men; it was indeed their concern with the role of the university in a rapidly changing society that helped to push them along the Radical path towards democracy and reform. This was the message of *Essays in Reform*, to which many of them contributed. Published in March 1867, in the middle of the Reform Crisis, it continued in a real sense the debate on democracy as it had been left by Mill in his *Representative Government* of 1861. In ideas and ethos it stands (together with its companion volume, *Questions for a Reformed Parliament*) as the quintessential document of the mid-Victorian intellectual avant-garde.

The twenty-two contributors to the two collections prided themselves on being a group, and they had much in common. Almost all of them were educated at Oxford and Cambridge in the 1850s where they generally distinguished themselves academically; eleven held fellowships at Oxford colleges and three at Cambridge – the *Essays* were in fact largely an Oxford enterprise. In origins they came from middle-class professional, often clerical, families, though one or two had links with the aristocracy. The friendships they built up at school and university were sustained in later life through common intellectual interests and professional work in London, often in journalism or law, which they were now able to combine with their college fellowships; an agreeable arrangement that was facilitated by the new railway links between Oxford and Cambridge and the metropolis opened in the mid-1840s. They also possessed a life-long addiction to club life – the Century Club was founded in London in 1865 especially to accommodate them; and, as with so many members of the Victorian 'intellectual aristocracy', they were prone to intermarriage (Annan 1955).

What made them reformers? The Oxford men particularly were undoubtedly influenced by the liberal atmosphere of their university in the 1850s when, as Mark Pattison wrote in a famous passage of hyperbole, referring to the aftermath of the Oxford Movement, 'Theology was totally banished from the Common Room and even from private conversation. Very free opinions on all subjects were rife; there was a prevailing dissatisfaction with our boasted tutorial system. A restless fever of change had spread through the colleges. . . .' (Pattison 1885: 244–5) The winds of change blew from many directions. A number of the contributors to the *Essays*, even when – like Leslie Stephen and Frederic Harrison – they had abandoned orthodox Christianity, remained deeply moved by the imperatives of evangelicalism with its emphasis on duty, moral seriousness and personal responsibility. Another important influence (often mediated through the ideas of Dr Arnold at a number of colleges was the Coleridgean ideal of a 'national community' led and revivified by a dedicated intellectual élite – the clerisy. A similar notion of élitism was part of the social philosophy of Auguste Comte, whose ideas were becoming known at Oxford in the 1850s mainly as a result of the personal influence of his disciple, Richard Congreve, tutor of Wadham. What Comtism offered to clever young Oxonians was not only the possibility of intellectual leadership and authority, but a new faith – the religion of humanity – and, for those of Radical temper, a commitment to the notion of the working classes as the instrument of social transformation. Many of the younger intellectuals of mid-Victorian England were influenced in some degree by Comtism, and one or two of the Essayists, notably Frederic Harrison and Godfrey Lushington, both ex-pupils of Congreve, became devotees of the Positivist Church. Above all, however, there was the extraordinary intellectual influence of Mill, based at this time mainly on his *Logic*, 'one of those books which capture the mind of a whole generation' (Annan 1951: 141). What Mill's ideas meant to his young disciples of the period has been well depicted by Henry Sidgwick, writing in old age: 'at the time it seemed to me the only possible ideal for all adequately enlightened minds. . . . What we aimed at from a social point of view was a complete revision of human relations, political, moral and economic, in the light of science directed by comprehensive and impartial sympathy. . . .' (Sidgwick and Sidgwick 1906: 39–40)

As a result, therefore, of their common background and experience, the ties of friendship and loyalties, and the influence of the *Zeitgeist*, 'the men of the 1860s retained in most cases as long as they lived, a common vocabulary and a common political agenda'. What this implied was a sharp awareness of the responsibilities of the universities to the wider society of which they were a part, and their own personal commitment to reform and change in order to overcome the alienation of groups and classes outside the ranks of the educationally privileged. Hence their leadership in the campaign for the abolition of religious tests at Oxford and Cambridge which, until finally successful with the Act of 1871, '. . . linked the Universities, Liberal politics, Nonconformity and the intellectual world of London' (Harvie 1976a: 141, 75). The university Radicals were not trying to disturb class relations but to bridge the gap between classes; to replace the deference paid to rank and wealth by a deference based on intellect. The coming of democracy would mean new territories for the cultural and intellectual imperialism of Oxbridge to conquer and evangelise.

Though they were primarily intellectuals, the 'university liberals' were not unaffected by the dramatic political events of their age. As very young men, one or two of them, Frederic Harrison and A. V. Dicey for example, had been deeply moved by the revolutions of 1848; and in the late 1850s and early 1860s they were all enthusiastic supporters of the cause of Italy and Poland. Above all, after some initial doubts, they gave strong support to Lincoln and the North during the American Civil War. Goldwin Smith, in particular, became the leading Oxford protagonist of the Union cause and, like Mill and Bright, he was associated with the Emancipation Society and the great public campaigns which they organised. In 1864 he persuaded Bright to visit Oxford, thus symbolically linking Oxford Radicalism and the democratic cause. 'I see the absolute necessity', he had earlier written to Cobden, 'of struggling for a great measure of Parliamentary reform, as the indispensable condition of every other measure of improvement and justice.' (Harvie 1976a: 120) This growing enthusiasm for democracy did not lead the intellectuals to reach out actively to the working classes or support the Reform organisations in 1865–67. For them, the general election of 1865 was important not because of the role of Bright or the Reform League, but because of the triumph of a number of men of their own kind standing in popular constituencies: Fawcett, Hughes and above all, Mill at Westminster. As the *Pall Mall Gazette* commented: 'the secret of success is not local wealth and proprietory influence . . . but an *entente cordiale* between the educated middle class and the more enterprising leaders in the great underlying masses of society' (Kent 1978: 47).

That *entente cordiale* was to be created principally by the pen rather than the public meeting. Characteristically, the *Essays in Reform* which resulted were, in origins at least, an attempt to reply to the anti-reform speeches of Robert Lowe directed against the Liberal Bill of 1866, and shortly afterwards published as a book: 'the most comprehensive case against democracy expressed in the House of Commons in the nineteenth century' (Briggs 1965: 244). For Lowe was himself an intellectual of the deepest dye – he had been a renowned Oxford tutor; and, disconcertingly, he used Utilitarian arguments to justify his opposition to democracy. Hence one of the main purposes of the *Essays* was to discredit the arguments of the opponents of reform, especially Lowe, and this was the task undertaken by G. C. Brodrick in the opening essay. Brodrick, more in sorrow than in anger, criticised Lowe's Utilitarian case against reform, based on its likely material consequences, by arguing that the notion of 'political justice' which moved the minds of the working classes but was ignored by Lowe, was just as much a part of the Utilitarian calculus as more material factors. The reformers' support for the vote, therefore, was also based on tests 'of experience'. In any case such arguments were strictly academic, the coming of democracy was inevitable: 'how frail are the barriers of reaction against the giant forces struggling to overcome them' (Guttsman 1967: 30–1). Similarly, as C. H. Pearson and Goldwin Smith pointed out in their respective essays on Australian and American institutions, the arguments adduced by the opponents of reform that democracy in those two countries meant the rule of 'money and the mob', and, by analogy, such would be the fate of this country if the vote was extended to the working classes, were false. The experience of Australia and the United States was a reflection not of democracy *per se*, but of their special history and circumstances.

More important in the *Essays* were the positive arguments in favour of extending the suffrage, though none of the contributors defended or expected a system of universal suffrage. One of the major justifications advanced was that such a reform would lead to the introduction of a 'new element' into the House of Commons; for the upper ranks of the working classes embraced those ideals of cooperation, unity and unselfishness which the House and the political system at large needed so desperately (Guttsman 1967: 43). Moreover, since the working classes possessed an acute sense of 'social progress' (in A. O. Rutson's phrase), their enfranchisement and entry into the Commons would force the members to take note of and tackle the vast array of social problems – health, housing, education, poverty – that cried out for redress. What in any case was the alternative? At the moment the governing classes could rely on a fair degree of goodwill on the part of the artisans for the established Constitution. Surely, therefore, it would be both wise and prudent to buttress that support by 'subtracting a portion of the besieging force and adding it to the governors'? (Guttsman 1967: 31) To oppose the workers' demand for the vote would be to expose society to even greater dangers. It would turn tolerance of the established order into hatred and suspicion, and force the workers back upon their 'instincts and passions' by failing to provide them with the opportunity for the exercise of moderation and reason that the franchise could ensure. 'If we will not teach them political wisdom, they will teach us political disaster', concluded Lord Houghton; 'the real danger', added Bryce perceptively, 'is not from the working classes, but from the isolation of classes' (Guttsman 1967: 59, 180).

The tone of these arguments clearly owed much to Mill; and indeed underlying the *Essays in Reform* was the Millite assumption that the individual's participation in politics was a good in itself, irrespective of its consequences. Bryce wrote (quoted in Guttsman 1967: 174):

It is undeniable that democracy . . . has a stimulating power such as belongs to no other form of government. By giving the sense of a common interest and purpose it gives unity and strength to the whole State; it raises the rich and powerful by obliging them to retain their influence not by privilege so much as by energy and intellectual eminence; it elevates the humbler classes by enlarging their scope of vision and their sense of responsibility.

Yet in terms of political reform the Essayists were much more within the mainstream of Radical doctrine than Mill. Hare's views on proportional representation were almost completely ignored by J. B. Kinnear in his article on 'Redistribution of seats', which supported the sort of traditional redistribution scheme based on equal constituencies later embodied in the Act of 1885. Similarly, Thorold Rogers on 'Bribery' (in *Questions for a Reformed Parliament*) strongly supported the ballot as one of the two essentials 'for the legitimate development of a representative system' (the other was the 'transfer of all electoral expenses from the candidate to the constituency' which Mill supported) and curtly dismissed Mill's theoretical objections to secrecy in exercising the vote (Guttsman 1967: 109). Nor was there any consideration of the vexed question of women's rights, a subject on which the contributors were hopelessly divided.

Even more important was the Essayists' scepticism towards Mill's views on the consequences of democracy. It was not only that they objected to schemes for giving representation to minorities because it undermined their ideal of national unity. They believed that Mill's arguments in favour of his various trip-wires against the power of a numerical majority – Hare's scheme and the rest – were misplaced. Mill argued that they were necessary in order to make it more difficult for such a majority to take over the state and use it in its own interests. But the Essayists argued that this view followed from Mill's over-simplified and over-intellectualised conception of British politics. What was important was not who possessed a numerical majority in voting power, but what were the determinants of voting behaviour – what forces really shaped the character of a political system; and in a society as deferential and as subtly organised as England's, wealth, rank and its concomitants were, and would continue to be, the greatest of these forces.

Leslie Stephen, for example, commented on what he called 'the occult and unacknowledged forces which are not dependent upon any legislative machinery'. 'When we consider', he went on, 'the enormous power which the upper classes can exert, either by the means of money or by the prestige of rank and birth, we may fairly doubt whether any extension of the suffrage would materially alter the composition of Parliament.' (Guttsman 1967: 82–3) Bernard Cracroft, in a highly original essay, attempted to show in detail how through the 'system of indirect representation' the power of the aristocracy in the House of Commons had remained almost unimpaired, despite forty years of social and economic change (Guttsman 1967: 118).

> They have a common freemasonry of blood, a common education, common pursuits, common ideas, a common dialect, a common religion, and – what more then any other thing binds men together – a

common prestige, a prestige grumbled at occasionally, but on the whole conceded, and even, it must be owned, secretly liked by the country at large. All these elements, obvious in themselves, but difficult to measure and gauge, go to make up that truly and without exaggeration tremendous content of power . . . which constitutes the indirect representation of the aristocracy in the House of Commons.

How could the democracy thwart this ancient and formidable power? Under any Reform Bill, Cracroft concluded, the same classes who wielded political power would continue to wield it. The real difference would be, he shrewdly added, 'that as the constituencies change, so will those who study their favours, and they will take problems, social and political, into consideration which they hitherto ignored' (Guttsman 1967: 118, 127).

Despite these insights, the practical influence of the *Essays in Reform* was negligible: they seem to have had no impact on the House of Commons or on the course of the Reform debates in 1867. They were, however, well received by the press and the reviews; even their opponents were impressed. Lowe admitted in the *Quarterly*: '. . . we owe some respect to the writers who have endeavoured to put into a permanent form the principles of the new order of things, and we take leave of them with the frank admission that though we cannot accept them for our teachers, they are undoubtedly our masters' (Lowe 1867). In this sense the achievement of the 'university liberals' was, as their historian suggests, 'the assimilation by the English upper middle class of the new vocabulary of political democracy' (Harvie 1976a: 13). It is doubtful whether their companion volume, *Questions for a Reformed Parliament*, published in April 1867, had even that elusive quality. While a number of the *Essays in Reform* revealed a considerable degree of insight and originality in political analysis, the later collection all too often displayed the baleful effects of the writers' limited experience and outlook; hence the timid and second-hand quality of much of the writing. While a number of essays featured some of the sacred cows of middle-class Radicalism – law, the land, education, the poor – there was no attempt to get to grips with any of the fundamental problems of an industrial society, or to go beyond the customary formulae of classical political economy. On the whole a rather worthy conventionality shrouded the *Questions for a Reformed Parliament*. 'We all assumed individualism as obviously and absolutely right', Bryce noted to Dicey fifty years later. 'We were not indifferent to the misfortunes of the poor, but looked on them as inevitable.' (Harvie 1976a: 159).

If *Essays in Reform* was the manifesto of the intellectual avant-garde, its journalistic right arm was undoubtedly the *Fortnightly Review*. The *Fortnightly* had been founded in 1865 by a group of liberal writers and publishers, including Anthony Trollope, Edward

Chapman and James Cotter Morison. Its purpose – as announced in its Prospectus – was 'to further the cause of progress by illumination from many minds' (Everett 1939: 332): and at first, under the editorship of George Henry Lewes, the new journal tried to maintain an eclectic and non-partisan tone. This proved difficult. Under the new editor, John Morley, appointed at the end of 1866, the *Fortnightly* became 'an organ of liberalism, free-thinking and open enquiry' (Trollope 1980: 191); and the superb vigour and brilliance with which Morley carried out his task, made the *Fortnightly* easily the outstanding Radical journal of the 1860s and 1870s. In outlook and sympathies John Morley may therefore be associated with the contributors to the *Essays in Reform*, though in some ways his background was different from theirs. He too belonged to the professional middle classes; his father was a surgeon at Blackburn and he was educated at Cheltenham College. On the other hand he came from a Nonconformist background (though his father soon abandoned Chapel for Church) and he was one of the very few intellectual Radicals of the time who had any personal experience of northern industrial England. Like many of the Essayists he was up at Oxford in the 1850s, but his career there was brief and disappointing. As a result of his 'loss of faith' Morley abandoned his intention of becoming a clergyman, whereupon his father refused to support him financially for a full honours course at Oxford and he took a pass degree in 1859 and went off to London. There, as an ambitious, hard-working and talented journalist and biographer, he soon achieved a growing reputation.

Morley was in many ways a touchstone for the influences and currents of thought of the age. Despite his rebellion at Oxford, he was never really able to shake off the moral impact of the 'stiff evangelicalism' of his birthplace (Morley 1918, vol. 1: 4). In the 1860s he was strongly affected by the ideas of Comte: partly through his friendship and respect for Frederic Harrison, partly because of his quest for a substitute faith that would embody his belief in order, progress and intellectual leadership. The biographies of the French thinkers of the Enlightenment that he produced in the 1870s reflect in many ways, as he admitted, the Comtist theory of history; and, like Harrison and the English Positivists, he believed in a real sense that the working class was the heir to all the ages. Yet in the end (like Mill) he was unable to stomach the certitudes of the full Positivist faith. 'I accept your statement of the Positive Problem', he wrote to Harrison in 1871, 'I do not accept your solution – certainly not Comte's new organisation, which I actively dislike . . . I believe I shall become more and more Millite, less and less Comtist. . . .' (Hirst 1927, vol. 1: 199–200) It was indeed Mill who was, finally, the most profound influence on Morley. As an undergraduate he was supposed to have known *On Liberty* almost by heart; and his unswerving allegiance to Mill's political philosophy – in his own rather *simpliste* interpretation – was enhanced by the personal friendship and sympathy of the great man after their meeting in London in 1865. Mill, he wrote to Helen Taylor after the philosopher's death, had 'the gift of intellectual fatherhood . . . the best and wisest man that I can ever know . . . whose memory will always be as precious to me as to a son' (Hamer 1968: 26). Morley established himself as chief incense-burner to the Saint of Rationalism, and in many ways the *Fortnightly* under his editorship was an intellectual memorial to the dead master.

Most of the liberal writers of the age contributed: poets and novelists such as Hardy, Meredith and George Eliot, as well as the more predominant group of writers on social, economic and political affairs – Bagehot, Harrison, Goldwin Smith, Beesly and Leslie Stephen. It was in the pages of the *Fortnightly* that Harrison's important articles on trade unionism first appeared, as well as the serialisation of Bagehot's *The English Constitution*, and later Morley's own *On Compromise*. As editor, Morley continued the policy insisted upon from the first issue, of signed articles, as compared with the tradition in the 'higher journalism' of anonymity. In this way he asserted the principle of personal responsibility, and at the same time encouraged vigorous and controversial writing. Morley's editorial direction thus helped to raise the status of journalism as a profession and, through its tone and the personnel of its contributors, placed the *Fortnightly* clearly within the orbit of the university Radicals.

Like them, Morley aimed to influence public opinion, and especially educated middle-class opinion, in favour of his ideals of progress and enlightenment; and, though the circulation of the *Fortnightly* remained tiny by modern standards – about 2,500 in 1872 – Morley claimed at about the same date that it had 30,000 readers 'of the influential class' (Kent 1978: 115). Like the Fabians of a later generation, it was men of influence and power whom he hoped to re-educate and prepare for the major task that would confront them as leaders of the new democracy. 'What we all have to seek', he told Harrison, 'is the modification and instruction of the current feelings and judgements of our countrymen. This is the only way to ripen them for change'. (Hirst 1927, vol. 1–188). Here he was thinking particularly of outstanding politicians with popular appeal who, suitably nurtured with *Fortnightly* ideals, would propagate them abroad, especially among the working classes. Hence the encouragement Morley gave to Joseph Chamberlain to publish his reflections on the Liberal Party in the *Review* in 1873–74. The *Fortnightly* would thus become an intellectual powerhouse diffusing through the different layers of society the ethos and ideas of the Radical élite it represented. Morley had always believed, as he later argued in detail in his élitist manifesto *On Compromise*, that the intellectuals were the creative force in society, the vanguard of progress. The coming of democracy – and here he joined hands with the Essayists – would reinforce and strengthen their distinctive role by uniting 'brains and numbers' (Morley 1867):

> For the future whoever attempts to estimate the direction and momentum of social tendencies in this country must count upon a close and ever-increasing sympathy between culture and democratic opinions. . . . The extreme advanced party is likely for the future to have on its side a great portion of the most highly cultivated intellect in the nation, and the contest will be between brains and numbers on the one side, and wealth, rank, vested interest, possession in short, on the other.

Despite his belief in the mission of the *Fortnightly Review* John Morley, like a number of his fellow intellectuals, was fascinated by the political life and stimulated by the example of Mill's candidature for Parliament in 1865. At the general election of 1868 he failed to secure nomination; but about a score of intellectual Radicals stood as Liberal candidates, and nine were elected, including just one contributor to the *Essays in Reform*, C. S. Parker. The number of such MPs increased in the elections of the 1880s. Morley himself was eventually returned for Newcastle in 1883, and the apogee of the intellectuals' success came at the general election of 1885 when twenty-five stood and eighteen were returned. Yet their political record was not very impressive. 'What', Matthew Arnold asked of these 'lights of liberalism', 'has been produced with their help? Really, very much the same sort of thing which was produced without it.' (Harvie 1976a: 9). Even the most successful of them in terms of political rewards, Morley and Bryce, loyal Gladstonians, holders of minor office, and eventually Liberal peers, were not very effective political figures. 'The inner conflict between the man of letters and the man of politics in Morley', suggested T. P. O'Connor, 'pursued and paralysed him all through his life' (Hammer 1968: 59); and this was true perhaps of his contemporaries and indeed some of his successors.

If these 'intellectuals in politics' found parliamentary life a chastening experience, those who remained outside, however successful they were in their chosen professions, discovered the political atmosphere of the 1870s and 1880s to be increasingly unpalatable. 'How is this wild force of democracy to be tamed?', asked Leslie Stephen in 1875, contemplating the fruits of the Second Reform Act (Stephen 1875). It was a question that haunted the minds of many intellectuals of the period, and helped to account for the revulsion against liberal political thought associated with the writings of Fitzjames Stephen and Henry Maine (Roach 1957). What worried them was the growth of 'socialistic' legislation by a House of Commons whose power – as

A. V. Dicey argued in his classic study of 1885, *The Law of the Constitution* – was now virtually illimitable (Cosgrove 1981), and the increasing identification of Gladstone with the 'passions' of the masses against the 'reason' of the educated classes. These fears led men like Leslie Stephen eventually to turn their backs on the Radicalism of their early life and abjure political interests almost entirely; it led men such as Dicey and George Brodrick to abandon the Liberal Party and end up as virtual Unionists.

The career of Brodrick is in fact almost a paradigm of the political development of many members of the Radical intelligentsia in the Age of Gladstone. In 1867 (as we have seen) Brodrick had contributed a forthright attack on Robert Lowe's criticism of democracy to *Essays on Reform*. Ten years later he had become one of the leading intellectual defenders of a tepid liberalism whose primary function was, he argued, to act as 'a stable regulator . . . a moderating and steadying force in the political machinery' against working-class pressure, fostered by Birmingham Radicalism, from below (Brodrick 1878). By 1883, at the height or Gladstone's second ministry, he was rapidly becoming disenchanted with democracy, and saw, unhappily, the verification of 'too many of the predictions' contained in those speeches of Lowe that he had denounced nearly twenty years before (Brodrick 1900: 222). Democracy had its obvious merits, Brodrick believed, but those necessary props which could alone restrain it within moderate bounds – the forces of privilege, authority and individuality – were being knocked away (Brodrick 1883). This was due not only to the prevailing scepticism in every department of thought, but to the degeneration of political principle into mere vote-catching. 'In a word, that which in France is called "opportunism" has become the guiding law of modern politics, and opportunism is but another name for subservience to democratic absolutism.' What then could counter the progress of democracy? Brodrick's answer was, by 'cultivating and elevating the nobler conceptions of citizenship and statesmanship'. 'If', he went on, 'Democracy will not endure Privilege and Authority, it must learn to yield ungrudging loyalty to intellectual and moral ascendancy.' (Brodrick 1883)

This *crise de conscience* within the ranks of the 'university liberals' was brought to a head by the Home Rule Crisis in 1886. Many of them opposed Home Rule because it seemed to be the apotheosis of all those features of democracy about which they were most uneasy; they drifted towards Liberal Unionism – 'a political party run by intellectuals for intellectuals' (Harvie 1976b). G. M. Trevelyan wrote in a well-known passage of his father's break with Gladstone in 1886: 'The intellectual and literary society of London and the Universities in which he had lived and moved all his life had been mainly Liberal; it now become mainly Unionist, nourishing hot detestation of Gladstone and moral reprobation of his followers.'

(Trevelyan 1932: 124) Another Cambridge man, Henry Sidgwick, wrote early in 1886: 'The anti-Gladstonian feeling seems growing and hardening at least among the people I meet . . . I am moved to write about politics, chiefly to mark, with some alarm, the extent of my alienation from current Liberalism. We are drifting on to what must be a national disaster and the forces impelling are Party organisation and Liberal principles.' (Sidgwick and Sidgwick 1906: 436)

The reaction by members of the sister university was even stronger. George Brodrick, now Warden of Merton, contributed an article to the *Liberal Unionist* 'designed to show the hollowness, as well as the wickedness, of Mr. Gladstone's attempt to set instinct above reason, and popular judgement against cultivated opinion' (Brodrick 1900: 328). It was an argument which was expressed, more fastidiously, by the greatest Oxford critic of the age – Matthew Arnold (Arnold 1886, 1887). Even Goldwin Smith, the idol of the university reformers in the 1850s and the scourge of the Whigs in the 1870s, threw himself into the campaign in 1886 as an ardent Unionist, impressed particularly – as befitted a man who was now a professor in the New World – by American experience. 'You fought for your Union against Slavery', he told an American friend, 'We are fighting for ours against Savagery and Superstition.' (Wallace 1957: 92) 'Threatened with disruption', he wrote in an article in the same year, 'the nation naturally and rightly rallies round its existing institutions'; parliamentary reform was now needed, he believed, to 'check, regulate and temper' democracy (Goldwin Smith 1886). And the constitutional argument against Home Rule received its most impressive and trenchant exposition at the hands of A. V. Dicey (Dicey 1886).

Brodrick, Goldwin Smith, Dicey: these had all been leading contributors to *Essays in Reform* in 1867. Only one notable Essayist who was alive in 1886 supported Gladstone and Home Rule – James Bryce – and even he did so 'in despair'. Out of the whole group of twenty Essayists then alive, eleven went Unionist, and only seven remained loyal to Gladstone. Here, in this Victorian *trahison des clercs*, we have the true 'paradise lost of Liberalism', in Fitzjames Stephen's evocative phrase; a loss rendered even more poignant by the fact that, as Christopher Harvie has suggested, the Essayists' shift in political allegiance was 'really a political miscalculation which most of them lived to regret' (Harvie 1976a: 175). Be that as it may, the Home Rule Crisis of 1886 ended the cohesion of the group of intellectuals associated in mid-Victorian England with the *Essays in Reform*, *Questions for a Reformed Parliament* and the *Fortnightly Review*.

Chapter 4

THE GROWTH OF MILITANT NONCONFORMITY

In a famous phrase Gladstone described the Nonconformists as 'the backbone of British Liberalism', but the process by which they became associated with the Liberal Party, and more particularly its Radical wing, was a slow and tortuous one. It is true that the history and traditions of 'Old Dissent' – the Independents, Presbyterians, Baptists and Quakers of the later seventeenth and eighteenth centuries – inclined them towards religious and political freedom; and in the 1790s some Dissenters, notably Drs Price and Priestley, were leading members of the Radical movement. In the early years of the nineteenth century, however, the English Dissenting communities were, at least politically, largely quiescent. This was partly due to their attempt to dissociate themselves from the charge of subversion in an age of war and social unrest; partly because of a renewed concentration on their evangelical mission. It was also the result of their own internal divisions, divisions which were worsened by the rise of Methodism, and the various offshoots which developed out of the main Wesleyan stem in the generation following the death of the founder in 1795. Moreover, mainstream Wesleyans were divided from their Dissenting brethren by their reverence for the Anglican Establishment and their sympathies with Toryism, as well as the 'no politics' rule imposed upon them by their 'Pope', Jabez Bunting. In any case, even if the penal laws against them remained idle, the character of the unreformed political system offered little scope for Dissenting political activity. This was borne out by the simple fact that they possessed only two MPs in the House of Commons in the 1820s, John Wilks and William Smith, the moderate leaders of the campaign for the removal of Dissenting disabilities.

Yet the character and outlook of Dissent was bound to be transformed by the reforming impulse of the age, and even more so by the extraordinary expansion in the number of Dissenters in the first half of the nineteenth century (Gilbert 1976). This was a phenomenon that affected mainly the ranks of the so-called 'New Dissent' –

the Methodists especially, but also branches of the Congregation-alists and Baptists. The result was that, as the famous Religious Census of 1851 revealed, by mid-century the Nonconformists (as they had begun to call themselves in the 1840s) numbered nearly 5 millions compared with less than 2 millions at the end of the eighteenth century, almost as many as the adherents of the Church of England. Geographically, this Nonconformist expansion was centred on the new industrial cities of the North and Midlands, Wales and scattered rural communities mainly in the West of England and East Anglia; London remained almost completely untouched. Socially, it embraced largely the middle classes and the artisans – the industrial proletariat and the very poor were largely unaffected (Inglis 1960).

This massive growth in numbers was accompanied inevitably by vigorous activity in all branches of Nonconformist life. Missionary and educational work increased; sectarian organization was devel-oped and improved at both local and national level – the Congre-gational and Baptist Unions date from 1831–32; 'defence' societies proliferated – though many were short-lived – as adjuncts to the senior, respectable, London-based organization of Dissenting Depu-ties formed in the early eighteenth century; new journals and news-papers appeared, all of which discussed social and political as well as purely religious topics, often – as with Miall's *Nonconformist* – from a liberal or Radical point of view (Salter 1953). Nonconformity in the first half of the nineteenth century was humming with new life and growing in wealth, influence and self-confidence; inspired by a communitarian culture which, despite the later notorious animad-versions of Matthew Arnold in *Culture and Anarchy*, its adherents found invigorating and fulfilling. Nevertheless, it was a culture which, as the autobiographical writings of Mark Rutherford clearly show, marked them off from the world of the religious and political Estab-lishment; a division symbolized by the differences between the aristocratic Anglican Rector, Rev. Augustus Debarry, and the Independent pastor, Rufus Lyon, in George Eliot's *Felix Holt the Radical*. The wider implications of the New Dissent were evident: a commitment to Nonconformity 'could be a symbolic rejection of the mores and values of a social system which ascribed status largely in terms of inherited advantages of landed wealth and family back-ground' (Gilbert 1976: 83–4).

The first hesitant political steps were taken in the 1820s when, under the shrewd leadership of William Smith MP, the various Dissenting communities combined together to press, successfully, for the repeal of the outmoded Test and Corporation Acts, though the final measure of 1828 was due more to the calculations of politicians faced by the greater threat of Catholic Emancipation, than to Dissenting pressure (Davis 1966). Nevertheless, the Act of 1828 was at least a symbolic victory, and was followed by 'a new agressive confidence' (Thompson 1972: 22). The Great Reform Bill of 1832 increased Dissenting political consciousness even more through the opportunities it presented for electoral influence in the boroughs. As the Duke of Wellington commented sourly: 'The revolution is made, that is to say, that power is transferred from one class of society, the gentlemen of England, professing the faith of the Church of England, to another class of society, the shopkeepers, being dissenters from the Church . . .'; though he added – a salutary warning against exaggeration – 'the gentry have as many followers and influence as many voters at elections as ever they did' (Thompson 1972: 83). It was at the local level in fact rather than in Parliament that the Dissenters made the greatest advance. The Municipal Corporations Act of 1835 gave them the chance for power in the new elected borough councils, which they successfully exploited in a number of provincial cities and towns; Manchester, Liverpool, Leicester – 'the metropolis of Dissent' – Colchester and later Birmingham, where powerful Nonconformist-commercial élites came to dominate municipal life (Patterson 1975; Briggs 1968).

What the Dissenters now wanted, was to turn the purely legal equality granted to them in 1828 into practical reality by the remedy of their major religious and educational grievances: the enforcement of compulsory church rate, restrictions on their control over births, marriages and burials, and the Anglican monopoly at Oxford and Cambridge. To achieve this programme of reform, the majority looked to their traditional allies, the Whigs, the party of religious equality, hoping that their growing social and political influence would act as a spur. But in the end the Dissenters' hopes went largely unrewarded: a Civil Registration Act gave them what they mainly wanted over births and marriages, the undenominational University of London got its Royal Charter – but that was all. Russell abandoned his attempt to deal with church rates, a subject which aroused passionate resentment in the 1830s owing to a number of well-publicized *causes célèbres* in which Dissenters were imprisoned for non-payment. By the later 1830s the ailing government of Melbourne and Russell lacked either the will or the power to do very much for its religious friends, especially as the Whig gentry on the back-benches were almost as stalwart defenders of compulsory church rate as their Tory counterparts. Inevitably, the Dissenting MPs and their allies drifted towards the Radicals. But if 'Dissent . . . had become a political phenomenon of startling potential', there was, as yet, severe limits on its political effectiveness. After 1832 there were still only a handful of Dissenting MPs, and the surface unity among the communities, skilfully built up in the 1820s, concealed sharp differences over policy towards Roman Catholics, and education – soon to come to the surface. Nor had they any electoral organization of their own, or a formidable and inspiring leader.

As Edward Miall asserted after the great Conservative victory of 1841 shattered the hopes of the Nonconformists even further, they were 'a disbanded army feared by no one' (Sellers 1977: 68, 70). It was Miall who offered a new strategy to his co-religionists, and the skill and fervour with which he developed it made him, in the 1840s and 1850s, the outstanding leader of militant Dissent.

Miall came from a London lower-middle-class family, and had been a Congregational minister in Leicester in the 1830s. In 1839 he gave up the pastorate and became (in his own phrase) a 'strolling agitator', devoting the rest of his life to the cause of militant Nonconformity as lecturer, author, journalist and, eventually, MP between 1852–57 and 1869–74. In 1841, believing that Nonconformity needed a more powerful mouthpiece for its views, he conducted a nation-wide campaign to raise money and support for the foundation of a new newspaper; the result was the *Nonconformist* of which he became editor. The timing was right: the new journal soon achieved a sound circulation and 'brought into the open an articulate broad-bottomed Nonconformist consciousness' (Binfield 1977: 111).

Miall's first purpose as editor was to stir his fellow Nonconformists from their complacency and political innocence by convincing them of the futility of relying for the redress of their grievances on the whims and favours of Parliament alone. 'What have you gained from your silence and morality? Not peace. . . . All parties agree in neglecting and oppressing you.' In any case, he argued, no real advance towards religious equality in practical matters could be expected while the greatest and most glaring example of religious inequality existed in all its pride and arrogance – the Established Church of England. Only the disestablishment and disendowment of that Church could really destroy the Nonconformists' status as second-class citizens. 'The primary object of the *Nonconformist*', he stated succinctly, 'is to show that a national establishment of religion is essentially vicious in its constitution, philosophically, politically and religiously; to bring under public notice the innumerable evils of which it is the parent; to arouse men . . . from the fatal apathy with which they regard its continuance and extension. . . .' He attacked the 'evils' of the Church Establishment with a venom and immoderate zeal unknown perhaps since the days of John Wade's *Black Book* at the beginning of the century. 'The whole thing is a stupendous money-scheme carried on under false pretences . . . a bundle of vested rights . . . an affair of livings and benefices, and baronial bishops. . . .' The Church of England was merely part and parcel of the aristocratic settlement of England – dependent upon it and supporting it; and the disendowment of its property – with due compensation – would only mean returning to the people of England the wealth that was truly theirs. Religiously, disestablishment would lead to gain rather than loss for the Church of England, for *true* religion was incompatible with state control (Miall 1884: 27–8, 51, 62).

Miall's religious Radicalism went further. Religious equality implied political equality: hence he supported the extension of the suffrage, and was sympathetic to the Chartist demands, especially as a fundamental reform of Parliament would make it more amenable to Nonconformist pressure. He was one of the middle-class Radicals who attended the discussions with the Chartists at the Birmingham Conference of 1842; and he supported Joseph Sturge's Complete Suffrage Union that emerged from it. Many Nonconformists of course, especially those associated with the Evangelical Associations, shied away from Miall's identification of Nonconformity with political Radicalism. But another reason for his attempted cooperation with the Chartists, was his wish to break down the barriers that existed, religiously as well as politically, between the middle and the working classes, especially as Nonconformity became more middle class in spirit as the nineteenth century progressed. As Miall noted sadly in his later study of *The British Churches and the British People* (1849), writing of his own community: 'Communion with God has not disposed them to communion with each other beyond the well-defined boundaries of class.' (Inglis 1963: 19) Yet though Miall saw keenly the nature of the problem, he had no real solution to offer. Even his Radicalism was in the end limited to support for household suffrage; and (as Clyde Binfield suggests) the priority he gave to sound principles and righteous conduct as the remedies for social improvement ultimately divided him from the aspirations of the working-class movement (Binfield 1977: 105).

The call for disestablishment remained a theoretical issue in the 1840s. It was the more immediate practical problem of educational policy that aroused the passions of the Nonconformist sects, and helped to impose upon them, once again, a rather fragile unity. Their approach to this question was based on the clear-cut if ultimately stultifying theory of voluntaryism; that is, they were opposed in principle to state control or interference in religion and, therefore, by extension, with what lay within the sphere of religion. The commitment to voluntaryism in education was thus, like its twin notion, disestablishment, a reaction against the slights of the 1830s, though it also reflected an aspect of the Nonconformist religious tradition. 'Education is a branch of civil liberty', as Priestley observed in the eighteenth century, 'which ought by no means to be surrendered into the hands of the magistrate.' (Kitson Clark 1950: 119) The voluntaries (as they came to be known) were of course supported by Miall; but their outstanding leader was Edward Baines, proprietor of the *Leeds Mercury*, MP for the city, and a moderate in politics.

Their first test came in 1843 when Sir James Graham, the Tory Home Secretary, included provisions for the compulsory part-time education of factory children in his proposed Factory Bill. This seemed to extend even further the educational powers of the Anglican clergy; and, though Graham retreated, his Bill was greeted with cries of protest from Nonconformists, including even the Wesleyans. It was, asserted Baines, 'educational dictatorship', 'a church extension scheme' in the words of the *Eclectic Review* (Ward 1972: 250; Machin 1977: 156).Graham bowed to the storm and withdrew the Bill.

It was the euphoria produced by this success, together with the inspiration of the Anti-Corn Law League's organization, that helped to produce in the following year, 1844, the Anti-State Church Society – 'the fulfilment of Miall's dream' (Thompson 1974: 214). The impetus for the society came from the provincial Nonconformists under the leadership of Miall; but they soon obtained the support of their London brethren, led by Rev. F. A. Cox, and in the Executive Council the latter acted as a moderating influence on his more militant colleague. The new society demanded: 'that the application by law of the resources of the State to the maintenance of any form or forms of religious worship and institutions, is contrary to reason, hostile to liberty, and directly opposed to the genius of Christianity' (Miall 1884: 96).Renamed after 1853 and known popularly as 'The Liberation Society', it was this new organization that became the first of the great, single-aim, militant Nonconformist pressure groups, committed to the disestablishment and disendowment of the Church of England, though it worked also for the attainment of other lesser Nonconformist objectives. The Society gradually established an effective organization, based on a central council concerned mainly with parliamentary and electoral affairs, and local committees, agents and lecturers responsible for propaganda and finance. Its expansion in the 1850s and 1860s owed much to the enthusiasm and vigour of its permanent secretary, Carvell Williams, appointed in 1847.

Another furore broke out in 1845 over the state's role in education, when Peel proposed to give a government grant to the Roman Catholic seminary, Maynooth College. This revealed once again the divisions within Nonconformity, since though the majority of Dissenters opposed the grant on the voluntarist principle of opposition to *any* state support for education, a moderate section, led by Rev. John Blackburn, an opponent of Miall and the Anti-State Church Association, was prepared to cooperate on friendly terms with the Anglican supporters of the Anti-Maynooth Committee. This attempt at a protestant 'popular front' was anathema to the militants. In addition, on this issue, the voluntaries were divided from such leading Radicals as Hume, Roebuck and Cobden – who burst out: 'We are all being plagued to death with the fanatics about the Maynooth grant. The Dissenters and the Church people have joined together to put the screw upon the members. However, I expect that Peel will carry his measure by a large majority.' (Morley 1903: 328)And so it proved: though, since the Tory Party was itself split on the issue, Peel had to rely on the votes of Whigs and Radicals to push the Bill through.

It was the Maynooth controversy that helped to widen the breach between Nonconformity and the Whigs, and led the militants to consider establishing their own electoral organization in order to increase their parliamentary strength. This move towards 'independence' was accelerated by the new educational proposals of Russell when the Whigs returned to office in 1846. The Prime Minister's plans to increase and reallocate the educational grants to the voluntary societies, and raise the number of HMIs, was – as in 1843 – interpreted by most Nonconformists as a further sop to the Church of England, though on this occasion the Wesleyans were prepared to go along with the government. A protest movement was again organized, but in the end the Bill went through by a massive majority. The Church of England gained the lion's share of the grants, and the Wesleyans received their portion. The government was again supported by a number of leading Radicals, including Cobden, who later complained to Baines, 'I suppose all parties agree that education is the main cause of the split among the middle-class Liberals.' (Morley 1903: 495) All this makes Professor Cowherd's identification of 'free traders' and 'voluntaries' in the 1840s as part of a new Liberal bloc, an exceedingly dubious one (Cowherd 1956: 163).

The most important outcome of the new round in the educational controversy was the formation of the Dissenters' Parliamentary Committee, under the chairmanship of Samuel Morley, to oppose the 'insidious encroachments of the State' and prepare for an independent role at the next general election. 'This design can be met and frustrated only by a firm enunciation of our principles in the House of Commons. The great battle of the age must be fought there.' This was followed by an appeal in June 1847 to the Nonconformist Electors of Great Britain, in which it was argued that, through independent electoral pressure, they might achieve a 'balance of parties' in the House of Commons (Hodder 1887: 101, 104). 'The connection between Dissent and Reform-club Liberalism', announced Miall, 'is at an end.' (Binfield 1977: 112) A foretaste of the new strategy had already been seen at the Southwark by-election of September 1845, when Miall himself stood in opposition to the official Whig candidate, Sir William Molesworth, a Radical, but opposed to voluntaryism. He was ignominiously defeated by 353 votes to Molesworth's 1942. Yet he remained undeterred. 'What we have done herein we have done advisedly . . . the time in our judgement is now come to pass on to another and more advanced stage of our undertaking. . . .' (Miall 1884: 126) The aim now was to widen rather than limit Nonconformist electoral action: by 1847, therefore, 'a specific, unaligned and determined Nonconformist party had at last emerged' (Sellers 1977: 73).

The strategy adopted by Miall, Baines and their friends in the 1847 general election, was to blackball all candidates who had voted either for the Maynooth Grant or the Russell Education Bill, and urge Nonconformists in their constituencies either to vote for a voluntaryist candidate – though only forty-six stood – or abstain. The thrust of the Electoral Committee's displeasure was directed mainly against Whigs and Radicals, and, in particular, at three MPs – Macaulay at Edinburgh, Roebuck at Bath and Russell in the City of London – who were regarded as especially blameworthy in their opposition to the voluntaryist position. As Machin notes, the Nonconformists did rather better in the end than they have been given credit for (Machin 1967). Though Lord John kept his seat, both Roebuck and Macaulay lost theirs. In addition, there were gains in the London boroughs, and at Bradford, though elsewhere in the West Riding Miall and Ernest Jones failed at Halifax and Joseph Sturge at Leeds, owing to Peelite support for the official Whig candidates. In Lancashire too, if there was no great advance, the voluntaryist group, including Bright, retained their seats. A reasonable estimate is that twenty-six voluntaries were returned, together with a further sixty members opposed to any future state endowment of religion (Machin 1967). 'The ice is broken', proclaimed the *Nonconformist*. 'The spell which sealed the eyes and paralyzed the will of the Nonconformist body is dissipated. They have had a taste of independence, and they will never forget it.' (Miall 1884: 128)

Yet their rejoicing was perhaps premature. If in the short run the voluntaries had improved their parliamentary position, the wider implications of the 1847 election were more damaging. For their electoral strategy had split wide open the 'auld alliance' with the Whigs; in the end, however, the Whigs – or their Liberal successors – were indispensable if the practical demands of the Nonconformists were to be met by legislation. In that sense, as Gash shrewdly notes, voluntaryism represented an emotional 'retreat from politics' (Gash 1965: 76). It also had a further effect. As we have seen, it helped to retard the 'natural' alliance between militant Dissent and Radicalism that was developing in the later 1830s and early 1840s. The general election of 1847 thus marks a further point in the fragmentation of the liberal forces in the Commons and in the country.

The consequences were to some extent seen over the next ten years, a decade which, on the surface, seemed an ebullient period for militant Nonconformity. The Liberation Society of 1853 was 'the epitome of rational agitation' (Vincent 1966: 68). It widened its influence at grass-roots level, mainly as a result of the work of Carvell Williams who became increasingly 'the master-mind of the society' (Thompson 1974: 231). It was a wealthy organization, mainly as a result of the support of northern industrialists; in 1855 its own news-paper, *The Liberator*, appeared. The society also began to re-estab-lish links with the secular Radicals both inside and outside the House of Commons. Moreover, in 1853 another great pressure group appeared, the United Kingdom Alliance, committed to a policy of temperance reform based on the principle of local option, 'a symbol rather than a serious proposal for solving the drink problem' (Harrison 1971: 383). The Alliance was supported mainly by Nonconformists and, like the Liberation Society itself, was thus an expression of Radical opposition to the Victorian Establishment, represented in this case by the great London brewers. Like the Liberation Society too, and even more systematically, the United Kingdom Alliance engaged in a policy of applying electoral pressure in the constituencies, and within the House of Commons its spokesman, Sir Wilfred Lawson, introduced an annual Permissive Bill which was as regularly thrown out.

In addition, the number of Nonconformist MPs increased steadily in the 1850s and re-established links with the Liberals in the House. In 1852 there were thirty-eight, including Miall who was returned for Rochdale. In 1857, following the setting up of a Nonconformist Elec-toral Committee to 'monitor' parliamentary action and opinion and influence elections, fifty MPs were returned, though Miall lost his seat in the Palmerstonian triumph of that year. Yet this growth was not reflected in any advance towards the promised land as far as Nonconformist aims were concerned. It was not merely that the demand for disestablishment, whether in Ireland or England, was not taken seriously by the House of Commons; even the growing agi-tation for the remedy of specific grievances, notably the abolition of compulsory church rate, got nowhere. Commons' majorities of between sixty and seventy in favour in 1858–59 had melted away to nothing by 1861, and small majorities *against* were recorded during the next two years. This reaction was partly due to the inevitable counter-attack mounted by Church of England defence organizations which had been gathering momentum since the 1830s, a movement bound to receive sympathetic attention in a still Anglican-dominated Parliament. It was also due to the confused state of party politics and principles during this period, and the Laodicean temper of a House of Commons dominated by the aristocratic erastianism of Russell and Palmerston. 'In the fifties', writes the historian of the Victorian Church, 'the union of church and state achieved an uneasy equilib-rium . . . the establishment was accepted as a practical and useful expression of Christain professions by the state and a public means to encourage Christian morality.' (Chadwick 1966: 479)

The conclusion drawn by Miall in 1863 was that the attempt to influence the Commons directly by working with and through the Liberals in favour of reform had failed; a new political strategy was needed. What he now proposed was that the Nonconformists should put their own interests first; they should exert pressure at constituency level to obtain the nomination of Liberal candidates who would be prepared to accept and work for the major Nonconformist demands. 'If this measure of justice be denied to us', concluded the Liberation Society minutes, 'that we resolutely withhold our cooperation – our votes and influence – whatever may be the consequences of our abstention to the Liberal Party.' (Mackintosh 1972: 123) The outcome of this policy of electoral blackmail was the return of a Radical Nonconformist bloc of eighty-seven at the general election of 1865. The Liberationists were thus putting 'principles' before 'party'; and it is true of course, as Thompson suggests, that the Liberation Society did not 'tie its fortunes directly' to the Liberal Party until after 1868 (Thompson 1974: 226–7). Yet one of Miall's hopes in proffering the new strategy of 1863 was that the foundation for a true *Liberal* Party could be created, 'strong in its own strength, capable of indefinite expansion, and vitalised and united by the broad principles which this Society aims to embody in legislation' (Hamer 1977: 103). That indeed is what the Liberation Society *was* helping to create at grass-roots level in the later 1860s through propaganda and organization, especially in Wales, where the local branches of the Society became in effect registration societies for the new Liberal Party in preparation for the general election of 1868 (Jones 1961).

There were of course other forces at work in 'the formation of the Liberal Party' in the 1860s: the growth of the artisan élite, enfranchised in 1867; the influence of the Liberal intelligentsia; the articulation of a new thrusting Liberalism though the cheap provincial press, dominated mainly by Liberal businessmen such as the Cowens, who controlled the *Newcastle Chronicle*, and the Leader family's *Sheffield Independent*. Above all, it was the contribution of the great Radical manufacturers, such as Titus Salt, Samuel Morley and William Rathbone, that was particularly important – the 'heroic element' in Victorian Liberalism (Vincent 1966: 35). The power of these men rested upon their wealth, their public positions, their self-confidence, their ability – and their wide-ranging interests. They were associated with a group of causes – philanthropic, political, social and religious – which took them far beyond the confines of the Liberation Society or even the House of Commons, into, for example, the world of trade unionism and labour politics. Samuel Morley, who had representatives of some seventy varying organizations at his funeral in 1886, was typical of the breed (Hodder 1887: 499——501). 'The world of controversial humanitarianism and the world of radicalism were linked in one way by a common tendermindedness in primary social attitudes, and in another by a stage army of interlocking directorships.' (Vincent 1966: 38) It was these men who, in the later 1860s became the real leaders of militant Nonconformity and provided the 'muscle' in parliamentary Radicalism. They thus displaced the more limited leadership of men like Miall – who was out of the Commons between 1857 and 1869 – Baines, and Bright, whose Radicalism was fast declining and who was unsympathetic in any case to Militant Dissent (Yarmie 1975: Ch. 7).

However potent the development of popular Liberalism during this period and whatever the successes of Nonconformity on the electoral front, a parliamentary 'leader' was needed if this power was to be transmuted through party into legislative action. For Nonconformity, one man seemed to be increasingly marked out to assume that role – W. E. Gladstone. They were impressed by his support for 'democracy' during the last years of the Palmerston government; his public expression of sympathy with Nonconformist attitudes over church rate; his condemnation of the Anglican Establishment in Ireland; and, above all perhaps, his moral and spiritual fervour. 'Dissenters', wrote one Nonconformist editor to him, 'have confidence in the deep feeling of religiousness which appears to imbue your public life and to make it a great and sacred responsiblity.' (Machin 1974) As Nonconformists moved closer to Gladstone, so he moved, cautiously, towards them. 'A liberal and kindly treatment of the Church by the State, and of Dissenters by the Church is what I desire to see', he stated in 1863. This new sympathy was consolidated by his meetings with moderate Dissenting ministers in the course of the following two years to discuss, *inter alia*, a practical programme of religious reform acceptable to both sides. The Dissenters' aim was, as Rev. Newman Hall their leader indicated deliberately to Gladstone, to obtain his '. . . more thoroughly understanding the views and motives of religious and thoughtful men who represent a large and not uninfluential section of the great Liberal Party' (Machin 1977: 325, 328). It was a prospect which seemed well on the way to fulfilment when the aspiring Liberal leader presented himself to the electors of south-west Lancashire in 1865 'unmuzzled'.

Nonconformity's cup seemed indeed to runneth over in the course of the next four years. The Second Reform Act gave Nonconformists the opportunity to increase their electoral influence, though this was offset by the lack of any fundamental redistribution of seats. In 1868 Gladstone pushed through his Church Rates Abolition Act, with the grudging acquiescence of the Conservative government. Basically a compromise shaped by Anglicans, which legislated for a situation already largely passed away in urban England, it was regarded nevertheless as a triumph for Nonconformist pressure and their ideal of social progress (Anderson 1974b). This was followed by a majority in favour of Gladstone's resolutions on Irish Church Reform, the resignation of Disraeli, and the general election of 1868. Since Gladstone appeared to be doing their work for them, there appeared to be no need for the Nonconformists to do anything in the election other than throw their weight enthusiastically behind their champion and the Liberal Party. Sixty-three Dissenters were returned as the mainstay of the Radical bloc on the Liberal benches. Gladstone, now head of a triumphant party, then became Prime Minister and proceeded to pass the great Irish Church Act in 1869, which disestablished and disendowed the Anglican Church in Ireland, though here again the Liberationists had no direct influence on the terms or passage of the Act (Bell 1969: 115). This was followed by the Endowed Schools Act in the same year, which limited Anglican control in such schools, and other minor concessions to Nonconformist susceptibilities. The tide appeared to be flowing strongly in their favour. Must not disestablishment of the Church of England follow in the not too distant future? And would not a Liberal government have to bow to the wishes of the Nonconformists in the field of elementary education, a subject which was being considered at that very moment by W. E. Forster, Vice-President of the Council on Education, a Quaker and a Radical? It was in fact the vexed question of education that was to bring to an abrupt halt the 'union of hearts' between Gladstone and Dissent, and lead within a year or two to a new outburst of militancy, the so-called 'Nonconformist Revolt'.

By this time, particularly after the report of the Newcastle Commission in 1861, it was clear to all unprejudiced observers that the religious societies, which had dominated English elementary education since the early part of the century, were unable to cope with the increasing numbers and social pressures of a rapidly developing industrial society; a situation which was underlined by the deeper implications of the Second Reform Act. Voluntarism was in effect dead; and both Baines and Miall (a member of the Newcastle Commission) now accepted the need for increasing state action to secure the educational needs of the working classes. It was in Birmingham, with its strong links between civic reform, Nonconformity and Radicalism, that this feeling was particularly acute and early in 1869 a meeting was held in that city to discuss the education question, with an eye on the new Bill now being prepared. It was attended by such characteristic figures as George Dixon, MP for the city and a leading light in the Birmingham Education Society, Jesse Collings, secretary of the same society, Rev. R. W. Dale, Congregational minister, J. T. Bunce, editor of the *Birmingham Post*, William Harris, secretary of the Birmingham Liberal Association and Joseph Chamberlain, a prominent local businessman and member of the Education Society. As a result, the National Education League was established with Chamberlain as head of the executive and Collings as secretary: a new militant pressure group had been born.

Chamberlain was the main driving force behind the policy and organization of the League in trying to shape the character of the

new Education Bill. The League's aim was simple – the establishment
of a system 'which shall secure the education of every child in the
country'. Its programme can be summed up in three words – free,
national and secular education, though there was no clear agreement
on the practical implications of either 'secular' or 'national'.Did
secular imply no religious teaching in schools, as Chamberlain and
free-thinking Radicals like John Morley believed? Did national imply
the dissolution of the voluntary schools? However, the League soon
established an efficient organization, with over 100 branches and a
substantial fund of more than £60,000 by the end of 1870 (Griffiths
1976). Yet it was a partisan organization. Despite its national pretensions, the League – as the names of its sponsors indicate – was
virtually controlled by a Birmingham Radical Nonconformist clique
who, while pursuing their educational campaign, were at the same
time, through the local Liberal caucus, striving to destroy the power
of the Conservatives and reactionary Liberals on the Birmingham
City Council.

On 17 February 1870, Forster introduced his Education Bill. Its
aim was, he said, 'to supplement the present voluntary system – that
is to fill up its gaps at least cost of public money' (Reid 1888,
vol. 1: 96). His object too was a national system of education – but
as speedily and cheaply as possible; and this meant combining state,
local and voluntary effort, and avoiding the issue of religious principle by the bland assumption that since all were agreed on the
religious basis of education, all would agree that this should be
determined by the local school boards. In the eyes of the League,
however, the Bill provided neither national education since school
boards were only to be elected where education was still deficient
after the voluntary societies had been given a year's grace, and
attendance was still permissive; nor free education – small payments
were imposed; nor secular education – since it was left to each local
school board to provide the religious education that it thought fit,
with consequent advantage to the Church of England. The wrath of
militant Dissent burst about the heads of the vice-president and his
leader. For the Nonconformists had misjudged Gladstone. He had
played very little part in the drafting and introduction of the Bill; but
on education matters he was, above all, a churchman, and had no
sympathy with the League's idea of allowing the voluntary schools
to wither away. Almost at once a Central Nonconformist Committee
was set up at Birmingham to fight the Bill, organized by Rev.
R. W. Dale and Rev. H. W. Crosskey, which worked closely with
the League and the Liberation Society. The machinery of militant
protest and pressure once again went into action. Petitions and public
meetings were organized, literature distributed; and on 9 March 1870
Chamberlain led a remarkable delegation representing all organiza-

tions and sympathizers – Robert Applegarth spoke for the trade unions – to London to meet Gladstone. The statesman listened courteously but without committing himself.

The debate was resumed on the second reading in late March, and then on the committee stage in July when – after a heated exchange between Miall and Gladstone – the government eventually accepted a number of important amendments. School boards were to be elected on a popular basis and could be set up if a town council or majority of ratepayers demanded it; the period of grace for the religious bodies was reduced to six months. The famous Cowper – Temple clause allowed only undenominational religious teaching in rate-aided schools, and by thus severing voluntary schools from rate-aid, induced Gladstone to raise their state grant – a bitter pill for the League to swallow. The government, believing, rightly, that they had made important concessions, then determinedly stood by the Bill as amended, and it passed through the Commons on 22 July, supported by Conservative votes – over sixty Liberals voted against it. A few days before this Chamberlain had written to George Dixon: 'It is not National Education at all – it is a trick to strength the Church of England against the Liberation Society.'[1] The Nonconformists therefore decided to carry on their opposition to the Act, and their case against it was soon enormously strengthened. For, unnoticed, clause 25 of the original Bill had slipped through the committee stage, and this clause allowed the local school boards to pay the fees of poor children in schools of the parents' choice, including voluntary schools. In this way the hated principle of rate-aid to the voluntary schools was given a new lease of life, and Anglican-controlled school boards were quick to seize this unexpected opportunity. The amount of money actually spent under the clause was trivial, but for Nonconformity clause 25 soon became the symbol of all they detested in the government's education policy. As a result the activities of the League became more political and more extreme. In 1871 at the third annual meeting of the National Education League, Dale declared (quoted in Adams 1882: 272–3):

> Every representative now sitting in Parliament for a Liberal
> constituency, every new candidate for Liberal suffrage, should be asked
> whether he is prepared to vote for the repeal of Clause 25. . . . A
> refusal, or an ambiguous promise, should be met with a clear and
> definite declaration that he cannot have our vote. . . . This may lead to
> the breaking-up of the Liberal Party. When the Liberal Party is false to
> its noblest principles, it is time that it *should* be broken up.

Once again, as in the 1840s, educational issues were prising apart the growing links between the Nonconformists and their political allies.

This policy of electoral blackmail was applied at by-elections, notably at Bath in 1872, nearly all of which were defeats for the government; and at a few places, Dundee and Greenwich for example, the League put up its own candidates, with the same result. Nevertheless, the ministry pursued its policies with an almost sublime tactlessness. Gladstone was concerned with the Irish University Bill, and Forster was determined, doggedly, to abide by the main principles of the Education Act. In 1872, 132 Liberals voted to repeal clause 25, and only 123 voted against, supported by 195 Conservatives. Chamberlain replied, in answer to the criticism that the League' campaign would let in the Tories: 'I think that is very probable. But, sir, what is that to us? What matters it to education – what matters it to the welfare and prosperity of the country, whether a Tory Government sits on the Cabinet benches or a Liberal Government passing Tory measures.' (Garvin 1932, vol. 1: 132) In June 1873, Forster' Amending Bill aimed at transferring from the school boards to the Poor Law Guardians authority to levy rates under clause 25 – the militant Nonconformists were furious. Chamberlain wrote (quoted in Garvin 1932, vol. 1: 137):

> With this knowledge of our opinion the Government has chosen
> deliberately to defy us . . . this conduct leaves us no alternative. . . .
> The great principle of religious equality must be accepted as part of the
> Programme of any Party which in future seeks our support and alliance
> . . . the Nonconformist Revolt, long threatened has at last begun, and
> parliamentary tacticians will do well to ponder its importance.

The education dispute inevitably overshadowed other Nonconformist demands. The United Kingdom Alliance, characteristically, opposed Bruce's Licensing Bill – preferring no loaf to half a loaf – and began their own bitter campaign against the government's tenderness to 'the Trade'. The long-term demand for disestablishment was given a fillip by the great reforms in favour of religious equality passed in 1868–69. In the debate on the Irish Church Bill of 1869 Gladstone had argued, in justification of the measure, that when a majority of the people of a country rejected a religious Establishment then 'the duty of the Legislature to interfere is imperative.'[2] The Liberationists believed that that test should be applied also to England. In the winter and spring of 1871 they organized a great campaign in favour of disestablishment, mainly in the north of England, with evident success, though they were of course preaching largely to the converted. In May a 'grand inquest' was held on the subject in the House of Commons as a result of Miall's disestablishment motion. Miall, in a deliberately moderate speech, expounded the now classical theoretical arguments in favour. Disraeli and the Conservatives were unimpressed by 'theory'; Gladstone and other Liberal front-benchers argued that disestablishment was simply not a practical proposition in view of the problems involved and the uncertainty of public opinion, a position which the Liberal leader stuck to through thick and thin. The motion was in fact defeated by 381 votes to 96, though the minority included such distinguished Liberals as Dilke, Fawcett, Trevelyan and Mundella. Nevertheless Miall was confident that he could see '. . . the rapid approach of what I may call a tidal wave of sentiment which will presently beat with overwhelming effect upon the union of the temporal authority with the spiritual in the constitution of governments'.[3]

In the debate Gladstone had insisted that before Miall converted the House of Commons, 'he must begin by undertaking the preliminary work of converting to those opinions the majority of the people of England' (Miall 1884: 316). The Liberationists once again responded to the challenge. But the next few years revealed if anything apathy rather than increasing support for disestablishment. The Press, even the Radical Press, dismissed the subject as one 'about which nobody cares a straw' (Ingham 1964). A deliberate attempt to appeal to the ranks of the working classes through the efforts of George Potter and George Howell, was an almost complete failure. It was a subject of supreme indifference to the majority of working men, and they gave it no high priority at a time when the 'Labour Laws' agitation was at its peak. Even the ranks of the faithful were growing greyer and wearier, as the failure to recruit younger converts and the falling off in subscriptions to the Liberation Society perhaps revealed. For the simple fact was that by 1871, especially after the passing of the Universities Test Act in that year, almost all the practical disabilities of the Nonconformists had been removed, and it had been the campaign against them rather than support for what Miall himself called the 'abstract' question of disestablishment, that had always formed the real stimulus for rank-and-file enthusiasm. Hence, paradoxically, 'as grievances were settled, the ultimate issue became more remote not closer at hand' (Thompson 1974: 232). In May 1873 Miall could muster only sixty-three votes for his disestablishment motion. The Liberationists accepted that they were now in no position to rally opinion against Gladstone and the Liberal Party; and they adjusted their electoral policy accordingly. There was to be no return to 1847. It was decided that no tests relating to disestablishment would be imposed by them on Liberal candidates at the next general election.

The National Education League too adopted a more moderate line a few months later, especially as it was evident that their pressure, though irritating, was having no impact on the government and the Parliamentary Party, and little on public opinion. 'Hardly any constituency is safe for a radical at the present time', commented Chamberlain in August 1873, after east Staffordshire, where the Liberal candidate was a League supporter, had been lost to a Conservative. 'I doubt if there are four boroughs in the kingdom where I could find a seat.'[4] In August John Bright, who had only recently returned to Parliament after a long nervous illness, partly due to an appeal from Gladstone and hoping perhaps to influence the government's education policy, agreed to accept the Duchy of Lancaster. 'I am afraid he has only come back to the House to prop the government', wrote Chamberlain to Dilke; he was not altogether wrong (Garvin 1932, vol. 1: 138). 'The present question', wrote Gladstone to Granville in September, '. . . is what we are to expect from Bright whose return to office we are making use of as a means of temporary reconciliation.' (Ramm 1952, vol. 2: 405) Nevertheless, despite their dubiety about Bright's position, Chamberlain and his friends in the League decided to call off their political campaign against the ministry 'as a *pledge*', as he wrote to Morley, 'of repentance and amendment' (Garvin 1932, vol. 1: 140).

The reprieve did little to help the government. In the spring of 1873 the Irish University Bill had been defeated on its second reading and Gladstone resigned, only to take up the burden again when Disraeli refused office. 'I felt reluctance personally', he wrote, 'from a desire for rest. . . . Also politically because I do not think that as a general rule the experience . . . of what may be called returning or resuming governments has been very favourable in its character.' 'Divisions in the Liberal Party', he went on, 'are to be seriously apprehended from a factious spirit on questions of economy, on questions of education in relation to religion, on further parliamentary change, on the land laws.' (Morley 1905, vol. 2: 63, 65) In the summer things got worse. Further by-elections were lost. Scandals were revealed in the administration of the Post Office, and both the Postmaster-General and the Chancellor of the Exchequer were forced to resign. On 22 October Bright in a speech to his constituents at Birmingham, denounced the 25th clause as 'an evil principle' and made a strong attack on those responsible for it; Forster replied a few days later at Liverpool and repudiated all that Bright had said (Garvin 1932, vol. 1: 141). At the end of 1873, therefore, confusion, disunion and virtual despair reigned in the ranks of the government. By the New Year, however, Gladstone was reaching a decision. 'The nation appears to think it has had enough of us', he wrote to Lord Granville on 8 January 1874, 'it is a question of measures then. Can we by any measures materially mend the position of the party for an impending election?' (Morley 1905, vol. 2: 89) The curious answer was – repeal of the income tax and other tax reductions; 'a rattling good Budget' would, Gladstone believed, win back public confidence and reunite the party. On 24 January the dissolution of Parliament was announced to a startled country.

The League was caught unprepared. The unexpected dissolution was described by the *Nonconformist* as 'a bolt from an unclouded sky that dished the Radicals' (Maehl 1963). For though, in the event, 149 supporters of disestablishment stood out of 425 Liberal candidates

and 300 were pledged to support the repeal of clause 25, the sudden-
ness of Gladstone's appeal to the country shattered the morale of the
Nonconformist bloc 'when their position in regard to the political
party with which they commonly act is one of some delicacy, and
requiring on their part unusual care and wisdom'.[5] How were they
to vote when faced with a Liberal candidate? Many clearly found it
impossible in the end to avoid the pull of traditional loyalties, some
abstained. The Liberation Society argued immediately after the election that with eighty to ninety MPs supporting disestablishment in
the new House of Commons, '. . . our cause has suffered no appre-
ciable damage'.[6] But the return of a powerful Conservative government with an overall majority of fifty, could hardly be regarded as
a victory, and many League supporters went down to defeat,
including Chamberlain, narrowly, at Sheffield. W. E. Forster was
repudiated by his own Liberal Association at Bradford, but fought
back powerfully and was re-elected, partly owing to Roman Catholic
and Conservative support. He had, however, effectively destroyed
his chances of becoming Liberal leader after Gladstone's resignation
in 1875 (Hurst 1972).

What then was the effect of the 'Nonconformist Revolt' on the
1874 election? Francis Adams, the historian of the National Education League, estimated that about twenty seats were lost to the
Liberals through Nonconformist abstentions at the polls (Adams
1882: 301). But it seems fairly certain that the importance of the
League generally as an influence on the Liberal débâcle has been
exaggerated. Nonconformist voters were after all concentrated in the
under-represented cities of the North and the Midlands; the majority
were not militant, and the 'Nonconformist Revolt' of Chamberlain's
rhetoric was one of officers rather than rank and file. Though there
were a large number of seats – thirty-four – where unauthorised
Liberals stood because of party divisions, Arthur Peel, the Liberal
Chief Whip, in a letter to Gladstone estimated that only thirteen were
lost due to these divisions.[7] For education was only one issue, and
not perhaps the most important, in the general election; the drink
question and working-class opposition to the Criminal Law Amendment Act were just as if not more significant. Perhaps the most
fundamental cause of all, however, was, quite simply, the swing of
the middle-class voter, alarmed by the rise of working-class
consciousness, to the Conservative Party, particularly in London
suburbia, as even Gladstone recognized in his resignation letter to
the Queen (Guedella 1933, vol. 1: 444–5). Frederic Harrison
summed it up in a letter to John Morley: 'I have been nearly all day
and every day at the Reform Club, and have seen candidate after
candidate return and tell the tale of his contest. The agreement is
wonderful. Tory organization and enthusiasm, middle-class conserva-

tism, personal hatred of ministers, rowdy hostility of the residuum class, and political apotheosis of Beer.'[8]

The 'Nonconformist Revolt' and the general election of 1874 raised wider questions for the future of Radicalism and the Liberal Party. On the limited issue of education itself, time seemed to prove the wisdom of the Education Act of 1870 and the narrowness and sectarianism of the attack upon it. Not that Nonconformist 'myths' were easily abandoned. Francis Adams (1882: 301) wrote:

> The defeat of the Liberal Party, calamitous as it proved in some respects, was not an unmixed evil. It has taught the country that no Government will be allowed to juggle with great principles with impunity. It also prepared the way for the reunion of the party on a more liberal basis with more assured purposes and with infinitely superior organization.

Despite this rosy view, there was something in it. In opposition, the Liberal Party tried to close its ranks. After the retirement of Gladstone in 1875, a review of educational policy was pledged by Lord Hartington and the party leadership. When in 1876 Lord Sandon's Act abolished the 25th clause and imposed a considerable measure of compulsory attendance, its effect was, says Adams, 'to destroy the *raison d'être* of the League as an Educational Organization', and it was wound up the following year (Adams 1882: 320).

Politically, the problems raised were even more profound. What was to be the future relationship of 'sections' and 'pressure groups' to the Liberal Party as a whole? And, even more fundamentally, what should be the purpose of the Liberal Party? These are perennial questions for parliamentary parties. For the militant Nonconformists the Liberal Party was there to serve their interests; it was for that that they gave it their time, their energy, their enthusiasm. Dale (1873: 7) wrote of the Liberal ministers:

> They have deliberately chosen to pursue a retrograde policy, and although we have cherished a hearty loyalty to the old leaders of the Liberal Party, our loyalty to the principles which both they and we are called to defend is stronger, more intense, deeper than our loyalty to them. We are at last thrown upon ourselves; for a time, perhaps for a few years, we shall have to act independently of the recognized leaders of the Liberal Party. The old union between them and us is now dissolved. . . .

The militants refused to recognize the wider interests embraced by Liberalism, especially in relation to the working classes, or the problems of Gladstone in maintaining balance and consensus within the Liberal Party and recognizing national as well as party responsibilities. In a sense, therefore, the disaster of 1874, much as they regretted it, was the logical result of the single-mindedness with which the leaders of militant Dissent pursued their mirage of 'independence'.

Their views were not shared by all Dissenters. Samuel Morley resigned from the Liberation Society after the general election of 1868 because he objected to the promulgation of schemes which are 'practically useless', and because he believed that denominational interests should be subordinated to the wider policies of the Liberal Party and the national good (Hodder 1887: 280). Indeed, it might be argued that the Nonconformists would have done better by a more conciliatory policy, as some of them recognized; the great reforms of 1867–69 and earlier in favour of religious equality, had after all only been achieved in cooperation with others. 'I am a Nonconformist', said Sir Jeremiah Colman, 'but I am a Liberal too, and I fear the latter will lose more than the former will gain.' (Hamer 1972: 7) In any case Nonconformity had not the power by itself to suborn the Liberal Party. As Hamer comments (1972: 7).

> The events of 1870–4 revealed the weaknesses of Nonconformity as a would-be section. Its resources for organization and agitation were not great, and it entirely lacked the means and potential for growth through influence over outside opinion that alone could make it practically effective if it wished to operate apart from, and even in opposition to, the Liberal Party. Nonconformity needed the Liberal Party – to get a parliamentary majority on its side – more than Liberalism needed it. . . .'

The implications of this were seen after 1874. During the years of Conservative rule the instruments of militant Nonconformity, the National Education League and the Liberation Society especially, began to realign themselves with the Liberal Party; their members began to work in and through the Parliamentary Party and the local Liberal Associations. The best future for militant Dissent lay, it appeared, in reform from within, in the creation of a more Radical Liberal Party. It was Joseph Chamberlain who now emerged into national prominence as the powerful champion of this popular Liberalism, centred once again on the city of Birmingham.

NOTES

1. 16 July, 1870; JC/5/27 (Joseph Chamberlain Papers).
2. Parl. Debs., vol. CXCIV, 23 March 1868, 211&.
3. Parl. Debs., vol. CCVI, 9 May 1871, 476.
4. To Morley, 10 August 1873; JC/5/50.
5. January 1874, A/LIB Minute Book 5 (Liberation Society Papers).
6. 20 February 1874, A/LIB Minute Book 5.
7. 26 February 1874; Gladstone Papers.
8. 16 February 1874; Frederic Harrison Papers, Box 2.

Chapter 5

JOSEPH CHAMBERLAIN AND THE RISE OF THE CAUCUS

There were sound reasons why Birmingham should take the lead. The city had a long history of cooperation between the middle and working classes in favour of Reform movements, going back to the days of Attwood's Political Union in the 1830s, and expressed later through Sturge's Complete Suffrage Union and the support given – by elector and non-elector alike – to John Bright's candidature for the city in 1857. It was a Radical tradition which arose out of the distinctive features of Birmingham society. In the first half of the nineteenth century Birmingham was a rapidly expanding manufacturing community, made up of numerous highly skilled trades engaged in producing the famous 'Brummagem ware' – guns, jewellery, metal goods of every description. These were generally based on small workshops, where relations between masters and men were close and harmonious, especially as the capable well-paid worker still possessed a chance of becoming a master himself. For the Birmingham artisan it was the chapel, the friendly society, the educational institute, that largely replaced the fellowship of the trade union, and the class-consciousness that often accompanied it (Tholfsen 1953–54). This communal unity was both sustained and expressed by the social and religious vigour of the dominant Nonconformist sects, particularly the Unitarians, and Unitarian families such as the Chamberlains and Martineaus formed 'the aristocracy and plutocracy of Birmingham' (Webb 1938, vol. 1: 150).

It was, therefore, an élite of middle-class businessmen who here, as elsewhere in provincial England, took the lead in the social and political life of the city. It was a leadership which the artisans both accepted and admired; for the middle classes embodied those ideals of respectability, self-reliance and economic advancement which they themselves aspired to. They also shared a common ideology of Dissenting Radicalism, and thus a mutual commitment to progress and reform. Yet in the mid-nineteenth century larger firms were beginning to emerge in Birmingham as a result of competition and rationalization – Chamberlain and Nettlefold, for example – and this produced new social tensions, and encouraged the rise of an independent working-class movement (Hooper 1978).

The Birmingham Liberal Association was founded in February 1865 by William Harris – 'the father of the Caucus'. Though it was more open in its membership than the older type of oligarchic association, it still remained basically middle class in composition and outlook, responsible primarily for the organization of the middle-class electorate – as in the general election of that year. What forced it to adopt a more popular and more Radical stance was the formation of a powerful branch of the Reform League in the city. Over the next two years the Liberal Association cooperated with the League in pushing for an extension of the suffrage, partly in order to bring the Birmingham workers back into the orbit of middle-class Radicalism. This cooperation led logically to the establishment of the Caucus (Hooper 1978).

After the passing of the Second Reform Act in 1867, William Harris remodelled the local Liberal Association on a popular but strongly centralised basis, ranging from the elected ward committees at the bottom, through the Central Committee of 400 (later enlarged as membership grew), which nominated parliamentary candidates, to the Central Executive, and the 'Council of Ten' at the top – the brains and will of the whole organization. The Caucus of 1867 was neither as original nor as much the result of malevolent calculation as its critics, both then and later, insisted. What was new about it was not so much its underlying aims or its methods – since, as we have seen, the middle and working classes in Birmingham had been cooperating mutually in reform politics since the 1830s – but the formalization of its machinery and its adaptation to an enlarged, mainly working-class, electorate, an electorate which tacitly accepted the leadership of the middle classes (Tholfsen 1959). The effectiveness of this new organization was seen when all three Liberals were returned at the general election of 1868 despite the fact that the Second Reform Act had given each elector only two votes; and – owing especially to the organizing genius of Francis Schnadhorst who succeeded Harris in 1873 – the Liberals easily won the school board and council elections in the same year. In 1874 the three Liberals were returned unopposed at the general election.

The real significance of the Caucus at this time lay in local rather than national affairs. In the mid-nineteenth century Birmingham was well behind other provincial cities – Liverpool, Leeds, Manchester – in the provision of civic amenities; and the Town Council itself – wedded to a policy of 'economy' and lacking men of vision and ideas – had a feeble reputation. The task of the Birmingham Radicals was to revolutionize this state of affairs by using the power – especially the financial power – of the Council as a major weapon in the cause of municipal progress, and thus help to make Birmingham 'the best governed city in the world'. The heightening of civic pride which would ensue, would enhance the prestige of Birmingham and the Town Council, and thus encourage men of ability to join its ranks and serve as its officers. All this implied 'a new vision of the nature and function of the corporation' (Hennock 1973: 172). The main political exponent of this 'civic gospel' was, of course, Joseph Chamberlain who joined the council in 1869. Its practical application was seen in his remarkable three years as Mayor between 1873 and 1876, when Birmingham's gas and water supply was municipalized, on the grounds that 'all regulated monopolies . . . should be controlled by the representatives of the people', a beginning was made to the great improvement scheme for rebuilding the centre of th city, and a considerable boost was given to its cultural and educational provisions. Ten years later, when he was a Cabinet minister, Chamberlain still argued that 'the most fruitful field before reformers at the present time is to be found in an extension of the function and authority of local government' (Boyd 1914: vol. 1, 165).

Much of this achievement was due to Chamberlain personally. But it was the financial and industrial boom of the late 1860s and early 1870s that provided the cheap money for his daring civic improvements. He was helped too by the party discipline imposed by the Caucus on the Liberal ranks. His civic gospel also had a strong appeal to many enlightened businessmen who had the time and energy to devote to council affairs – Chamberlain himself sold his interest in the family firm in 1874; and, by ousting the discredited 'old gang' from the council chamber, they helped to apply a new spirit in local administration. Their practical talents were reinforced by the idealism and inspiration of an outstanding group of Nonconformist ministers, beginning with George Dawson who, in his writings and sermons of the 1840s and 1850s, outlined some of the basic ideas of the civic gospel well before Chamberlain appeared on the scene. His message was continued by his disciples and successors, H. W. Crosskey and R. W. Dale, both of them closely connected with leading members of the Caucus. They urged their congregations to live out their Christianity through active involvement in civic affairs, in order to attack the fundamental evils of poverty, ill health and ignorance. 'A strong and able Town Council', wrote Dale, 'might do almost as much to improve the conditions of life in the town as Parliament itself.' (Briggs 1968: 206) It was an awareness of the link between local government and educational progress – particularly through the device of rate-aid – that drove many Birmingham Radicals, including Chamberlain himself, towards membership of the Council. Thus: 'Religion provided the inspiration and business sense the practical driving force of the civic transformation.' (Briggs 1952: 70)

Despite later criticisms – especially the lack of adequate provision for working-class housing – the transformation was a real one. 'I think I have now almost completed my municipal programme', Chamberlain wrote to Collings on 6 June 1876. 'The Town will be parked, paved, assized, marketed, Gas-and-Watered and *improved* – all as the result of three years active work.' (Garvin 1932, vol. 1: 202) It was a fitting swan-song. Within a fortnight, owing to the retirement of George Dixon, Chamberlain was returned, unopposed, as an MP for Birmingham.

The new member was now forty years of age. He had spent twenty years in business, since he had first come to the Midlands from London in 1854 at the age of eighteen to work for the screw-manufacturing firm of Chamberlain and Nettlefold, founded by his father. This background, together with his family's traditional Unitarianism, made it almost inevitable that he would end up as a Radical. But what kind of Radical? Chamberlain's Radicalism was not based on any set of intellectual or moral principles, as with Mill or Bright, or influenced – in style or substance – by the religious ethos of militant Dissent. Nor, despite his dabbling in 'good works' in Birmingham in the earlier 1860s and his later invocation of 'socialistic legislation', was he moved emotionally by the plight of the poor or the inequalities of the social system. He was after all a rich man who relished worldly success, and his appearance and life-style let no one forget it. Chamberlain's Radicalism was that of the self-made, rational capitalist. He abhorred inefficiency and idleness, and their progenitors – tradition, deference, the cult of the aristocrat and the amateur in politics and administration. But he also despised much of the claptrap and impracticability of conventional Radicalism. His political persona was cold, hard and unsentimental. He prided himself on being the man of action – practical, clear-headed, down-to-earth; determined to achieve the simple Utilitarian aim of the greatest happiness of the greatest number by applying pragmatic solutions to specific problems, locally and nationally, using the materials that lay to hand.

Chamberlain's work on the Birmingham Town Council seemed to show what could be done to raise the standards of a whole community through the application of clearly thought-out, imaginative schemes of civic improvement. It also displayed his outstanding qualities as an administrator and a political leader, prepared to use constructively and ruthlessly the powers granted to him by the people – and the party machine. For Chamberlain the two were virtually synonymous. 'The aim of the caucus', he said, 'is essentially democratic. It is to provide for the full and efficient representation of the will of the majority, and for its definite expression in the government of the people.' (Briggs 1968: 209) And it was 'Radical Joe' who embodied that will. The populist rhetoric he indulged in at Birmingham to justify his domination was almost more important for the future of

Radicalism than the achievement itself. As he admitted to Dilke in 1876, writing from his Birmingham mansion, he possessed 'almost Despotic authority here'[1]; and there is little doubt that he relished it, both for its own sake and for what he could achieve with it. As Beatrice Webb (who almost married him) noted (1938, vol. 1: 147):

> By temperament he is an enthusiast and a despot. A deep sympathy with the misery and incompleteness of most men's lives, and an earnest desire to right this, transform political action into a religious crusade; but running alongside this genuine enthusiasm is a passionate desire to crush opposition to his will, a longing to feel his foot on the necks of others, though he would persuade himself that he represents the right and his adversaries the wrong.

He was the only outstanding Victorian Radical who understood the relationship between power and policy. 'A man worth watching and studying', Gladstone shrewdly noted in 1877, '. . . of great tenacity of purpose: expecting to play an historical part, and probably destined to it.' (Ramm 1962, vol. 1: 43)

Well before he entered the House of Commons in 1876 Chamberlain had pondered on the role of Radicalism and the future of the Liberal Party. As we have seen, his first experience of a national political movement was as leader of the National Education League after 1869; but within a few years his developing Radicalism was tiring of the education issue alone and his mind was already turning to wider issues – land reform, trade unionism, the county franchise. The League was important though, because it brought him new friends and contact with deeper national issues, and both made him more Radical. Jesse Collings put him in touch with Joseph Arch and agricultural trade unionism, and strengthened his interest in land reform; Dilke introduced him to the London Radical world and won his support for the county franchise and sympathy with 'republicanism'; Frederic Harrison advised him on the problems of labour. Above all, there was the influence of John Morley whom he first met in July 1873 as one of the London delegates at the National Education League's Annual Conference; 'decidedly a leader for an English progressive party', commented Morley to Harrison, welcoming Chamberlain into honorary membership of the 'party of humanity' (Hirst 1927, vol. 1: 276). A month after their first meeting Chamberlain sent Morley an eloquent analysis of the weaknesses of contemporary Radicalism[2]:

> The object just now should be to state as clearly as possible the programme of the party of the future, and *to make a party thereby*. At present there are only individual Radicals, each specially interested in some part of the whole, but with no connecting organization or idea of united action. There are Leagues and Associations and Unions but no party; and there never will be or can be till we choose out the most

important of all the questions debated and weld them into a connected scheme which all or most of us may accept as our programme. I have long felt that there is not force enough in the Education question to make it the sole fighting issue for our friends. From the commencement it has failed to evoke any great popular enthusiasm.

Morley, an expert on 'the future', was bound to be impressed. From the start he had had his own doubts about the capacity of 'the Chamber of Mediocrity' elected in 1868 to act as a vehicle for Radical reform. Though he soon modified his views, his opposition to Gladstone's government was renewed as a result of its education policy, and, though an agnostic, he became as bitter an opponent of the Education Act as the militant Nonconformists. In his articles in the *Fortnightly* on the controversy (republished as *The Struggle for National Education* in 1873) he saw it as a conflict – not only against the lay and clerical Establishment – but for the soul of the Liberal Party. Morley was now well established as the editor of the *Fortnightly Review*, and its pages provided Chamberlain with the opportunity of appealing to a wider, educated Radical opinion.

The first fruits of this collaboration of metropolitan and provincial Radicalism was Chamberlain's article, 'The Liberal Party and its leaders', printed in the *Fortnightly* for September 1873, in which he detailed his criticisms of the party's leadership and policies. The Liberal Party was now a despondent and declining body, argued Chamberlain, because the leaders had abandoned the invigoration of true Liberalism for measures of 'compromise and weakness'. The government was bankrupt as far as future policy was concerned; on all the great issues of the day it was 'inarticulate or indefinite' and 'deaf to the growing desire for radical reforms which occupies the minds of the mass of the people'. Those laws it *has* passed, have betrayed its friends – Nonconformists and trade unionists – and heartened its enemies. The time had come, therefore, to break the stranglehold of the 'respectable Whigs' in the Liberal Party and adopt a policy of out-and-out Radicalism. This new Radical Liberal Party would be based on a union of all the dissident elements, and have as its programme the 'four F's': free school (no fees, and repeal of the 25th clause); free church (disestablishment); free land (abolishing the ancient laws restricting the sale of land); free labour (legalising peaceful picketing). What Chamberlain thus offered was a 'policy and a programme' wide enough and Radical enough to reinvigorate the Liberal Party, win back its natural allies, and inspire the country (Chamberlain 1873). But it was also an attempt to 'concentrate' and strengthen Radicalism itself on the lines outlined to Morley in his letter of 19 August. This would pave the way for a 'reconstructed' Liberal Party in which Radicals like Chamberlain would have greater power – a premonition in fact of the NLF of 1877.

Morley was enthusiastic about the article, which caused something of a stir in political circles, and had already sent a copy of it to his friend, Frederic Harrison. Harrison welcomed Chamberlain's plan for widening the programme of the Education League, especially as his main concern was with the grievances of the trade unions. 'In the act of affecting the general current of politics and the reorganization of parties', he wrote back, 'I think a broad platform essential, and I believe Chamberlain is worthy of the occasion.' But, he pointed out, the working classes had little interest in the '25th clause' agitation, 'they will not budge for a section squabble or what looks like it. . . .' Moreover, he continued, 'the question arises – do the League and the middle class Nonconformists and secularists ranged round it really accept the workmen's demands as to anti-unionist laws'.[3] Harrison had here put his finger on one of the major weaknesses of the Morley – Chamberlain conception of a Radical popular front in 1873. Could trade unionists and Nonconformists work together? This seemed unlikely. It is true that a number of trade unions had supported the League from its inception, but after the passing of the Education Act in 1870 their interest waned rapidly, especially as they had their own 'revolt' – over the Labour Laws – to worry about. Nor, as we have already seen, were they any more enthusiastic for the cause of disestablishment. Moreover, the 'Labour Laws' agitation had the effect of stimulating the trade unionists' class-consciousness, and therefore tempted them to see many of the leaders of the Education League as businessmen first and Radicals second. For their part, it was the extremism of current trade union opinion that worried middle-class Dissenters. The *Nonconformist*, for example, though prepared to support the legalization of trade unions, jibbed at approving peaceful picketing (Mayor 1967: 89–91).

This clash between the middle-class Radical Establishment and a growing working-class consciousness affected Chamberlain himself. By 1873 some labour leaders were already suspicious of the activities of the caucus; they bitterly resented, for example, its failure to nominate working men as candidates in local elections, as in the Birmingham school board contest of 1870, even though Chamberlain boasted that 'three-quarters of the great committee of the 600 are working-men' (Garvin 1932, vol. 1: 258). In December 1873 Henry Crompton wrote to George Howell suggesting that Chamberlain be invited to the Sheffield TUC to be held at the beginning of 1874, but nothing came of it.[4] Ironically, when the TUC did meet, it was at the very moment when Chamberlain was campaigning to obtain the second Radical nomination for the city, and only a week or two before Parliament was dissolved. But Congress gave no endorsement to his four-point programme, nor elicited any particular interest in his plans for reconstructing the Liberal Party. During the Sheffield contest Chamberlain fought on the platform of the 'four F's',under the aegis of the breakaway Sheffield Radical Association organized by the ubiquitous local Radical, H. J. Wilson (Fowler 1961: 45–6). Chamberlain certainly received strong support from many local working men, but leading trade union leaders, such as George Howell, backed his Liberal rival, A. J. Mundella, and it seems clear that as one of the leading 'irreconcilables' Chamberlain antagonized many middle-class Liberals (Hurst 1972). He lost narrowly to the moderate Radicals, Mundella and Roebuck. But the election was ominous for the future of Chamberlainite Radicalism. As the campaign showed, his personality and ideas divided rather than united the Liberal Party.

The electoral disaster of 1874 confirmed Chamberlain's gloomy forebodings about the future of the Liberal Party. It was defeated not because it was too Radical, but because it was not Radical enough. What was still needed, therefore, was a reorientation of the party in a Radical direction, and its acceptance of a unifying and inspiring programme. But what programme? 'Free Church and Free Labour', he wrote to Morley in March 1874, 'are the best available wedges for forcing the gates of Conservative obstruction . . . and we must have both on our side.[5] He developed his ideas in a new article in the *Fortnightly*, 'The next page of the Liberal Programme', published in October. Chamberlain now accepted that things had changed since his earlier polemic. The '25th clause' was a dead issue, and 'free education' still unpopular. Radical land reform was obviously unacceptable to the party leadership. All the signs were that Disraeli was clearing the ground for the legalization of peaceful picketing, which he achieved in the following year. Out of the 'four F's' only 'free church' remained. Chamberlain placed disestablishment at the head of the Radical programme as the one issue that might now unite and revivify the Liberal Party (Chamberlain 1874).

There were, he believed, sound political reasons for this. In 1874 the 'ritualist controversy' weakened the intellectual cohesion of the Church of England, and even Gladstone admitted that year that 'the Establishment . . . is not strong enough to bear either serious secession or prolonged parliamentary agitation' (Morley 1905, vol. 2: 110). Then too the new popular Liberal Associations springing up throughout the country needed a new rallying cry after the disappointments of recent years. A programme of disestablishment and disendowment would also appeal to the working classes, resentful of the wealth and privileges of the Established Church, especially if 'the vast sums now held by the Church be applied to the public good' (Chamberlain 1874). And the Liberation Society was again on the move. The years between 1875 and 1877 represented the culmination of the Society's campaign in favour of disestablishment when, as one of its leaders said, 'there was an amount of interest and excitement on the subject which led us to hope, not certainly for immediate action, but for greater prominence being given to it both inside the circle of Dissent and in the Liberal Party itself' (Guiness Rogers 1903: 214).

Once again, as in 1873, Morley enthusiastically endorsed Chamberlain's programme. 'It is now clear on all sides', he wrote in the *Fortnightly*, 'that the Church question is . . . the next page of the Liberal programme. . . . It will no longer be possible for the party organs to put aside the supporters of Disestablishment as dreamers and busybodies.' (Morley 1875) 'The Church question', he wrote to Harrison, 'is the only one I care about in politics.' (Hirst 1927, vol. 2: 4) His friend replied with his customary realism[6]:

> I . . . agree very much that the removal of the Church is the only first class question as yet provided with a programme. I hesitate to follow you at present if you mean to make this the basis of a revived Liberal Party. It may become so, but in other hands than those of our friends of the [Liberation] Society. What I doubt is whether it is a *practicable* basis for any party beyond that clear and determined band. Whilst it is for the most defined and living part of the Radical movement, it is also the part which is of all others confined to a section of the movement. A new Liberal movement on a basis which Glad., Hartington, Forster, Lowe and the rest abhor is a thing I doubt. . . . I do not [as yet] see in it the elements of reviving the Liberal Party'.

Chamberlain was soon inclined to agree. Lord Hartington, who succeeded Gladstone as Liberal leader that year, partly because of the Radicals' detestation of Forster, was antipathetic to disestablishment, as indeed was a majority of the Parliamentary Liberal Party. The working classes were clearly as unenthusiastic as ever. Equally galling was the fact that the Liberation Society stubbornly refused to abandon its separate organization in favour of working for Radical policies within the Liberal Party. Nevertheless, Chamberlain was allowed to chair its Annual Conference in May 1876. By that time it was perhaps too late for the cause of disestablishment. That very month the Bulgarian massacres were taking place. The foundations were already being laid for the 'Bulgarian Agitation' of 1876, a movement that was to transform profoundly the fortunes of both Radicalism and the Liberal Party, and help to push disestablishment – as Gladstone foretold – into 'the dim and distant future'.

The debate on the Eastern question, writes its historian, was 'the most clearly defined public conflict in English history on the fundamental problem of the moral nature of the state' (Shannon 1963: 23). The Bulgarian Agitation directed against Disraeli's Eastern policy appealed to the whole of Nonconformity as the embodiment of their profoundest beliefs, in Christian morality, reason and progress. At a time when their practical grievances had been remedied and disestablishment was still an 'abstract question', the Agitation gave the

Nonconformists the opportunity to direct their superabundant moral energy into a pure, unsullied, humanitarian crusade – rather like the Spanish Republican cause to the European Left in the 1930s. The attitude of the middle-class secular Radicals was similar. They too were moved by moral considerations and the belief that Turkey was the antithesis of all that nineteenth-century civilization stood for, as well as general hostility to Conservatism and suspicions of Disraeli's motives, tinctured, for some, by a dash of anti-Semitism. It was Radicals such as Mundella, Freeman, the Oxford historian, and, above all, the popular journalist, W. T. Stead, who whipped up the Agitation; Gladstone only appeared on the scene later (Shannon 1963: 90). But there were important dissidents in the Radical ranks. The anti-Russian tradition, so important during the Crimean War, was still strong, and affected men such as the Newcastle MP, Joseph Cowen, a passionate supporter of the European national movements, and Charles Dilke (Jones 1885). Working-class radicals on the whole remained aloof, though George Howell and Henry Broadhurst, convinced Gladstonians, became strong supporters of the movement. John Bright, always worried about the possibility of British intervention in a European war, was a reluctant member of the Agitation. Among the intellectuals, Morley, as a belligerent anti-Christian, tried to maintain a neutral position, and his friend, Frederic Harrison, adopted in public the official anti-Agitation Positivist line, though in private, as so often, his admiration for Gladstone made him more sympathetic.

What of Joseph Chamberlain? He had entered the House of Commons in June 1876 at the very beginning of the Agitation; but his attitude to the movement in the first few months of its life was rather cool – reminiscent more of the line adopted by Lord Hartington and the Whigs than that of his fellow Radicals. Possibly he was put off by the unctuousness of the campaigners' rhetoric; and, never a Radical of the Manchester School, was more sympathetic to the claims of *realpolitic* advanced by the government's supporters (Jay 1981: 36–7). In the end, however, characteristically, his public stance was based not on moral or foreign-policy considerations, but on his assessment of the domestic political scene. He realized that, as a potential, national Radical leader, he could not afford to be out of step with the sentiments of the rank and file, and in the autumn of 1876 he emerged as a leading opponent of the government's Eastern policy. Furthermore, the Agitation had generated a high degree of passion and enthusiasm which could be tapped for Chamberlain's personal and Radical schemes, while the growing prestige of Gladstone as the outstanding leader of the movement and hero of the Nonconformists, could, rightly handled, be used for the same ends. 'Though I don't believe I am more Gladstonian than you', Chamberlain wrote to Dilke on 10 October 1876, 'at this time I can't help thinking he is our best card . . . if he were to come back for a few years (he can't continue in public life for very much longer) he would probably do much for us and pave the way for more. If G. could be induced formally to resume the reins it would be almost equivalent to a victory.'[7]

By the beginning of 1877 Chamberlain was determined to regain the initiative and place himself in the centre of the political stage. This he had failed to do in the House of Commons, partly because of the difficulty of welding the wayward group of Radicals into an effective bloc. 'There is literally no Liberal and no Radical Party in the House of Commons', he wrote. 'Those who call themselves Radicals are as much divided among themselves upon questions of cardinal importance as they are separated from the Whigs.' (Judd 1977: 78) In collaboration with William Harris he therefore floated the idea of a national union of Liberal organizations centred on Birmingham. Early in 1877 a general invitation was sent out from the Caucus to popular Liberal Associations throughout the country, inviting them to send delegates to an inaugural meeting at Birmingham on 31 May 'in order to facilitate the public discussion of political questions and to more effectively promote the adoption of liberal principles in the government of the country' (NLF 1877: 3). The move seemed well timed. The Radical enthusiasm engendered by the Bulgarian Agitation was still in full spate. Popular Liberal Associations had by now been established in many great cities, such as Leeds, Sheffield, Bradford, Manchester and Newcastle, and though they differed from the Caucus in details, the Birmingham Radicals 'supplied the associations with both an ideology and an organizational model' (Hanham 1959: 133). Moreover, the stimulus for such a national organization was already at hand in the National Education League which, after it was deliberately wound up by Chamberlain early in 1877, bequeathed its pattern of organization, its sectarian passion and much of its personnel to the new Federation (Herrick 1945). 'We are just going to issue the League dissolution circular', wrote Chamberlain to Morley in February 1877, 'announcing at the same time the formation of a Federation of Liberal Associations with headquarters at Birmingham and the League officers as chief cooks. I think this may become a very powerful organisation and proportionately detested by all Whigs and Whips.'[8]

The inaugural meeting took place at Birmingham as planned. Chamberlain acted as president, backed up by his local acolytes, and set the tone of the proceedings with his call for 'clearer aims and more decisive action' to 'revive the drooping fortunes of Liberalism'. 'We hope', he declared, 'in the first place to secure local representative associations, and then to weld them together into a central organization, itself representative in its turn of these popular associations, and forming what I may call a national convention to promote Liberal objects.' (NLF 1877: 16) A constitution and statement of policy was drawn up for the new National Liberal Federation incorporating most of Chamberlain's ideas. This declared (NLF 1877: 7):

> The essential feature of the proposed Federation is the principle which must henceforth govern the action of Liberals as a political party – namely, the direct participation of all the members of the party in the direction of its policy, and in the selection of those particular measures of reform and of progress to which priority shall be given. This object can be secured only by the organization of the party upon a representative basis; that is, by popularly elected committees of local associations, and by the union of such local associations, by means of their freely chosen representatives, in a general federation.

The meeting was not a complete success. Only about half of 100 or so delegates agreed to join the Federation owing to fears for the local autonomy of their associations, and of the pressure groups, only the National Education League, as we have seen, agreed to give up its independence and merge itself into the larger organization. The new Federation, however, was dominated by Birmingham men. Chamberlain was elected president; William Harris, chairman; Jesse Collings, hon. secretary, and Francis Schnadhorst, paid secretary; three sub-committees were set up, and a central office in Birmingham. By 1879 the new secretary's organizing genius had brought in over 100 Liberal Associations, though nearly all were in the provinces and hardly any in London. The new organization was thus virtually the creature of the Birmingham Radicals, as indeed it was intended to be.

Curiously, Gladstone attended the inaugural meeting of the Federation and spoke in the evening. 'Reached Birmingham at 3.15', he noted in his diary. 'A triumphal reception. Dinner at Mr. Chamberlain's. Meeting 7 to 9.30, half occupied by my speech. A most intelligent and duly appreciative audience.' (Morley 1905, vol. 2: 178) His presence there, in the very citadel of Radical Nonconformity, was a response to Chamberlain's invitation, and Chamberlain's motives in urging him to attend were transparently clear. He intended to reshape the Liberal Party in his own image, and the presence of Gladstone – increasingly the personification of Radical hopes and ambitions – at the Birmingham meeting might help him to do that. Lord Granville warned Gladstone against going. 'I presume', he wrote, 'that Chamberlain's object is not to reorganize the whole Liberal Party, but to strengthen the young liberal and more advanced portions of it, and to secure you willing or unwilling as its leader.' Gladstone was not unaware of Chamberlain's motives. But he *was* sympathetic to his plans for improved Liberal organization which, as he indicated to Granville, was necessary both for its own sake and 'will tend powerfully to promote the unity of action in which we are still more deficient' (Ramm 1962, vol. 1: 40–1). This emphasis on *action* was vital for Gladstone. Any opportunity must be seized for hammering the government's Eastern policy – and where could one find a better platform than at Birmingham? 'I believe I can do some good there by minimising the difference which preceded the last debate', he suggested to Granville. 'I consider the general position to be better than ever defined, and to be this, that the Government will only be kept even decently straight by continuous effort and pressure from without. . . . From the Birmingham meeting there will be a ramification, through the Liberal Delegates assembled there, stretching all over the country. . . .' 'Good ends', as he had earlier informed the cautious aristocrat, 'can rarely be attained in politics without passion: and there is now, the first time for a good many years, a virtuous passion.' (Ramm 1962, vol. 1: 38–9, 3).

This hints at Gladstone's own special reasons for going to Birmingham. For in the previous year, he had, under pressure, emerged as the greatest supporter of the Bulgarian Agitation. He soon found, sadly, that the Liberal Front Bench and official Anglicanism were lukewarm in support, whereas many Radicals and the whole of Nonconformity were solidly behind him. This impressed Gladstone profoundly; he never forgot what he called their 'noble support', and his visit to Birmingham in 1877 is, in a sense, a public gesture of accord and appreciation for English Dissent which did much to heal the rift that had developed between them over his earlier education policy. It is also something more. It is, as Professor Shannon has argued, in its attempt to rebuild the moral rapport with the masses that had been broken in 1874, a stage on the road to Midlothian and the resumption of the Liberal leadership (Shannon 1963: 92). Gladstone's presence then at the inaugural meeting of the NLF symbolizes this new *rapprochement* between the great Liberal and Nonconformity, and helps to explain his flirting with such Radical ideas as extending the county franchise. It was indeed in his article on that subject in *The Nineteenth Century*, November 1877, that he described the Nonconformists as 'the backbone of British Liberalism'. On their side too the Nonconformists began to see Gladstone once again as their personification of Christian statesmanship. As a prominent Congregationalist wrote: 'Political dissent covers the entire area of international relations, and here Mr. Gladstone is recognized by the Nonconformists as one of the very few statesmen who feel that the law of Christ is to govern nations as well as individuals.' (Glaser 1957–58) But, as far as their demands nearer home were concerned, the Nonconformists found that they had been captured by Gladstone for his ends and not theirs. It was the Eastern question, Guiness Rogers regretfully suggested, that checked and diverted the movement for disestablishment when it was in full flood (Guiness Rogers 1903: 214).

It was the formation of the NLF that really sparked off the grand debate on the merits and defects of 'the Caucus'. For Joseph Chamberlain and his friends the Caucus of 1877 meant a democratisation of the Liberal Party by, as he wrote, 'the direct participation of all its members in the direction of its policy and in the selection of those particular measures of reform to which priority shall be given' (Chamberlain 1877). Such a conception of party organisation implied an attack on the domination of the Whigs within the party, as reflected in both the leadership and the Whips' Office, and a demand for renewed energy, enthusiasm and purpose within contemporary Liberalism. 'The opponents of the Caucus are not to be convinced', wrote Chamberlain to Morley, 'they hate it for its virtues – because it puts aside and utterly confounds all that club management and Pall Mall selection which has been going on for so long and which has made of the Liberal Party the molluscous, boneless, nerveless thing it is.'[9] As expected, the Whig leaders were suspicious of Chamberlain's new creation. Lord Granville (as we have seen) warned Gladstone against attending its inaugural meeting; and Lord Hartington, the party leader, refused to recognize the Federation at all. He told Granville (quoted in Holland 1911, vol. 1: 245):

> I do not feel at all certain that we ought to give our adhesion to this federation scheme . . . it is almost certain to put the management into the hands of the most advanced men, because they are the most active. . . . There is a good deal of the American caucus system about it, which I think is not much liked here; and though we have all been preaching organization, I think we may sacrifice too much to it.

If these arch-Whigs damned the Caucus with faint praise, other critics were more forthright in their denunciations. It was argued that the democracy of the Caucus was a sham since control was bound to fall into the hands of the professional wire-pullers with the time and energy to devote to the running of the political machine. The Caucus thus gave power to a ruthless (and probably corrupt) faction, who not only manipulated the whole Federation in the interests of Birmingham, but through their control of voters, parliamentary candidates and policy, would eventually dictate to Parliament itself (Marriot 1882). Both the defenders and the opponents of the Caucus overstated their case. Certainly, Chamberlain's more extravagant claims on behalf of the democracy of the Caucus were patently absurd, since in practice if not in theory, as in any similar political organisation, power was bound to fall more and more into the hands of the most powerful members of the Executive Committee. There is obviously much truth in the harsh judgement of one modern commentator: 'The popular form of the party Organization merely enables the latter to penetrate deeper into the masses for the purpose of capturing them more easily, and not for giving them independence.' (Ostrogorski 1964, vol. 1: 303). On the other hand it would be foolish to exaggerate the real power and influence of the Caucus. It was not really representative of Liberal opinion in the country at large, its writ barely ran outside Chamberlain's bailiwick in the Midlands and selected cities in the north of England. Its income was tiny; and, despite its propaganda, there was, as its historian suggests, at the outset no 'clear agreement as to what the real objects of the Federation were to be' (Watson 1907: 7–8). Nor, in the end, did it really exert much control over the actions of the party leaders.

The arguments of his critics were irrelevant to Chamberlain: the product either of prejudice or pedantry. For him the Caucus was a practical political organization to be justified by its results. Its purpose was twofold. First, it would concentrate and unify Radicalism by transcending individual Radical demands in a larger national organisation, which would sort out priorities in policies and present them to the party leaders as the expression of majority Liberal opinion – the raw material of a party programme. Second, it aimed to scare (or bluff) the Whigs and moderates in the Liberal Party into accepting Radical men and Radical measures by emphasising the truly representative character of the Caucus as compared with the Parliamentary Party, and its achievement in the regeneration of Liberalism; just as the Labour Left invokes the transcendental democracy of the labour movement to tame the pretensions of the Parliamentary Labour Party.

But for Chamberlain, unlike some Radicals, the ultimate purpose of the projected radicalization was to strengthen rather than weaken Liberal leadership and government – especially as he hoped eventually to control both; 'to forge a relationship between Radicalism and power' (Hamer 1972: 51). Much of Chamberlain's speechifying about the aims of the Caucus was thus mere persiflage. There was no real agreement on what its 'programme' was: the various policy counters – the county franchise, disestablishment and the rest – changed their position on the Radical board with amazing celerity. Besides, they were overshadowed by the dominating concern with foreign and imperial affairs after 1876 – the Eastern question, Afghanistan, South Africa, Egypt. Nor, despite his veiled threats to Lord Hartington ('Can the leader of the Liberal Party afford to ignore altogether so large a section of it?') was Chamberlain as hostile to the Whigs' leadership as he made out, especially as his personal position in the House of Commons was a weak one. He told Collings in 1878 that the best chance of success for the Radicals now lay 'rather in a hearty alliance and attempt to influence our present leaders, than in the formation of any new party' (Hamer 1972: 55). The Caucus thus became the predestined instrument of

'Radical Joe's' personal ambition; the counterpart of the modern trade union leader's block vote, by means of which he could engineer a 'forced entry' into any future Liberal government.

In the country the fortunes of Radicalism seemed to be in the ascendant in the years between the formation of the NLF and the general election of 1880. In that election the Radicals believed they had two supreme advantages. First, control of the electoral organisation of the NLF. Second, the support of Gladstone who was now regarded as almost an 'honorary Radical' – 'the impersonation of all that is hopeful, bold and belligerent in Liberalism' (Dunckley 1880). This was of course a consequence of Gladstone's leadership of the Bulgarian Agitation, and the subsequent pattern he was able to impose on the election through the Midlothian Campaign – the appeal to 'morality' in foreign policy and the exaltation of 'the nation' against 'the classes' (Lloyd 1968). It meant that – as in 1868 – the Liberal leader received the wholehearted support of Radicals and Nonconformists. The Liberation Society, for example, decided that 'except in Scotland, the question of Disestablishment should be held in abeyance in order to avoid divisions in the Liberal ranks'[10]; an act of self-abnegation that later earned the public praise of Gladstone himself. It was the 'moral' attack on the Conservative government's foreign and imperial policy that conjoined with the effects of agricultural and industrial depression to give the Liberals their great victory in 1880 (Lloyd 1968: 38).

The results of the general election seemed to offer the Radicals the fulfilment of their hopes. The Liberals obtained a majority of more than 100 over the Tories, and roughly a third of the Parliamentary Party were Radicals. Chamberlain claimed for the Caucus that 'In 67 contested boroughs it was victorious in 60. In 10 counties it won in every case.' (Fraser 1966: 33) The claim was somewhat exaggerated, but both friends and enemies were impressed. Yet the fundamental fact about the general election of 1880 was that it was 'Mr. Gladstone's victory.' As he himself said, 'it made me again leader whether I would or no' (Morley 1905, vol. 2: 158), a position which was formally recognised when he was appointed Prime Minister for the second time. The enormous prestige Gladstone had built up since 1876 enabled him then to bend the party to his own will, and eventually embark upon a new crusade – this time over Ireland. This was something which Lord Hartington would never have had the strength to do if he had continued as leader; and Gladstone's triumph in 1880 meant, therefore, Shannon suggests, 'the ruin of Radicalism' (Shannon 1963: 273). This was indeed implied almost as soon as Gladstone formed his new administration. For only one member of his Cabinet of eleven was an out-and-out Radical, Chamberlain at the Board of Trade, and Dilke – slower off the mark than his Birmingham colleague – had to make do with the under-secretaryship at the Foreign Office. Even these appointments were made by the Prime Minister reluctantly and with an ill grace.

Chamberlain's acceptance of a Cabinet post, though gratifying to him personally, was an equivocal victory for the cause of Radicalism generally. It meant that he had now abandoned the attempt first adumbrated in 1873 either to reconstruct or set up a rival counter to the established Liberal Party. Now he was committed to the traditional path of personal advancement *within* the old party. Bereft of his commanding leadership, the Caucus relapsed into a state of suspended animation.

NOTES

1. 30 January 1876; Dilke Papers, vol. XII.
2. 19 August 1873; JC/5/50.
3. 21 August 1873: Frederic Harrison Papers, Box 2.
4. 30 December 1873; George Howell Collection.
5. 13 March 1874: JC/5/54.
6. 27 December 1875; Frederic Harrison Papers, Box 2.
7. Dilke Papers, vol. XII.
8. 6 February 1877; JC/5/54.
9. 29 September 1878; JC/5/54.
10. A/LIB Minute Book 6, 12 April 1880.

Chapter 6

THE MAKING OF THE RADICAL PROGRAMME

'Like the rest of the world, I am full of curiosity as to the composition of the new Government', wrote Chamberlain to the Radical journalist, T.H.R. Escott, a few days before its formation, 'but above all as to its policy. One or both must be radical – or there will be the devil to pay in a short time.[1] But by 1883 none of the major demands of the Radicals had been achieved, and even uncontentious reforms, such as Harcourt's Government of London Bill, failed in the end to receive ministerial backing. This was partly a result of the electoral campaign of 1880. If it was 'Mr Gladstone's victory', it was a victory that was won against 'Beaconsfieldism' rather than for anything positive, concerned with foreign and imperial rather than domestic issues. The Liberal Party came into power in 1880 with no definite programme other than a vague commitment to franchise and local government reform. Indeed, Gladstone himself thought only in terms of clearing up one or two outstanding problems inherited from his predecessor – mainly in imperial affairs – before returning once again to the peace and quiet of his books and tree-felling at Hawarden. His teasing obsession with old age and retirement added yet another element of uncertainty to the problems of his second ministry. As Chamberlain realised quite clearly, it was the extraordinary pre-eminence and political unpredictability of the Grand Old Man himself, rather than the mere numerical majority of the Whigs within the Cabinet, that stood as the greatest barrier to Radical advancement. 'He would be King Stork, and . . . some of us frogs would have a hard time of it under him.' (Garvin 1932, vol. 1: 288) Hence Chamberlain's continual frustration, his leaks to the Press, perpetual threats of resignation, and appeals to the public over the heads of his Cabinet colleagues.

The Radicals themselves were partly to blame for their position in 1880. They too like the rest of the Liberal Party had put victory and unity first in the election campaign; and once victory had been achieved they found themselves with a plenitude of policies but no agreement as to which should be given priority or how they were to be obtained. This disagreement also helped to emphasise the perennial disunity within the ranks of the parliamentary Radicals below the gangway – 'a miserable lot', according to Labouchere (one of them) 'who seem ashamed of their opinions' (Thorold 1913: 206). Even more important was the fact that these Radicals were cut off from their former associates and potential leaders – more especially Chamberlain – now in the government; a rift which widened immeasurably as Irish and imperial difficulties came to the fore in the 1880s, involving delicate problems for the Radical conscience. It was the domination of these complex, emotional and time-consuming issues in the early years of Gladstone's second ministry that ultimately helps to explain why demands for domestic reforms were ignored or postponed. Such a situation was almost inevitable, as the Radicals themselves recognised, given the appalling inefficiency of the legislative machinery of the House of Commons, even after the procedural reforms of the early 1880s passed to deal with Irish obstruction (Guiness Rogers 1884).

It was the Irish question, as always, which posed the most agonising questions for the Radicals. It 'acted as a kind of surgical knife on Radicalism, cutting through the rhetoric of professed ideals and laying bare the nerve system and bone structure of the entire movement' (Heyck 1974: ix). The urban, Protestant, progressive tradition of English Radicalism provided no clear guide-lines for comprehending the problems of a Catholic agrarian community, especially when accompanied by the depredations of the Land League and the contempt for English parliamentary traditions displayed by the Irish Parliamentary Party. The middle-class Radicals were as ignorant of Ireland and as subject to the same prejudices and *idées fixes* as other Englishmen; the benefits of the Union and the fallacies of the Home Rule case were to them almost self-evident. Moreover, the Irish question was both an irritant and a distraction, diverting the Liberal government's attention away from its predestined role – the achievement of the Radical Programme in England. If the problem of Ireland had to be tackled, then the solution lay (in Chamberlain's phrase) in 'a wise and liberal policy of reform', especially that most cherished of Radical nostrums, land reform. This would destroy the *raison d'être* of agrarian agitation and undermine the credibility of the Home Rule party. Hence the Radicals were at one in supporting Gladstone's further attacks on Irish landlordism, culminating in the great Land Act of 1881. This piece of legislation, by granting the 'three F's' – fair rents, free sale, fixity of tenure – the major demand of Davitt and the Land League, seemed to provide for many Radicals a once-and-for-all panacea for Irish problems; hence their dismay and anger at Parnell's cavalier attitude towards the Act. As Chamberlain commented: 'I am convinced that Parnell does not want the Government to succeed. He fears that the settlement of the land question would be the death-blow to his Home Rule agitation.' (Garvin 1932, vol. 1: 326)

The real division in the Radical ranks came not over the question of reform, but over that of coercion – the introduction by the Liberal government of special powers to deal with crime and violence in Ireland. This was strongly supported by Forster, the Irish Secretary, and was the main purpose of the Bill of 1881 which preceded the land legislation of that year – a measure that was only passed after a bitter and protracted struggle by the Irish members. Though Chamberlain had argued consistently in favour of conciliation before coercion, in the end (like Bright) he firmly supported Forster's policy. He believed that law and order – and therefore the British fiat in Ireland – must be maintained at all costs, even if it meant the proscription of the Land League and the arrest and imprisonment of Parnell, actions which followed hard upon the heels of the new Coercion Act. This was an attitude which was for the moment shared by the majority of Radicals both inside and outside Parliament, including, significantly, the leaders of the TUC (Webb and Webb 1920: 362–3). This gave some credibility to Chamberlain's claim that the working classes were with the government over coercion. 'Parnell is doing his best to make Irish legislation unpopular with English radicals. The workingmen do not like to see law set at defiance, and a dissolution on the "justice to Ireland" cry would under present circumstances be a hazardous operation.' (Heyck 1974: 58)

Chamberlain defended himself to his Birmingham constituents in June: 'For my part I hate coercion . . . But then we hate disorder more'; and at Liverpool in October: 'I say to Ireland what the . . . Republicans of the North said to the Southern States of America. The Union must be preserved. Within these limits there is nothing which you may not ask and hope to obtain.' (Garvin 1932, vol. 1: 337, 345) In private he was even more outspoken and brutal. He wrote to Morley: 'We are agreed that it is impossible to concede the present demands of the Irish party – that national independence cannot be given to Ireland. It is, therefore, war to the knife between a despotism created to re-establish constitutional law, and a despotism not less completely elaborated to subvert law and produce anarchy as a precedent to revolutionary change.'[2]

Not all Radicals were prepared to see the issue in such stark terms. An important minority in the House of Commons, led by Cowen, believed that coercion was 'evil, unjust and impolitic' (Jones 1885: 65). They were backed up outside the House by groups of London working-class Radicals who, in disgust at official Liberal policy, joined Hyndman's Democratic Federation, though his extremism soon drove them out (Thompson 1964). In addition, middle-class intellectuals such as Harrison and the Positivists and, above all, John Morley, were just as violent in their opposition to coercion.

Morley, now editor of the *Pall Mall Gazette* as well as the *Fortnightly Review*, became the outstanding critic in the Press of the government's policy. He complained to Gladstone that with the best will in the world he found it difficult to support the policy of coercion in Ireland, since it undermined fundamental Liberal values and produced (yet again) 'a crisis for Liberalism' (Hirst 1927, vol. 1: 110–11). But Morley not only denounced coercion (and in a famous article in the *Pall Mall Gazette* early in 1882 called for Forster's resignation and his replacement by Chamberlain); he also courageously expressed sympathy with the demands of the Land League, believing that the principle of 'justice for Ireland' far outweighed the importance of the law and order issue. He replied passionately to Chamberlain's earlier letter: '. . . in my heart I feel that the League has done downright good work in raising up the tenants against their truly detestable tyrants', even though he accepted that violence and intimidation often accompanied its activities.[3] For his part, Chamberlain became increasingly uneasy at the fissures produced in the Radical ranks by his hardline attitude, and admitted frankly to Dilke that the Irish question was 'a horrible imbroglio and for the moment I do not see my way out of the fog' (Jay 1981: 58).

The dramatic events of 1882 introduced no new issues of principle into Radical disputes with the government or among themselves over the Irish question. In the spring of that year Joseph Chamberlain, with the tacit support of Gladstone, helped to arrange the 'Kilmainham Treaty' with Parnell. By this agreement the Irish leader was to be released from prison, and in return would use his influence to end the 'No Rent' campaign organised by the Irish tenants; the British government also intimated that it would help with rent arrears. For Chamberlain, the main purpose of the Kilmainham Treaty was to build up support among the Irish for the Liberal Party, and especially its Radical wing. And Parnell had his own personal and public reasons for supporting such an arrangement. It would 'in my judgement', he wrote to Chamberlain, 'be regarded by the country as a practical settlement of the Land Question and would enable us to co-operate cordially for the future with the Liberal Party in forwarding Liberal principles and measures of general reform' (Chamberlain 1953: 50). The release of Parnell and the consequent resignation of Forster as Irish Secretary was followed by a more sympathetic understanding between Gladstone and Parnell. This spirit was not entirely destroyed by the Phoenix Park murders and the passing of another Crimes Act, backed by the new Irish Secretary, G. O. Trevelyan. These events convinced most Radicals, including Chamberlain, that coercion was no longer acceptable as a long-term solution to the troubles of Ireland.

The Liberal government also inherited formidable problems in Africa. These were subtly related to the Irish question; not only because African issues were used as counters in the internal Cabinet wrangling over Ireland in 1880–81, particularly by Chamberlain, but because many Radicals saw British policy in Africa as similarly oppressive – a continuation in fact of Beaconsfield's 'imperialism' (Schreuder 1969: 177–9; Robinson and Gallagher 1961: 69–71, 92–3). In the Transvaal, for example, which had been annexed by Britain in 1878, Gladstone was faced with a growing nationalist demand from the Boers for an immediate return to independence now that the threat from the Zulus had been destroyed. Worried by their moral obligations to the natives and tempted by the prospects of a South African Confederation, the Liberals hesitated. But the shock of the Boer uprising and the British defeat at Majuba Hill (February 1881), together with pressure from the Radicals in the government, pushed Gladstone towards a quick settlement, and the Boers gained their independence (subject to a vague British suzerainty) by the Pretoria Convention in the same year. Thus in the Transvaal conciliation appeared to have triumphed.

In Egypt, on the other hand, a quick neat solution seemed beyond the government's grasp. There, during the previous Conservative administration, the British had already increased their 'informal' influence through the purchase of the Suez Canal shares, and the establishment of the Anglo-French Financial Commission to supervise Egyptian finances and arrange payment of the foreign debt. Ironically, it was the Liberals who now blundered into direct military intervention in Egypt in 1882. This was the result of a confused and often contradictory set of motives – strategic, financial and humanitarian – following the outbreak of a nationalist revolt in the country, the withdrawal of the French, and the deaths of about fifty Europeans in anti-foreign riots in Alexandria. 'It is a nasty business', commented Lord Granville, the Foreign Secretary, 'and we have been much out of luck.' (Chamberlain 1974: 33)

The occupation of Egypt produced a real moral crisis for the Liberal Party: it marked 'either the Liberals' coming-of-age as imperialists, or, the betrayal of every principle for which the party professed to stand' (Thornton 1959: 57). John Bright resigned from the Cabinet in July 1882 in protest at the bombardment of Alexandria, more out of habit than conviction. His place was taken by Dilke who was appointed President of the Local Government Board. Chamberlain (who was dubbed by Granville 'almost the greatest jingo' over Egypt) supported Hartington in favour of intervention, on the grounds that the safety of the Suez Canal must be maintained to secure the route to India, and reparations exacted for the damage and loss of life during the riots. As he pointed out to Gladstone (who stressed, characteristically, Britain's 'civilising' mission in Egypt): 'Liberal opinion in the country will be extremely restive at the idea of armed intervention either for the maintenance of the control in the interests of the Bondholders, or for the enforcement of restrictions on the right of the Egyptian people to manage their own affairs.' (Chamberlain 1953: 72).

But it was precisely those aspects of the situation that Radicals outside the government found so evident and so reprehensible. For Labouchere, the Egyptian campaign was 'a Bondholder's War' (Thorold 1913: 180); and John Morley (who had originally acquiesced in intervention) saw the later involvement in Egypt as the result of 'financial cupidity, bastard Imperialism, and . . . truculent philanthropy' (Hirst 1972, vol. 2: 196). Frederic Harrison, in letters and articles in the early 1880s, used the Egyptian example to develop a crude but vigorous attack on 'economic imperialism'. 'High interests of state', he wrote to Morley, 'are the pretext for intervention. But the true object is to get the gamblers 7% paid a little longer till the great financiers of Europe can get out their unified stock . . .'[4] Over the Egyptian imbroglio, however, the Radical opponents of the government gained even less public support than they did over Irish coercion. The Anti-Aggression League, formed in 1881 by Harrison and his friends to oppose intervention in Egypt, soon melted away, mainly because, as Harrison saw, few Liberals were prepared deliberately to oppose Gladstone whatever doubts they might have about the wisdom of his policy (Harrison 1911, vol. 2: 123).

Wolseley's victory at Tel-el-Kebir and the military occupation of Egypt created new problems rather than solved old ones. What action should be taken by the Liberal government now that it found itself, to its own astonishment and embarrassment, the master of Egypt? On this issue the Cabinet was as divided as it had been over the invasion itself. Should they stay or withdraw? 'Scuttle and bankruptcy' versus 'protectorate and guarantee', as Chamberlain sardonically noted (Gwynn and Tuckwell 1918, vol. 2: 94). Given the appalling internal problems of Egypt and the diplomatic ramifications spreading from the original invasion, both courses were open to serious objections. The situation became even more complicated in 1883 when widespread revolt broke out in the Sudan, and the government found itself faced with a replay of the original scenario – withdrawal or intervention? The Radicals were bitterly opposed to a forward policy in the Sudan, a position which in principle Gladstone too supported. Some seventy Radicals, including John Morley who was now member for Newcastle, supported Labouchere's motion of censure on the government in March 1884 over the decision to send Gordon to the Sudan. By that time, however, the Cabinet had at last faced up to the reality of its position on the Upper Nile. 'We have done our Egyptian business', as Gladstone said in a famous retort to Chamberlain at this time, 'and are an Egyptian Government.'

(Gwynn and Tuckwell 1918, vol. 2: 46) It was a consummation that had only been achieved at the price of confusion, weakness and division within the Liberal Party over the previous three years.

By 1883 Chamberlain was acutely aware of the restlessness of the Radicals over the government's dismal record on reform and its illiberal policies in Ireland and Egypt, policies which both he and Dilke had supported. One of the results was that, as Sir Edward Hamilton, Gladstone's private secretary, suggested, the influence of the Radicals within the party was probably less then than it had been in 1880 (Bahlman 1972: 302). 'The Radicals in the Cabinet were now only Dilke and myself', noted Chamberlain, 'and we found our views ignored or outvoted by the majority of our colleagues. In the country, however, our opinions were endorsed by at least four-fifths of the Liberal Party.' (Chamberlain 1953: 88) What was now needed was a vigorous campaign to revive the flagging spirit of Radicalism. 'The country . . . is ripe for a new departure in constructive Radicalism', Chamberlain told Dilke, 'and only wants leaders. So if we are driven to fight we shall easily recruit an army.' (Gwynn and Tuckwell 1918, vol. 1: 516) The basis for such a *démarche*, he believed, now lay in parliamentary reform – the county franchise and equal electoral districts, for parliamentary reform was 'the root of all others . . . the settlement of which will give the greatest possible stimulus to all the reforms which the Liberal Party have in their hearts to carry' (Lucy 1885: 47). Once the rural labourers were enfranchised and the constituencies remodelled, then the Radicals could capture the new electorate, dominate the party after Gladstone's inevitable retirement, and proceed to their task of political and social reconstruction.

This was the purpose of Chamberlain's national campaign of 1883. He was preparing the ground for a later decisive struggle with the Whigs by once again seizing the political initiative, even if this meant breaking established conventions on collective responsibility. 'I have a difficult part to play', he wrote to Labouchere in December. 'I expect I shall get the sack sooner or later, and my object is to get the whole machine as far forward as possible before the smash comes.' (Fraser 1966: 53) He appealed above all to the Radical faithful by displaying his refurbished Radical credentials, while at the same time distancing himself from the failures and weaknesses of the government of which he was a notable member. The demand for parliamentary reform was therefore accompanied by vigorous attacks on the old Radical *bêtes noires* – the aristocracy ('who toil not neither do they spin'), the House of Lords and the Established Church – even the monarchy did not entirely escape. More important was the new emphasis on social reform. 'Just now public opinion is all on social questions', Chamberlain wrote to Escott (now editor of the *Fortnightly Review*) apologising for the failure to produce an agreed Radical statement on foreign policy[5]. He himself contributed an article that year to the *Fortnightly Review* on 'Labourers' and artisans' dwellings'. Here Chamberlain was responding to, rather than initiating, a public mood of concern over working-class housing conditions, generated by the efforts of slum parsons, muck-rakers and socialists, reaching its apotheosis in the Royal Commission on Housing of 1884 – and then dying away. It was a theme which was closely linked with the attack on 'the landlord', typical of the early 1880s – a period of fierce agricultural depression – as developed in the work of Henry George particularly and the plethora of land reform societies that flourished during these years (Lynd 1968; Perkin 1973; Martin 1974). It was these 'great social questions', Chamberlain hinted to his audiences, that would be taken up by a future Liberal government (Lucy 1885: 54).

Gladstone was worried by the tone of Chamberlain's speeches (to which the Queen inevitably brought his attention) and, more importantly, by his concern that they might create the impression in the public mind that the Cabinet was committed to policies which were still being considered, or be used to pressurise those ministers who were unenthusiastic about Radical reform. This was a point of some importance, since Hartington was threatening to resign over the franchise question, believing that the extension of the vote to rural Ireland would be disastrous for the Union. 'My difficulties in keeping things together at the moment are very great', lamented Gladstone to Chamberlain. But the nice questions at issue between them over the freedom of speech of Cabinet ministers were for the moment smoothed over (Garvin 1932, vol. 1: 407).

This was helped by the fact that by late 1883 the Prime Minister was a convinced supporter of the county franchise, and by exerting moral pressure was able to carry Hartington with him. Gladstone's plan, which was strongly supported by Chamberlain, was to deal with the franchise issue first, leaving the complicated question of redistribution to a later date. But the original Bill, though it easily passed through the Commons, was blocked in the Lords, as Salisbury believed, probably correctly, that franchise extension without redistribution would give an unfair advantage to the Liberals. This enabled Chamberlain to whip up a new campaign in the summer of 1884 on the basis of 'the Peers versus the People'. It fizzled out, since the party leaders were busy arranging a compromise behind the scenes based on the passing simultaneously of an agreed 'package' – the county franchise plus redistribution. The great Acts of 1884 and 1885 which secured this seemed to be a Radical triumph. At last the principles of manhood suffrage, and equal electoral districts based largely on single-member constituencies, had been secured.

'As soon as the success of the Reform Bill was assured I began seriously to prepare for the general election', wrote Chamberlain, 'and especially to frame, with the assistance of other prominent

Radicals, a programme for the Liberal Party in the new Parliament.'
(Chamberlain 1953: 108) This programme was formulated in a series
of articles 'on Radical policy and methods' published in the *Fortnightly Review* between 1883 (rather earlier than Chamberlain indicates) and 1885, with the active cooperation of the editor, Escott,
and subsequently published as a book, *The Radical Programme*, in
July 1885. *The Radical Programme* thus stands in a similar relationship to the parliamentary Reform Acts of 1884–85 as *Essays in
Reform* and *Questions for a Reformed Parliament* do to the Second
Reform Act of 1867. It is an appeal by 'the advanced party' to the
Liberals – and the nation – to recognise and adapt to the social
implications of the extension of democracy. 'At last', wrote Chamberlain in 1885 in his preface to the *Programme*, 'the majority of the
nation will be represented by a majority of the House of Commons,
and ideas and wants and claims which have been hitherto ignored in
legislation will find a voice in Parliament, and will compel the attention of statesmen.' (Chamberlain 1885: v) Chamberlain contributed
no article to the symposium himself; but the main contributors,
Morley, Collings, Escott, Adams, were his friends and allies, and the
topics covered in the *Programme* – housing, agricultural labour,
disestablishment, education, taxation and local government – provide
a reasonable conspectus of Chamberlainite Radicalism in 1885. The
book was thus also an attempt by Chamberlain – successful but short-
lived – to reassert his intellectual and political ascendancy over the
Radical movement, as a prelude to his bid for domination within the
Liberal Party.

The Radical Programme breathes an air of confidence and optimism; the Radicals believed that the future was theirs. It was they
who would gain most from the massive creation of new seats in the
great towns and cities – the most important aspect of the 'revolution
of 1884'; for such centres were bound to become strongholds of
Radical power and influence. 'The great towns as they now are',
wrote Escott, 'constitute the source and centre of English political
opinion. It is from them that Liberal legislation receives its initiative;
it is the steady progress exercised by them that guarantees the political progress of the country.' Moreover, the establishment of single-
member constituencies would end the old practice by which a Whig
and a Radical were run together in two-member seats, and who could
doubt that, in an age of rising democracy, this would favour the
choice of Radical candidates? 'The buffers on which timid Liberalism
has hitherto relied against advanced Liberalism will henceforth
disappear.' (Chamberlain 1885: 5; 7–9) Nor, given the reverbera-
tions of the new electoral system in the counties, were Radical
chances there as hopeless as they traditionally appeared.

But the political revolution of 1884–85 – profound as it was – was
but the prelude to the major social transformation that must surely

follow. 'The era of purely political legislation is at an end for a time
. . . it is social legislation which will afford a field for the energy and
constructive skills of Radical statesmen in the future.' Within the
pages of *The Radical Programme* is contained a practical programme
of reform for a future Liberal government. At the heart of this
programme is an attack on landlordism – in a wide sense – coupled
with the Chamberlainite emphasis on the local authorities as the main
instrument of social progress. The emphasis in land reform has now
moved away from the old Radical concern with 'free trade' in land
by an attack on entail and primogeniture, to the new notion of a
direct attack on the great estates by legislation and thus the creation
in the countryside of a new class of smallholders – the famous 'three
acres and a cow'. In addition, by taxing the landlords' 'unearned
increment', society would reclaim part of the wealth which it has
created, and this could be used to raise the appalling standards of
the rural community. But the aim of land reform is not just to
improve conditions in the countryside. Even more importantly, its
purpose is to attack, indirectly, the even greater problems of urban
unemployment and deprivation. By providing a reasonable security
and comfort for the rural labourers it would help to check the drift
from the land to the towns and cities, which only exacerbated the
social problems of the urban working classes (Chamberlain 1885: 61,
217, 104).

This emphasis on social change in the countryside is closely linked
with the need for local government reform in Great Britain and
Ireland, more particularly the establishment of elected county councils. By setting up a nation-wide pattern of elected local authorities
and introducing at the same time a system of 'progressive taxation'
at the centre and a more efficient rating system locally, the councils
could become the agencies for the provision of those social reforms
so desperately needed – free education and slum clearance especially.
Nor was the question of disestablishment – the subject of a long
article by John Morley – unrelated to these tasks. Its triumph was
now virtually a foregone conclusion. 'As we trace back the course of
events, the most reluctant eye sees them all tending uniformly and
with growing momentum to the secularisation of the State and the
emancipation of the Church.' Disendowment would accompany
disestablishment, and this too would unleash new financial resources
'for the purposes of national usefulness'. These separate proposals
for changes in landownership, taxation, local government and the
Church, thus provided an interlocking programme of Radical reform;
together, they 'sound the death-knell of the *laissez-faire* system'
(Chamberlain 1885: 127, 44, 13).

The Radical Programme was denounced as 'socialism', as indeed
its authors had expected. But it is difficult to see the programme as
socialist in any realistic sense. The emphasis on the establishment of

smallholdings was the very opposite of socialism, and Chamberlain was a violent opponent of land nationalisation which he denounced as 'veiled confiscation'. 'The Socialists and the land nationalisers wished to extinguish private ownership in land', as Hamer comments, 'Chamberlain and his associates wished to extend it.' (Hamer 1971: xii) The authors of *The Radical Programme* certainly supported what they termed 'socialistic legislation'. But by this they meant an acceleration of the well-established principle of state intervention 'on behalf of the weak against the strong, in the interests of labour against capital, of want and suffering against luxury and ease'. The state had 'the right and duty . . . to fix within certain broad limits the extent, and to control the conditions of private ownership'. The concern with 'progressive taxation' is part of the same pattern, though this did mark a break with the old Cobdenite emphasis on economy and retrenchment (Chamberlain 1885: 17, 57).

The Chamberlainite Radicals believed firmly that their programme would act as a spur to real individual and especially local effort. 'The socialistic measures now contemplated would preserve in their normal vigour and freshness all the individual activities of English citizenship, and would do nothing more spoliatory than tax . . . aggregations of wealth for the good of the community.' (Chamberlain 1885: 13) Chamberlain was a convinced believer in the merits of free enterprise and private capitalism, except in very special circumstances. His plea for cheapening the costs of slum clearance by lowering the compensation paid to local landowners was coupled with an unmerited confidence in the ability of private enterprise to provide a sufficient quantity of working-class housing at reasonable rents (Chamberlain 1883). The measures proposed in *The Radical Programme* only continued lines of policy already laid down by previous legislation: 'it was the last fling, rather than the death-knell, of the established social order' (Fraser 1966: 46). In that sense, as Escott shrewdly insisted in a contemporary tribute, Chamberlain was one of the strongest defenders of the 'rights of property', so long as property recognised its duties and responsibilities. 'The truth is', he wrote, 'that, like Mr. Gladstone, Mr. Chamberlain is . . . one who makes for Conservatism. He is a controlling force in a democratic era.' (Escott 1884)

This observation underlines the truth that *The Radical Programme* was an appeal by urban middle-class Radicals to members of their own class, rather than to the rural labourers or the industrial proletariat. It urged them to support reform in order to preserve the established property system; to reduce class hostility rather than exacerbate it. Chamberlain was therefore providing an alternative to the socialism of the Social Democratic Federation (SDF) and the Fabians. Hence, once again, the concentration on the figure of the landlord as the scapegoat for the ills of modern society, and the singular absence from the *Programme* of any discussion of the contemporary industrial system. 'The Radical today', said J. E. Williams of the SDF, 'was the "Artful Dodger" who went up and down the country telling the people to take hold of the landlord thief but to let the greater thief, the capitalist, go scot free.' (Clegg et al. 1964: 53) It was a taunt which the middle-class Radicals could only greet with embarrassed silence. It went to the very heart of their traditional creed.

With parliamentary reform out of the way, and with a general election inevitable in the not too distant future, Chamberlain struck while the iron was hot. In January 1885, at Birmingham, he launched a new phase of the Radical campaign. His purpose was plain. 'We will utterly destroy the Whigs', he told Morley, 'and have a Radical government before many years are out.' (Howard 1950) It was not so much the contents of his speeches which aroused alarm; apart from references to the payment of MPs and a graduated income tax they did not go beyond what had already been outlined in the *Radical Programme* articles in the *Fortnightly Review*. It was their tone that was so outrageous, particularly the taunting references to the 'rights of property'. 'But then I ask', he said at Birmingham, 'what ransom will property pay for the security which it enjoys? What substitute will it find for the natural rights which have ceased to be recognised?' (Lucy 1885: 104) In later (and less well-known) speeches his views became more circumspect – and more revealing. A week later, at Ipswich, he asserted (quoted in Lucy 1885: 107–8):

> I hope I may be able . . . to show that the interests of rich and poor are not hostile interests, but that, in pressing as I do for a more practical acknowledgement of the duties of property, I am putting the rights of property on the only firm and defensible basis . . . I asked the other day what ransom will property pay for the natural rights which have ceased to be recognised. I will put the same question now in a different form. What insurance will wealth find it to its advantage to provide against the risks to which it is undoubtedly subject?

Once again, as in 1883, Gladstone was concerned about the constitutional propriety of Chamberlain's speeches. He himself had suffered virtually a physical and mental collapse during the latter part of 1884 as a result of the agonising problems of Egypt, Gordon and the Sudan; and this led to hints of a palace revolution, backed by Hartington, Chamberlain and Dilke, to replace him (Cooke and Vincent 1974: 29–33). The murder of Gordon in January 1885 followed by the capture of Khartoum, delivered another shattering blow to the already battered reputation of the government – a blow from which it never really recovered. Curiously, the Prime Minister's morale revived as a result of these events and, throwing aside thoughts of retirement, he aimed to reassert his authority over the Cabinet. In tortuous letters to Chamberlain, he stressed the difficulties that could arise, particularly for party unity, through his advancing policies that were still undiscussed and controversial (Chamberlain 1953: 114–15). But Chamberlain said in reply that he was only expressing personal opinions, not intended to commit individual ministers or the Cabinet as a whole. More forcefully, he argued that times had now changed (Chamberlain 1953: 116–17):

> Popular government is inconsistent with the reticence which official etiquette formerly imposed on speakers . . . .. Now the Platform has become one of the most powerful and indispensable instruments of Government. We are within sight of a General Election when, for the first time, two millions of men, hitherto without representation, will be called upon to exercise their political rights; and it is of great importance that these vast masses of people . . . should be assured that their interests are a constant object of concern to the Liberal Party and the Liberal Government.

As a Cabinet colleague noted of Chamberlain at this time: 'He proclaims his own policy, and bids for the favour of the coming democracy, as if he were an independent politician.' (Cooke and Vincent 1971: 52)

The 'coming democracy' did not seem all that impressed by Chamberlain's winter campaign. Moreover, there were dangers for the Radical leader in running too far ahead of his more timid colleagues. As Hamilton observed: 'It will be many years before the Radical party in this country will be strong enough to stand by itself without the aid of moderate Liberals and Whigs. So if Chamberlain does not mind, he will find himself stranded. . . .' (Bahlman 1972: 776) There was, however, another alternative available: an alliance with Parnell and the Home Rule Party based on a settlement of the problem of Irish self-government. Such an agreement would have enormous advantages. It would give the Liberal Party powerful and much-needed allies in the forthcoming general election since, as a result of the 1884 Reform Act, the Irish Party was bound to dominate the whole of Ireland outside Ulster. It would also help the Radicals in their inter-party conflict with the Whigs, which would become crucial if, as expected, Gladstone retired after the election. It would also have the additional advantage of removing the Irish 'obstruction' and thus pave the way for the implementation of the Radical Programme. Chamberlain's project therefore arose not from altruism, but entirely from his assessment of the state of party politics in Britain.

Plans for providing a greater degree of self-government for the Irish had been in the air since 1883, when a scheme for establishing county councils had foundered owing to Cabinet divisions. Now, in the latter months of 1884, following the Reform Act, a small Cabinet Committee mooted a plan for an enlarged system of internal self-government involving county councils and some sort of elected

'National Council' for Ireland. Chamberlain went even further. In December he proposed, in addition to county councils, an elected 'Central Board' which should have a major legislative, as distinct from just administrative powers. For Chamberlain, this proposal was conceived as a generous but 'safe' concession to the Irish – an alternative to the Home Rule solution which he so bitterly opposed. The scheme was presented to Parnell using Capt. O'Shea as an intermediary, and O'Shea – for his own opportunist reasons – made out to Chamberlain that the Irish leader was more amenable to such proposals than he really was. Parnell *was* prepared to consider any plan for providing a greater degree of self-government in Ireland. What he was not prepared to do, was to sacrifice Home Rule – to which he was totally committed – for its sake. No form of self-government, he reiterated in January 1885, was 'a substitute for the restoration of our Irish parliament'. On this rock Chamberlain's plan, and therefore the Irish alliance, foundered, though the complicated negotiations, which also brought in Cardinal Manning and the Irish bishops, continued until the summer (Howard 1952–53).

As far as the Liberal government was concerned, Chamberlain's Central Board scheme became linked with the problem of a renewal of the Crimes Act and thus a continuation of coercion. Both questions further divided an already demoralised Cabinet. 'The Cabinet', wrote Harcourt, 'seems like a man afflicted with epilepsy, and one fit succeeds another, each worse than the last . . . Every one wishes to go at once. But how, and why, and on what pretext?' (Gardiner 1923, vol. 1: 527) The government was soon to receive its quietus. On 9 May the Cabinet rejected the Central Board scheme by one vote, much to Gladstone's disgust. For Chamberlain it was the last straw. Only the previous year the Cabinet had failed to provide firm backing for his Merchant Shipping Bill. His loyalty to the government, fast-fading, was now utterly at an end. On 20 May he and Dilke resigned in exasperation at the impasse over coercion. This action was shortly overtaken by events when, on 9 June, the government was defeated by a combination of Irish and Conservative votes, for Parnell now believed that he had more to gain from the Tories than the Liberals. Gladstone resigned, and was succeeded by a 'caretaker government' under Lord Salisbury until a new general election could be held in the autumn.

Chamberlain was now 'unmuzzled' and therefore free to promote his own ideas with less restraint. As he remarked to Hamilton, he had 'programmes enough and to spare' (Bahlman 1972: 884). In the summer he launched his own personal 'Radical Programme' in a series of belligerent speeches in the north of England and London. At Hull, on 5 August, he spelt out in more detail the main reforms proposed in his January campaign, and, deliberately trailing his coat, he re-emphasised the evils of inequality of wealth and the responsibilities of 'property' (Lucy 1885: 161–72). Lord Hartington repudiated Chamberlain's programme as 'socialism', and defended the rights of property in a notorious speech at Waterfoot a few weeks later. The Whig leader was in turn denounced by the Radical as 'a political Rip van Winkle' (Lucy 1885: 188). It has been suggested that for Chamberlain this war of words was related more to 'the political tactics of the moment' than to programmes of social reform (Cooke and Vincent 1974: 11). For during the summer months of July and August Gladstone was in Norway recuperating after illness; once again the question of his retirement loomed over the party. Chamberlain's campaign during these months was therefore a deliberate bid for the party leadership by an attempt to destroy the political pretensions of his only possible rival – Lord Hartington – and capture the new electorate. Yet war *à outrance* with the Whigs had its own dangers: by antagonising moderate opinion in the party it might imperil Chamberlain's own chances of the leadership – a point he had discussed with Hamilton two months earlier (Bahlman 1972: 884). Chamberlain's speeches in September began, therefore, the process of retreat from the full Radical Programme: now his three main points were free schools, compulsory land purchase and fiscal reform (Simon 1970). The graduated income tax and payment of MPs were dropped, and, though there were still references to disestablishment (especially for his Scottish audiences) it was not regarded as an early priority for any future Liberal government (Howard 1950).

There was, in any case, an even greater reason for circumspection. In early September Gladstone returned to England and made it clear that he intended to stay on as party leader. He issued his own election address, emphasising four areas of reform: procedure, local government, land and registration. Two of these (local government and land) were part of Chamberlain's programme, but the rest was dismissed by Gladstone; 'the average opinion of the party', he told Chamberlain, 'ought to be the rule of immediate action' (Chamberlain 1953: 130). For Gladstone, his lack-lustre manifesto was of no great importance; its purpose was to unify the party for the future not of England but of Ireland. 'Only the Liberal party can (*if* it can)', he wrote to Chamberlain on 9 September, 'cope with the great Irish question which may arise three months hence . . . It is my duty, and my desire, to avoid collision with either wing of the party.' (Chamberlain 1953: 121) Chamberlain's reaction to all this was in a letter to Dilke on 20 September. 'The Manifesto is, as I expected, bad – it is a slap in the face to us . . . I am now going to tell him frankly that . . . I will not join any Government with a programme confined to his four points. . . . His reign cannot be a long one . . . If we chose to go into direct opposition we might smash him, but the game is not worth the candle. . . . ' (Garvin 1933, vol. 2: 95–6) He followed this up by publicly stating, in his famous 'Ultimatum' speech at Victoria

Hall, London, on the 24th, that he would not join a Liberal government which excluded free education and smallholdings from its platform: these were the two 'unauthorised' elements in Chamberlain's programme (Lucy 1885: 225).

Even Morley, rapidly emerging as a devoted Gladstonian, dismissed the speech as 'melodramatic', and protested to Chamberlain against 'deliberate isolation on personal grounds from the rest of the party at a moment when there is no great *practical* issue ... on which radicals take a line of their own' (Barker 1975: 27). In private at least Chamberlain was not prepared to disagree. The process of backtracking continued. He was conciliatory to Hartington, stressed the need for party unity, and in a private visit to Gladstone at Hawarden in early October, spoke of 'reducing to an absolute minimum his idea of necessary conditions' (Ramm 1962, vol. 2: 405). The reasons for this are not far to seek. From Chamberlain's point of view it would be madness to cut himself off from Gladstone and the moderate Liberals if the GOM was able and willing to take the party into the general election, with a good chance of winning. Like Hartington also, Chamberlain needed Gladstone's 'umbrella' to shelter him from the hazards of a new and unknown electoral terrain. Besides, Gladstone was (as in 1880) almost 'an honorary Radical': 'on the greatest issue between us and the Whigs Mr.G. is on our side', he told Dilke (Barker 1975: 13). There was something in this. For though Gladstone was in many ways antipathetic to Chamberlain – 'his socialism repels me', he said – he was even more disillusioned with the conduct of 'the timid or reactionary Whigs' (Ramm 1962, vol. 2: 393, 461–2). Hence, if elected, either through pressure or blackmail, Gladstone could do the Radicals' work for them; if he decided to retire, then Chamberlain had a good chance of achieving the vacant place.

In the run-up to the election in mid-November there was a lot to be said, therefore, for a policy of conciliation and moderation – in public if not in private – if it could be maintained. Unfortunately, in the last few weeks before polling took place, Chamberlain made a series of blunders. Under pressure from the Liberation Society and the newly formed National Liberal Federation of Scotland who were campaigning on behalf of Scottish disestablishment, Chamberlain brought the disestablishment issue to the forefront of his campaign (Savage 1961). It was a gift to the Conservative opposition, who were able to link it with the Radicals' earlier references to disendownment and therefore cash in on the cry of 'the Church in danger'. Moreover, the emphasis on free schools (and disendowment) antagonised the Roman Catholic clergy who were fearful for the position of their own institutions if fees were abolished in the board schools. At the eleventh hour, therefore, Chamberlain's electioneering became dominated by religious and educational issues from his Radical Nonconformist past, issues which he believed were vote-winners, 'designed to power the engine of urban noncomformity manufactured by the Redistribution Act' (Barker 1975: 37).

The results of the general election of 1885 were a severe disappointment to both Gladstone and Chamberlain who had hoped for and expected an overall Liberal victory. In the event the Liberals won 335 seats, the Conservatives 249 and the Irish 86; and the immediate victor was Parnell who had not only obtained his primary aim – to hold the balance of power in the House of Commons – but, as expected, had utterly destroyed the power of the Liberal Party in Ireland into the bargain. In the counties in England and Wales, on the other hand, the Liberals did remarkably well: their numbers went up from 54 in 1880 to 133 in 1885 – giving them about 30 more county seats than their Tory opponents. This has generally been attributed to Chamberlain's land policy – his wooing of the agricultural labourers with 'three acres and a cow'. It has been suggested, however, that economic issues were more important: the labourer voted Liberal because he was frightened by the growing Conservative support for 'fair trade', a policy of protection which might, if successful, increase the cost of living (Pelling 1967: 16). In some areas too, there appears to have been a reaction against the overweening domination of squire and parson, a resentment which the rural labourer could now express for the first time through the vote (Simon 1975).

The other outstanding feature of the election was the heavy Liberal losses in the boroughs. It is true that they still maintained their lead in the largest industrial cities, but in London, Lancashire and the middling boroughs generally, they did badly. This was due to a variety of causes. Lord Richard Grosvenor, the Chief Whip, complained that Chamberlain's 'extremism had frightened away shoals of what I call the 'floating balance', the men who turn an election' (Howard 1950). Certainly, as Radical friends reported to Chamberlain, the disestablishment issue was a major handicap in their contests. 'The shopkeepers are very hot on the church question', wrote Dilke from London, 'which has turned many of our men. Even my nonconformist friends come to me to implore me to pledge myself against disestablishment', which indeed he did (Simon 1975). 'Free schools' too, with its implication of higher rates, proved to be 'very awkward', as Morley pointed out.[6] Gladstone himself wrote to Grosvenor that the main factors in the defeat were: 'Fair Trade + Parnell + Church + Chamberlain . . . I place the *causi damni* in what I think their order of importance.' (Hammond 1964: 398) This was a fair estimate. The Catholic working men in England obediently voted Conservative in accordance with Parnell's instructions; though the anti-Liberal stance of the Catholic clergy over the free schools issue also seems to have been important (Howard 1947). There is also evidence to suggest that, as in the countryside, economic factors were significant. The industrial working classes in the cities were strongly influenced by the unsatisfactory state of trade; and to some of them at least Chamberlain was important not so much as the author of the 'Unauthorised Programme' (in which they had little interest) but as the ex-President of the Board of Trade who had done little to improve their prospects of employment. In some parts of industrial Britain the gospel of fair trade was bound to be tempting (Brown 1943). Clearly, beneath the great abstractions of the politicians, bread-and-butter issues were again of major importance in an election.

What can be said about Chamberlain's role in the campaign of 1885? A recent biographer describes it as 'one of the highwater marks' of his career (Judd 1977: 124): but more detailed analyses of the election are much more scathing (Cooke and Vincent 1974: 13–14; Simon 1975; Barker 1975:28–40). Despite appearances to the contrary, Chamberlain's campaign was aimed at winning the urban, and especially the metropolitan, vote: he was well aware that the Greater London area now returned ninety-five members! It was sensible, therefore, in tune with Escott's arguments in *The Radical Programme*, 'to lay the foundations of his new party upon what he imagined was the bedrock of urban Liberalism instead of upon the shifting sands of rural sentiment' (Barker 1975: 37). But the Radicals' interpretation of the effects of the Redistribution Act was largely wishful thinking. If they gained at the expense of the Whigs – the Tories overtook them both. For the cities were carved up in 1885 on largely 'class' lines, and 'villa Toryism' – now separated out in its own constituencies – was easily captured for the Conservative Party (Cornford 1963–64). Moreover, the policies offered by Chamberlain to the urban electorate, especially in London – free schools, small-holdings, disestablishment – not only antagonised moderate Liberals and divided and embittered Radicals, they also had no real appeal to the economically hard-pressed working classes. The vital issues of trade and employment, in a period of social and economic disloca-tion, were largely ignored. Even 'Radical Joe's' earlier denunciations of urban landlordism and an inequitable tax system were played down in favour of his own sectarian formulae. Hence: 'the 1885 elec-tion left his reputation in rags. . . . He had shown that he did not know about the things he was supposed to know about – the induce-ments that would win the popular mind.' (Cooke and Vincent 1974: 13)

Chamberlain was left nonplussed and bereft of ideas. 'We are dreadfully in want of an urban "Cow"', he wrote to Harcourt on 6 December. 'The boroughs do not care for our present programme and I confess I do not know what substitute to offer them.'[7] Nor was his judgement about the political future any more prescient. Though, after the election, the Parliamentary Liberal Party contained more

Radicals than ever before, it was Gladstone who, with their blessing, carried on as party leader for his own obscure purposes. A few weeks before the election he had assured Chamberlain that, 'An instinct blindly impresses me with the likelihood that Ireland may shoulder aside everything else.' (Chamberlain 1953: 132) This was perhaps a self-fulfilling prophecy – but so it proved.

NOTES

1. 22 April 1880; Escott Papers.
2. 18 October 1881; JC/5/54.
3. 19 October 1881; JC/5/54.
4. 3 June 1882; Frederic Harrison Papers, Box 2.
5. 3 December 1883; Escott Papers.
6. 12 October 1885: JC/5/54.
7. JC/5/54.

Chapter 7

HOME RULE AND THE DECLINE OF RADICALISM

It was clear during the autumn of 1885, while Gladstone was brooding at Hawarden, that his mind was turning more and more towards some kind of Home Rule as the great 'constructive measure' that Ireland required (Ramm 1962, vol. 2: p 411). The outcome of the general election of 1885, in which the Irish Parliamentary Party won virtually every seat in southern Ireland, confirmed this growing conviction. 'I consider that Ireland has now spoken', he wrote to Hartington on 17 December, 'and that an effort ought to be made by *the government* without delay to meet their demands for the management by an Irish legislative body of Irish as distinct from imperial affairs. Only a government can do it, and a tory government can do it more easily and safely than any other.' (Morley 1905, vol. 2: 503). Gladstone's hope was utterly destroyed, however, by the publication on the very same day of the news of his support for Home Rule, as a result of the deliberate action of his son, Herbert Gladstone. Herbert believed that Chamberlain and Dilke were planning to block any possibility of his father re-emerging as Prime Minister, and the only way to forestall them was by flying the 'Hawarden Kite' and forcing Gladstone to re-enter the political arena immediately. Shortly afterwards Salisbury finally quashed any possibility of the Conservatives conceding to Parnell's demands. On 26 January 1886, therefore, the Liberal and Irish members combined together in favour of Colling's famous 'three acres and a cow' amendment, and defeated the government. Almost a score of Whigs voted with the Conservatives and seventy-six Liberals abstained; the disruption of the Liberal Party was already under way.

It was Gladstone, therefore, and not Salisbury who faced the formidable task of forming a government to introduce Home Rule for Ireland; a task undertaken in the worst possible circumstances, since nearly all his colleagues had been left completely in the dark about his change of attitude. Whatever Gladstone's motives: whether he was moved primarily by a sense of 'justice for Ireland' – the leitmotiv of Hammond's classic study (Hammond 1964); or by a determination to use the Home Rule issue to unite the party under his own leadership (Cooke and Vincent 1974: 55); or by a mixture of idealism and expediency (Steele 1970–71); his commitment to the principle of Home Rule widened the breach in the Liberal Party. Hartington and most of the Whigs refused to join the government; the appointment of Morley – now a rabid Home Ruler – as Irish Secretary, was a clear signal of what lay ahead. Dilke was 'unavailable' owing to his involvement in a notorious divorce scandal. Chamberlain and Trevelyan did join, reluctantly, but the former's confrontation tactics only precipitated the GOM's hasty production of a Home Rule Bill, and both resigned at the end of March when it was brought before the Cabinet, accompanied by a Land Purchase measure (Vincent 1977: 229). The Radical leadership was now in complete disarray. Over the next few months, following the introduction of the Home Rule Bill into the House of Commons in April, a complicated sparring match of lunge and feint, advance and retreat, took place around the body of the Bill between Gladstone and Chamberlain and their supporters and opponents. In the end, however, though the GOM was prepared to reconsider details of the Bill, such as withdrawal of the Irish members, and abandon the unpopular Land Purchase Bill, the fundamental differences between the two sides remained. 'I do not see the bridge over which even the Prince of Opportunists can pass', Granville (almost the only Whig to remain loyal to Gladstone) commented sardonically (Ramm 1962, vol. 2: 421). In the final vote in the House of Commons on the night of 7–8 June 1886, ninety-three Liberal Unionists, led by Hartington and Chamberlain, combined with the Conservatives to defeat the Bill.

What was the attitude of the Radicals to the Home Rule Crisis? The majority of parliamentary Radicals supported the Bill: out of about 160 Radical MPs 4 abstained and only 32 voted against. This was not because many of them were committed theoretically to the principles of Irish nationality and self-government; Morley was virtually the only important Radical who adopted that position. Like most loyalist Liberals they were moved by more pragmatic considerations: they trusted Gladstone and were content to follow his lead. Harcourt believed, in April, that 'the tendency of the Party is to rally to Gladstone, and they will do so the more in proportion as he appears to be ill used.' What also pushed them in this direction, was the fact that by 1886 Parnell's policies seemed to have destroyed any escape route between coercion on the one hand and Home Rule on the other; and the Radicals no longer had any stomach for a policy of coercion, especially when confronted with the Irish electoral results. 'The number of people who sufficiently understand the dangers of Home Rule', wrote Harcourt sensibly, 'to feel that it must be repelled *at all costs* is small', and he himself believed that, on balance, it should be tried (Gardiner 1923, vol. 1: 583, 554). Moreover, Gladstone's scheme had the one great merit of removing the Irish MPs from the House of Commons, and therefore contained the possibility of ending the Irish 'obstruction' and opening up again the channels of Radical reform.

The traditions and prejudices of the Radicals made them averse anyway to the arguments of the Unionists based on imperial unity, national defence or the maintenance of the established social order – especially when mouthed by Tory landowners, Whig aristocrats or City financiers. The instinct of many Radicals was expressed by Dilke, whose long personal friendship and political support for Chamberlain made his decision a particularly painful one, when he wrote to him on 5 May: 'As to the future, the 2nd. Reading will be a choice between acceptance of a vast change which has in one form or the other become inevitable, and on the other side Hartington–Goschen opposition, with coercion behind it. I am only a camp follower now, but my place is not in the camp of the Goschens, Hartingtons, Brands, Heneages, Greys. I owe something, too, to my constituents.'[1] All these attitudes were supported to a greater or lesser degree by the Radicals in the country. The labour movement supported Gladstone over Home Rule; so, eventually, did the majority of Nonconformist leaders, with the notable exception of the Birmingham men, R. W. Dale and H. W. Crosskey. The NLF also swung to Gladstone: not a single Liberal Association was irretrievably lost to the Home Rulers (Griffiths 1976). Only the bulk of the Radical intelligentsia (as we have seen) fled for cover to the Unionist camp.

This general Radical consensus on Home Rule thrusts into high relief the apostasy of Chamberlain, and makes his behaviour during the Crisis perplexing and controversial. So perplexing indeed, that one historian has been reduced to explaining it ultimately in terms of the Radical leader's 'authoritarian personality' (Heyck 1974: 147–8). There is no need perhaps to go so far. Certainly Chamberlain's attitude towards Irish affairs before 1886 was not markedly different from that of most Radicals, as his support for Irish reform and ultimate opposition to coercion shows. Yet behind Chamberlain's Radical gestures was a bleak dogmatic view of the Irish problem and the likely consequences of Home Rule which he never questioned. It was a view that was strengthened by the excesses of the Irish in the 1880s and (as he believed) the callousness and duplicity of their leaders over the Central Board scheme and the general election of 1885 especially, actions which he reacted to with bitter personal resentment.

Implicit in Chamberlain's approach was the view that the Irish were unfit to govern themselves – at least in important matters. He was prepared to go far, as his Central Board scheme shows, in giving the Irish what he believed they wanted – or at least what was good for them: as he said, 'the widest possible self-government . . . consistent with the integrity of the Empire' (Chamberlain 1953: 151). But he was not prepared to make the jump from devolution to Home Rule, even if a majority of Irishmen clearly wanted it; to do this would be to place the wishes of a minority above the interests of the majority of the people of the United Kingdom. It was not so much that the Empire would be disrupted if Home Rule succeeded, or that British trade would suffer grievously from an Irish protectionist policy; but rather that Britain's prestige and security would be imperilled. For Gladstone's scheme would lead, he insisted, 'in the long run to the absolute national independence of Ireland, and that this cannot be conceded without serious danger and the heaviest sacrifices on the part of Great Britain' (Heyck 1974: 132). In any case he convinced himself, even in the eye of the Home Rule storm, that such purely political considerations were irrelevant. It was the land question that was 'the foundation of Irish discontent (and) should be settled first. If it were settled, I doubt if Home Rule would any longer be a burning question.' (Chamberlain 1953: 229)

It is impossible to doubt the sincerity of Chamberlain's views on Home Rule, but it is also difficult to believe that he was unmoved by political calculation in the decisions he took in 1886. These were determined in the last resort by his view of Gladstone, and once again his belief in the imminent retirement of the GOM was crucial. During his second ministry Gladstone had treated him with an extraordinary lack of tact and sensitivity. He was loath to admit him to the Cabinet in 1880; in 1882 he twice failed to consider him for the post of Irish Secretary without any real justification. Even in 1886, when Chamberlain was anxious to become Colonial Secretary, he was given the Local Government Board but without any strong backing for a policy of reform. Chamberlain felt, with considerable justification, that he was being deliberately slighted, and that Gladstone's raising of the Home Rule issue in the winter of 1885–86 was a considered attempt to sweep the 'Unauthorized Programme' under the carpet. It was Gladstone, therefore, who was now the main obstacle to Radicalism! There was, however, one way out of this ignominious position: the cynical policy projected by Labouchers in his letters to Chamberlain in the early months of 1886. 'The Radical game', Labouchere argued, 'is to go with Mr. G. on Irish matters, and to use him in order to shunt them and, if possible, the Whigs . . ..'[2] 'For my part', he continued later, 'I would coerce the Irish, grant them Home Rule, or do anything with them, in order to make the Radical programme possible. Ireland is but a pawn in the game.'[3]

Despite the superficial attractions of such a strategy, there were for Chamberlain two fundamental objections to support for Home Rule on these terms. It meant, first, his subordination to Gladstone once again, with no guarantees for the future, and that he was loath to accept. In addition, he was well aware of the antipathy of the British public to the Irish, and therefore to Home Rule, a theme he constantly stressed in private correspondence in the 1880s. He replied to Labouchere's first letter: 'I believe the anti-Irish feeling is very strong with our best friends – the respectable artisans and the non-conformists.'[4] There was much to be said, therefore, for breaking with a party that seemed bent on self-destruction, and building up his reputation from a position of independent strength outside, 'I think I shall win this fight', he told Dilke, 'and shall in the long run have an increase of public influence.' (Jay 1981: 136) Once the situation had settled down and the GOM had retired, then he could await the inevitable call to the Liberal Party leadership. As he wrote to his brother on 8 March 1886: 'The immediate result will be considerable unpopularity and temporary estrangement from the Radical Party. . . . I shall be left almost alone for a time. . . . But in time the situation will clear. Either Mr. G. will succeed and get the Irish question out of the way or he will fail. In either case he will retire from politics and I do not suppose the Liberal Party will accept Childers or even John Morley as its permanent leader.'[5]

In the end of course things did not work out quite as Chamberlain imagined. The Home Rule Bill *was* defeated in the House of Commons; the Unionists *did* win a tremendous electoral victory; but the GOM stubbornly refused to bow to the inevitable. By the time Gladstone did retire as Liberal leader, in 1894, the political situation had been completely transformed, and Chamberlain's hopes of succeeding to that position had long since faded.

Despite the disasters of 1886, the years immediately following the Home Rule Crisis were a time of hope and opportunity for the Radical loyalists. The sacrifice of Joseph Chamberlain and his small and dwindling band of Radical Unionists seemed a price well worth paying for the almost total secession of the Whigs and their allies from the Liberal Party. It is true that the number of Radical MPs had declined absolutely since the general election of 1885. But the group of some 145 Radicals who sat in the House of Commons up to 1892 represented about 70 per cent of the Parliamentary Liberal Party, and, as seen by the Liberal votes on such issues as Welsh disestablishment and opposition to the House of Lords, the Parliamentary Party during these years was increasingly Radical in temper (Heyck 1974: 154–5). As Gladstone himself admitted to the NLF in 1887, the withdrawal of the Liberal Unionists had meant 'an enormous stimulus to advanced opinion all through the country and throughout the ranks of the Liberal Party' (NLF 1887: 47). The appointment of Arnold Morley (son of the great Nonconformist manufacturer) as Chief Whip in 1886 in succession to Lord Richard Grosvenor, seemed a symbolic recognition of that change.

The increased Radical influence was seen above all in the revival of the NLF after 1886. Francis Schnadhorst, secretary of the NLF since its inception in 1877, had deserted his master, Joseph Chamberlain, over the Home Rule issue, and helped to swing the Federation against him. In the summer of 1886 following the general election, he was appointed to the secretaryship of the Liberal Central Association, in addition to the post he already held, and a few months later the headquarters of the NLF was transferred from Birmingham to London, alongside the Association's premises in Parliament Street. This meant that the great Birmingham wire-puller was now a member of the inner party hierarchy and the most powerful man in the national organization of the Liberal Party; in effect Gladstone's protégé in equating Liberalism with firm adherence to the Home Rule line. Fifty new Liberal Associations joined the NLF in 1886. By 1888 most 'Unionist' Associations had been won back to the Gladstonian Party; Birmingham itself was recaptured in that year, and Dale, Crosskey and Harris – former Unionists – crept back into their old Association.

The NLF became an increasingly national organization: in 1889 it claimed that 'it practically embraced the whole sphere of Liberal organization and activity' (NLF 1889: 12). In 1886–87, mainly owing to Schnadhorst's efforts, North and South Wales Liberal Federations were formed and affiliated to the National Federation. In Scotland too, where divisions within the Liberal ranks over Home Rule had been particularly deep, a new united Scottish Liberal Association was formed in December 1886. Though it insisted on remaining independent of the English Federation – a source of weakness as it turned out – it was captured by the Scottish Radicals, and by 1892 it had promulgated a programme well in advance of that produced by its English counterpart at Newcastle the previous year (Kellas 1965).

In London also – hitherto outside the orbit of the old Birmingham-dominated Caucus – and where the Liberal Party had fared particularly badly in the elections of 1885–86, there were important organizational developments. In 1887 the London Liberal and Radical Union was formed and affiliated to the NLF. This was mainly a middle-class and Nonconformist association – the secularist working-class Metropolitan Radical Federation preferred to remain outside (Thompson 1964). But under the guise of 'Progressivism', and with prodding from the *Star* newspaper and the London socialists, it produced a fairly advanced programme of Radical reform for the metropolis and made great gains in the elections for the newly created London County Council (LCC) in 1889. Even in the adjacent Home Counties – largely barren terrain for the Liberal Party – a new party division was formed in 1887 and affiliated to the NLF. That same year the Liberal Publications Department was created as a propaganda agency, dominated mainly by the Radicals, notably Acland and Bryce.

The increasing influence of Radicalism within the Liberal Party was seen in policy as well as organization, and here again the work of the NLF was particularly important. Though Irish Home Rule was given clear priority, a long list of resolutions on other topics was accepted at the annual conferences of the Association between 1886 and 1891, amounting to a programme 'ripe' for consideration by a future Liberal government. The disestablishment of the Church of England had by this time been accepted as impracticable as an immediate objective. But as a result of pressure from the increasingly militant group of Welsh Liberal MPs, led by Stuart Rendel–themselves reflecting a growing tide of national feeling in the Principality–by 1887 the disestablishment of the Welsh Church was placed second only to Irish Home Rule in the NLF's resolutions (Morgan 1963: 77–80). The Scots, more divided and isolated from the English Radicals, had to wait until 1891 to get their own claim accepted (Kellas 1964). 'Wales and Scotland are running a race one against the other and both are pressing me', commented Gladstone sourly (Barker 1975: 123). In addition, further resolutions were accepted by the NLF based upon, or developing out of, the traditional Radical demands in favour of land, tax, local government, and temperance reform.

None of this activity was new: the NLF had always been adept at passing resolutions. What *was* new and significant was that the Federation was now patronized by the party leadership: Harcourt and Morley often spoke at the annual conference, and, even more portentous, Gladstone himself addressed all but one of those held between 1887 and 1891. In Gladstone's mind this was perhaps mainly a graceful acknowledgement of the Radicals' steadfastness over Home Rule, though it also provided him with a key platform to maintain enthusiasm and devotion to the Irish cause and lambaste the government's coercion policy. It also meant that, inexorably, he moved leftwards. 'One man one vote', tax reform, free trade in land, the 'rights of labour' – all were accepted; by 1891 the GOM had even swallowed Welsh disestablishment.

The culmination of this 'radicalization' of the Liberal Party and the growing 'union of hearts' between the NLF and Gladstone, was the 'Newcastle Programme' of 1891. This endorsed: Home Rule, Welsh disestablishment, more powers to the LCC, public control of schools, 'one man one vote', the establishment of district and parish councils, and the concession of compulsory powers to local authorities to acquire land for smallholdings, etc. An 'omnibus' resolution, moved by Sir Wilfred Lawson, was also passed, and this approved: free trade in land and taxation of land values, the direct popular veto on the liquor traffic, Scottish disestablishment, reform of death duties, rates reform, taxation of mining royalties, a 'free breakfast table', extension of the Factory Acts, and the 'ending or mending' of the House of Lords (NLF 1891: 6–8). There was nothing original about these resolutions, most of which had been passed at earlier conferences. But the Newcastle meeting was regarded as something of a landmark in the progress of Liberalism because this time the detailed programme was apparently endorsed by the party leadership, though it is fair to say that Gladstone accepted its spirit rather than its letter, and, as his speech to the conference makes clear, he supported some points of the programme and ignored others (NLF 1891: 105–9). Nevertheless, the NLF could feel satisfied that it had spelt out to the party leaders those questions 'with regard to which the mind of the party as a whole has been made up', and which could therefore form the basis for the work of the next Liberal government (Watson 1907: 12).

Despite these developments, the advance of Radicalism after 1886 was more apparent than real. Compared with the era of Chamberlain, the Radicals lacked any outstanding leaders. Harcourt's Radicalism merely reflected his adaptation to circumstances; he was, as always, primarily concerned with party unity. Morley was now a notable member of the Liberal Front Bench and, like his chief, committed above all to Home Rule. Dilke was mistrusted; Labouchere, who acted as the ostensible leader of the extreme Radicals in the Commons in the later 1880s, was destructive and negative as a politician. This only emphasized the eminence of Gladstone. 'Talk of the Liberal Party', said Morley. 'Why it consists of Mr. G. After him it will disappear and all will be chaos.' (Hamer 1972: 141) But Mr. G. had made it clear that he remained as leader only to deal with the Irish question, and this meant that after 1886– as before – Ireland stood at the heart of Liberal politics. By 1891 Gladstone *had* accepted that other questions were 'ripe for solution'. But the party's absolute commitment to Home Rule, and the alliance with the Irish Party which that implied, meant that the carrying out of any large-scale plan of English reform by a future Liberal government would be fraught with difficulty, especially if it failed to obtain an overall majority. In any case, how were priorities to be organized among the competing claims of the Newcastle shopping-list?

The NLF was something of a paper tiger. It ignored priorities in its domestic policy commitments, thus rendering the task of the party leadership more rather than less difficult. It also failed to face up to the problems of 'labour' that were so intrusive in an era of socialism, New Unionism and industrial depression, both from the point of view of policy and the selection of parliamentary candidates. On the latter point, in reply to working-class criticism, the executive of the NLF protested, rather lamely, that it had no power to influence the choice of candidates by the local constituency associations. Yet it was essential to recapture the working-class vote if the Liberals were to regain power. At the moment however, as Sidney Webb insisted, Radical working men were disillusioned with the Liberal Party. 'Even such of them as can be induced at the election to vote for the Liberal candidate, are in the party but not of it. There is an almost universal conviction among them that its aims are not theirs, and that its representatives are not those whom they would have chosen.' The Liberals needed to offer the workers something more than 'trivial improvements in legal and administrative machinery' (Maccoby 1953: 58–9).

The Newcastle Programme had indeed a musty air: its contents were largely derived from mid-Victorian Radical orthodoxy, and there was no real concessions to the interests of the industrial working class. The attempt by George Lansbury and Sidney Webb to get a resolution accepted by the NLF in favour of the eight-hour day – the symbol of the new labour philosophy – was rejected by the executive on the grounds that opinion in the party on that issue was still 'in a state of flux' (NLF 1891: 43). This was true. But it was also true that a strong anti-labour pressure was exerted by the powerful industrialist group within the Federation, especially through the influence of the Leeds ironmaster, Sir James Kitson, president between 1883 and 1890, and a formidable figure thereafter (Barker 1975: 150). Hence the suspicious attitude of many labour leaders. As one of them (T. R. Threlfall) wrote of the Caucus: 'as it exists today it is too narrow and too much hampered with class prejudice to be a reflex of the expanding democratic and labour sentiment (Pelling 1965: 223).

The caution of the NLF over these contentious issues was repeated in the upper echelons of the party. Though there was considerable support in the Parliamentary Party for the miners' eight-hour day, Gladstone demanded 'circumspection' on the general eight-hour question (NLF 1891: 109), a position supported by Harcourt. Morley was a defiant and bitter opponent, as he indicated with typical outspokenness to his constituents at Newcastle (Morley 1918, vol. 1: 326–7).

To approve the eight-hour day, he said, would mean 'thrusting an Act of Parliament like a ramrod into all the delicate and complex machinery of British industry' (Hamer 1968: 257). In the wider sphere of social thought Morley, characteristically, represented all the contradictions and hesitations typical of those men of goodwill who inhabited (in Beatrice Webb's phrase) 'the "no man's land" between the old Radicalism and the new Socialism' (Webb 1938, vol. 1: 210). Despite Mrs Webb's later contemptuous dismissal of his ignorance, Morley *was* aware of the grim conditions among the London working classes and deeply concerned with the social question, partly through his contacts with the younger intellectual Liberals in the House of Commons (Webb 1938, vol. 2: 353; Morley 1918, vol. 1: 323–4). He accepted a greater role for the state in dealing with social problems – at one point he supported free school meals for needy children – and in his 'Clerkenwell Programme' of 1888 advocated such modish progressive reforms as local taxation of ground rents and the ending of the leasehold system. But in the end his obstinate commitment to economic individualism, together with his native caution and loyalty to Gladstone, made him draw back from such unsettling ideas as old age pensions or the break-up of the old Poor Law. Even the Newcastle Programme he regarded as a dangerous move 'towards the Extreme Left' (Hamer 1968: 280).

The NLF, and parliamentary Radicals of the type of Morley, Labouchere and Lawson, no longer represented 'the advanced party' in any significant sense. Even within the Parliamentary Liberal Party, younger men such as Haldane, Asquith, Grey and Atherley-Jones, were demanding a more constructive Liberalism; less emphasis on Home Rule and disestablishment and more concern with the fundamental problems of the age, particularly those relating to the working classes. Here were the first stirrings of the 'New Liberalism' (Atherley-Jones 1889). Outside the House of Commons the 'old' Radicals were faced with even greater competition from the socialists, especially the Fabians – 'loose, superficial, crude and impertinent', according to Morley – who in many ways were setting the pace in English thinking on social problems (Barker 1975: 192). Moreover, the recent integration of the NLF into the central party machine, and the growing accord between the Federation's grassroots membership and the party leadership over policy, meant that much of the Radicalism of the Newcastle Programme entered into the mainstream of Liberalism. Instead of Radicalism taking over the Liberal Party – as Chamberlain had once hoped – it was the Liberal Party that was now swallowing up Radicalism.

The implications of all these developments were seen in the run-up to the general election of 1892, and the record of the Liberal administrations that followed. By 1890–91 the Liberals were in a stronger electoral position. The tide of by-elections ran strongly in their favour, especially in rural areas where the labourers – apathetic towards Home Rule – were wooed with the prospect of allotments and parish councils (Tuckwell 1905: 220). The fall from power and subsequent death of Parnell during these years as a result of his involvement in the O'Shea divorce scandal, followed by the disruption of the Irish Party, weakened but did not break the Home Rule Alliance. It also revealed, dramatically, that the smouldering embers of 'the Nonconformist conscience' could still be stirred into flame when faced with a conflict between private morality and political expediency (Glaser, 1960–61).

As far as policy was concerned, the Conservatives had done something, through their legislation in favour of land purchase in Ireland and free schools, to remove two particularly prickly issues from the arena of Liberal debate. But the problems that faced Gladstone and the party leaders in devising a programme for the forthcoming general election that was practical, popular and at the same time acceptable to all the special interests within the Liberal Party, was formidable. In the end the Liberals really fought the election of 1892 in support of Gladstone and Home Rule, together with vague commitments to 'reform' in England.

The results of the general election were a disappointment. The Liberals gained more than fifty seats, and made an important recovery in London (where Burns and Hardie achieved spectacular victories at West Ham and Battersea) due mainly to socialist and trade-union, rather than middle-class, enthusiasm (Thompson 1967: 97–8). The rural swing failed to materialize, except in East Anglia; and, though the 'Celtic fringe' was now even more impressively Liberal, the Unionists were well ahead in English constituencies and thus achieved a fifty-seat lead over the Liberals. Nevertheless, with the support of the eighty-strong Irish Party, Gladstone had a clear majority, and was therefore able to form his fourth ministry in August 1892.

The GOM now had no alternative – even had he wished to – but to proceed with the introduction of a new Home Rule Bill. This was obviously not enough to satisfy the hungry Liberal lions. Gladstone therefore indicated to the Cabinet that he was prepared to introduce 'the more concise and telling parts' of the party's English programme, though this clearly could not cover the immediate demands of all the Liberal supplicants. As he burst out in reply to Tom Ellis, remonstrating on behalf of the Welsh members: 'Does he think Welsh Disestablishment can be carried at the same time with a Home Rule Bill and other claims?' (Barker 1975: 261, 242) In the end the government's programme did amount to a fairly long list, covering 'one man one vote', local government reform, education and concessions to labour, but *not* Welsh or Scottish disestablishment – they were to be left to the private members.

As expected, the passage of the Second Home Rule Bill through the House of Commons took up much time and labour; it only reached the Lords in September 1893, where it was inevitably and overwhelmingly crushed. Gladstone would have liked to have dissolved and appealed to the country, as in 1886; but his colleagues – divided by their own personal animosities and anxious to save something from the wreck of their programme – refused to agree. The GOM carried on for another seven months, growing ever more aloof, embittered and difficult to work with.

The Lords, meanwhile, well aware of the Liberals' lack of an overall majority and brushing aside their threats of future reprisals, had no compunction about opposing other important parts of the ministry's programme. Knowing what the inevitable result would be, major items in the Queen's Speech were either withdrawn – as with the Employers' Liability Bill – or passed only after they had been emasculated by the Upper House. Such was the fate of the 'parish councils' section of the Local Government Act of 1894. Some uncontentious measures *were* passed: in the industrial field, by A. J. Mundella, who created the Labour Department at the Board of Trade; in education, by Arthur Acland; and by Asquith at the Home Office, who strengthened the Factory Inspectorate and introduced a new Factories and Workshops Act. But though they were useful reforms, the legislative achievements of the government as a whole hardly justify the accolade – 'one of the most successful reforming governments of the nineteenth century' (Barker 1975: 253).

Tired, disillusioned and at odds with all his colleagues over the naval estimates, Gladstone eventually retired in March 1894; and, to the dismay of Harcourt – who had hoped to become Prime Minister – he was replaced by Rosebery, the Queen's not the party's choice. This only added to the demoralisation of the government. Harcourt's 'death duties' scheme in his Budget of 1894 had profound radical implications, as both Premier and ex-Premier noted with concern. But two great traditional pillars of Radicalism, the Local Option Bill and Asquith's Welsh Disestablishment Bill, faded away in the spring of 1895, in the last dying days of the government. The '*genus irritabile* of Wales' (in Harcourt's phrase) had, however, already been somewhat placated by the setting up of a federal university and a Royal Commission on Land, as well as limitations on the patronage of the Welsh Church (Morgan 1963: 123).

None of this was of any great interest to the Prime Minister – his *métier* was foreign and imperial policy. Rosebery's position had been a difficult one from the start. He was bitterly opposed by Harcourt, his leading colleague in the House of Commons; and, as a Liberal peer, he felt trapped and isolated in the Upper House. He was intelligent enough to see the need for the party to break the Gladstonian mould and adapt itself to the contemporary world, but he seemed temperamentally incapable of doing much about it. Vain and sensitive, it was Rosebery's growing feeling of personal frustration and impotence rather than the more fundamental weaknesses in the government and party, that led him to seize upon a trivial defeat in the House of Commons on 22 June 1895 and resign office. He thus abandoned, thankfully, his *damnosa hereditas*. A few weeks later the Liberals were crushingly defeated at the general election and remained out of power until the end of 1905. They were reduced to less than 200 MPs, and the Unionists had an overall majority of around 150. Leading Radicals such as Morley, Caine, Lefevre and even Harcourt, lost their seats, and the electoral result was a shattering blow to Radical morale.

The shock of defeat did little to solve the disputes among the Liberal leaders after Harcourt and Morley returned to the House of Commons in by-election victories in 1896. The feuds were in fact worsened by differences over foreign policy, in which Gladstone sided with the anti-Rosebery faction: abruptly in October Rosebery resigned as leader of the Liberal Party. Harcourt therefore became at last *de facto* leader; but it soon became only too apparent that he was incapable of remedying the deep-seated malaise that afflicted the party. His inept performance over the Jameson Raid inquiry convinced his colleagues that he possessed none of the qualities of real leadership, and there were moves against him in the NLF. In December 1898, therefore, Harcourt also resigned, to be followed a month later by John Morley – depressed with politics and actively at work on his life of Gladstone – who retired from the Liberal Front Bench. These resignations paved the way for the emergence of the dark horse, Henry Campbell-Bannerman, who became Liberal leader early in 1899, and committed himself, with eventual success, to the restoration of the party's unity and self-confidence (Stansky 1964).

The problem of the leadership was to some extent at least a reflection of deeper doubts and divisions within the Liberal Party itself over policy, aims and tactics. What was its *raison d'être* in a post-Gladstonian world? This was the question that haunted the minds of Liberal politicians and publicists in the last years of the nineteenth century. In this process of painful self-examination the years 1894–95 were, suggests Professor Hamer, crucial. 'The sudden removal of the two factors which had disciplined and concentrated Liberal politics over the eight years since 1886', he writes, '– Gladstone's leadership and the preoccupation with clearing the Irish "obstruction", restored to view the basic disorganization of Liberal politics. Sectionalism re-emerged, rampant and uncontrollable.' (Hamer 1972: 185) It is this reversion to 'faddism', with each Liberal section pursuing its own hare oblivious of the rest of the field, that Hamer sees as one of the major sources of Liberal weakness in later Victorian England. It is a view that has been criticized by other historians, who have stressed the positive as well as the negative aspects of faddism (Barker 1975; Morgan 1971: 25). Yet, as Hamer insisted, his thesis was one that was advocated by a number of acute contemporary observers. 'I can't help feeling', wrote Herbert Gladstone in 1895, 'that defeat may be good for us. We are plagued with obstinate faddists who are too strong for the leaders, and except for Ireland I could wish to get rid of them through defeat.' (Hamer 1972: 207)

Some of these faddists, particularly the members of the Liberation Society and the United Kingdom Alliance, were associated peculiarly with traditional Radicalism; but, in the last years of Victoria's reign, these causes were no longer upheld with the vigour and dedication that had sustained them a generation earlier. The Liberation Society had insisted on the eve of the election of 1895 that 'We must continue to require from all Liberal candidates distinct pledges in favour of Disestablishment in both Wales and Scotland. Nor need there be any reservation of opinion on our part on the question of Disestablishment in England also. . . . The tendencies of the times are in favour of the change we have so long been advocating!' This was Cloud-cuckoo-land. The Liberation Society was clearly in decline. Its membership and financial resources were dwindling, and few younger men now came forward to carry on the work of the older leaders who were passing away – Crosskey died in 1893 and Dale two years later (Mackintosh 1972: 294). Much of the activity of the Society had already been taken over by the nationalist-minded movements in Wales and Scotland, and their demands had become official Liberal policy. This in itself was a reflection of the weakness of the Liberation Society: its original purpose – the disestablishment of the Church of England – was, after 1895, accepted as virtually a dead issue.

The United Kingdom Alliance did exert greater political influence in the decade following the Home Rule Crisis. But this was only achieved by the Society abandoning its earlier aloof attitude and recognizing the domination of the Liberal Party within the field of temperance reform; 'the temperance question was now the Liberals' – or it was nobody's' (Hamer 1977: 291). It therefore accepted the Liberal government's commitment in its Local Option Bills of 1894–95. Even this in the end did the Alliance little good. The Bills were abandoned; but the Liberals' meddling with temperance reform was regarded by some as a contributory cause of the débácle of 1895, since it antagonized the brewers even more and tied them closer to the Unionist Party.

In similar fashion, such relics of the old Chamberlainite programme as allotments and free trade in land, were regarded as boring and irrelevant in an age dominated by urban and industrial problems; while it seemed absurd to consider the complexities of electoral or Lords' reform at a time when the Unionists dominated both Houses of Parliament. It was not that all these causes were abandoned by the Liberal Party: most of them re-emerged to be considered at one time or another during the years of domination after 1906. But they no longer occupied the forefront of the Liberal mind. Even the NLF reacted against faddism. It replied to the criticism that the party had been hamstrung in 1895 by the Newcastle Programme, by arguing that it had not produced a party programme in 1891 but a series of resolutions; it was Gladstone who turned them into a rigid programme and hung it round the party's neck. In this way the NLF implicitly abandoned for the future any pretence of advising the leadership on policy; and thus undermined even further its dwindling influence (NLF 1898: 40–2).

Other movements emerged during these years to replace the declining impulse of traditional Radicalism and make their own contribution to the grand inquest on the future of Liberalism. Liberal Imperialism began as an attempt to provide a new coherent philosophy for the Liberal Party based on a commitment to 'national' rather than 'sectional' issues – the 'clean slate' versus 'faddism'. Led by Lord Rosebery and supported by the brilliant trio of Asquith, Grey and Haldane, the Liberal Imperialists argued in favour of a combination of 'sane imperialism', 'national efficiency' and 'social welfare', all resting on the foundation of a stronger and more responsive state (Matthew 1973). But they were and remained an élite, out of touch with grass-roots Liberal feeling – as their over-zealous support for the Boer War revealed – and in no position therefore to convert the party as a whole to their creed. Liberal Imperialism too ended up as a fad, a position which was formalized by the foundation of the Liberal League in 1902.

In the long run, of greater importance for the future of the Liberal Party were the ideas of the mixed bag of younger politicians, publicists and academics associated with the 'Rainbow Circle' and *The Progressive Review* in the later 1890s. Their concern with the reconstruction of Liberalism based on 'an enlarged and enlightened conception of the functions of the State', linked up with the similar concern with social policy displayed by the influential Radical journalists, H. J. Massingham and J. L. Hammond, editors of the *Daily News* and *The Speaker* respectively (Emy 1973: 106, 133). Here we have the real centre of the New Liberalism. Of particular importance in this rethinking were the writings of L. T. Hobhouse and J. A. Hobson (Collini 1979). Using ideas drawn from many strands of thought, they attempted to construct a unified Liberal philosophy that eschewed both socialism and Conservatism, and supplied a rational defence for what has been called 'pragmatic collectivism' (Clarke 1978: 56). In this way, it has been argued, the New Liberalism became an 'Ideology of Social Reform', and thus provided the intellectual basis for the social legislation of the Liberal governments of 1906–14 (Freeden 1978).

All this marked a decisive break with the concerns and assumptions of the earlier generation of Radicals. On one issue, however, these older men were able to speak out with something of their former fire and confidence – and that issue was the Boer War. The opponents of the war covered a wide spectrum of political feeling: left-wing Liberals, Keir Hardie and the members of the ILP, a few Nonconformist ministers such as John Clifford, even the maverick Liberal Unionist, Leonard Courtney (Porter 1968: Ch. 3). The traditional Radicals, notably Labouchere, Morley and Harrison, adopted the same anti-war stance. To them the issue was simple and clear-cut; one which they understood and were familiar with from the past, and even perhaps relished – once the old bandwagon of committees, petitions and public meetings began to roll. Their arguments against the war were a response less to the realities of the South African situation, than to memories of battles fought long ago.

For Morley, as always, the issue was a moral one. As he told a hostile audience at Manchester in September 1899, the war was one between 'the strongest power in the world', hand in glove with the millionaires, and 'a little republic' (Morley 1918, vol. 2: 86–7). For Harrison, as over Egypt in 1881, England's role was 'that of an Empire scrambling for half a continent at the bidding and in the interest of cosmopolitan gamblers and speculative companies in search of bigger dividends and higher premiums'. Some went back even further. 'Where Mr. Gladstone stood in 1850', proclaimed G. W. E. Russell at a public meeting of the Transvaal Committee, 'we stand now – for national faith and honour.' (Koss 1973: 66, 81)

Their opposition to the Boer War represented the final political gesture of the Victorian Radicals as a group – and it was an honourable one. Those who survived into the new century found themselves faced with public men (and women) and issues with which they had little sympathy. In Campbell-Bannerman they possessed a party leader who in many respects shared their outlook. 'As I go on', he wrote early in 1900, 'I get more and more confirmed in the old advanced Liberal principles, economical, social and political with which I entered Parliament thirty years ago.' (Hamer 1972: 288) During the next few years C-B and Herbert Gladstone (Chief Liberal Whip, 1899–1905) worked together to reunify and revivify the Liberal Party as a 'broad church' movement, embracing and tolerating all sections; and, through the overhaul of organisation and finance, and the Lib/Lab pact of 1903, to prepare for the next general election. But the new party leadership deliberately made no attempt to formulate a definite party programme which could bind a future Liberal government; their attitude was one of caution, flexibility and waiting upon events. As it turned out, the Unionist government did their work for them by projecting great emotive issues – imperialism, education, tariff reform especially – which were bound to arouse Liberal passions and stimulate the Liberal revival in the country at large.

What this meant, therefore, was that though there was a strong commitment to social reform by many younger Liberal candidates in the general election of 1906 (Russell 1973), the electoral verdict of that year was largely a negative one; it expressed a revulsion against Unionism rather than for a New Liberalism or any as yet unspecified set of Liberal policies. 'The Liberal programme was to the best of my belief', wrote John Morley, 'mainly due, in the huge extent of it to furious detestation of Balfour and his tactics. No great issue was really settled.' (Koss 1970: 214) All this, together with the character of the Liberal leadership, meant that the policies of the Campbell-Bannerman administration of 1906–8 were shaped more by the legacy from the Victorian past, than by any new directions in ideas or tactics. For a variety of reasons the weight of 'the dead generations' rested also upon C–B's successors. If the great ministry of Asquith, Lloyd George and Churchill represents in many ways the triumph of New Liberalism, it is marked also by a dogged commitment to the Radical Programme of the 1890s which in the end was largely successful. The years 1905–14 represent therefore the culmination of Victorian Radicalism.

NOTES

1.   JC/5/24.
2.   1 January 1886; JC/5/50.
3.   31 March 1886; JC/5/50.
4.   3 January 1886; JC/5/50.
5.   JC/5/II.
6.   A/LIB, Minute Book 8, 1 July 1885.

Chapter 8

VICTORIAN RADICALISM IN THE LIBERAL ERA, 1905–1914

It is in their policies of social reform that many would see the greatest achievement of the Liberal governments of 1905–14, a view that has been reinforced by the quest of recent historians for the 'origins of the Welfare State' and their fascination with social theorists of the New Liberalism. There is obviously much justification for this assessment. The package of well-known social reforms passed during this period, ranging from the provision of free school meals for needy children by the Act of 1906 through to the National Insurance legislation of 1911, seemed to many contemporaries, and later historians, to mark a decisive break with earlier attitudes towards the role of the state in the social field, especially when coupled with such measures as the miners' eight-hour day and minimum wages Acts of 1908 and 1912. A major advance towards 'collectivism' had been accomplished. Certainly, the new social legislation rested upon the principle of *national* action to deal with the problems of poverty, ill health and unemployment among ordinary workers outside the Poor Law system. It thus undermined, implicitly, the old Victorian belief in the responsibility of each individual for his own welfare and 'signified a permanent change in the politics of welfare legislation' (Gilbert 1966: 157). Above all perhaps, conditioned by the social thought of the Fabians and New Liberal publicists such as Massingham, Hobson, Masterman and Hammond, a section of the Liberal Cabinet, led by Lloyd George and Winston Churchill, came to believe that social evils were remediable – in contrast to the pessimism of their Liberal predecessors. 'There is a tremendous policy in Social Organization', wrote Churchill in 1908 when he was at the Board of Trade. 'The need is urgent and the moment ripe. . . . The expenditure of less than ten millions a year, not upon relief, but upon machinery, and thrift stimuli, would make England a different country for the poor.' A programme of old age pensions, labour exchanges, etc. could, he added, 'be carried triumphantly, and that they would not only benefit the state but fortify the party' (Churchill 1969: 863).

Yet, despite the enthusiasm of Lloyd George and Churchill during the key years 1908–11, there were severe limits on what was accomplished by the Liberals: it was a 'social service' rather than a 'welfare' state that was established before 1914, in an *ad hoc* and piecemeal way. The principle of universality in social benefits was not yet accepted, despite Churchill's Fabian rhetoric about the 'national minimum'; the benefits provided were meagre and (for the non-aged worker) were expected to be self-financing; the Poor Law system still remained outside the new structure of social provision as an awful warning and example of older and still influential principles of deterrence and strict accountability. Even more importantly, the new legislation was intended to alleviate the impersonal harshnesses of the established social and economic system – not to undermine it; to increase working-class independence and thrift, and, through the various devices affecting unemployment, to achieve the smoother working of the free market economy (Harris 1972). The New Liberalism then, 'was not an abandonment of individualism but a reinterpretation' (Hay 1975: 35).

It is understandable, however, that the older Radicals were worried by the implications of the new legislation. John Morley, their outstanding representative in the governments of Campbell-Bannerman and Asquith, commented in 1908, on the eve of the collectivist deluge released by his colleagues: 'We are drawing to the edge of that formidable Maelstrom, the Social Question. And opinion is not in the least ripe.' (Hamer 1968: 354) The language was touchingly Gladstonian. So often were Morley's opinions. On the question of unemployment he remained stubbornly pessimistic: 'at the end of a lifetime of study and thought', commented Churchill, 'he has come to the conclusion that nothing can be done' (Churchill 1969: 755). Old, vain, disdainful of his younger colleagues and isolated in the India Office until 1910, Morley was never prepared, however, to push his scepticism about many of the proposed reforms to total opposition – though he threatened resignation time and time again. In the unfamiliar terrain of 'the Social Question' it was often the political implications of the new social legislation that he was most concerned with. Like other Radicals of his generation, Frederic Harrison and James Bryce, for example, he was alarmed by the growth of socialism – 'the key to our politics' – and believed that in their obsession with the interests of labour, the Liberal Party stood in danger of losing middle-class support. 'If anybody thinks that we can govern this country against the middle classes he is wrong' (Fowler 1912: 505); a view which seemed confirmed to some extent by the general elections of 1910 when the middle classes in southern England returned to their natural allegiance to the Unionist Party (Blewett 1972).

The social legislation of the Liberals was linked with and financially dependent upon the system of public finance where, even before the Liberals took office in 1905, a crisis had been brewing. This was the result of a rapid increase in public expenditure at national (and local) level in the later nineteenth century due to the increasing provision of public services, while the basis of taxation remained narrow and regressive. In 1905 about 60 per cent of revenue still came from indirect taxes and income tax was only 1s. in the pound! If public expenditure continued to rise, as it was certain to do given the Liberals' eventual support for naval rearmament and social reform (in fact it doubled between 1900 and 1914), the question was bound to be asked: how was such expenditure to be financed? The answer provided was as much a political as a fiscal one. For having utterly rejected tariff reform and the argument put powerfully by Chamberlain that it provided an effective way of financing social reform, the Liberals had to show that their increased expenditure *could* be realized within a free-trade system, without imposing any new financial burdens on their supporters among the middle and working classes. This implied, almost inevitably, a greater emphasis by Liberal Chancellors on direct taxation aimed, deliberately, at 'the rich'.

Something had already been done to that end by earlier Liberal ministers: Harcourt in 1894 had introduced death duties and even contemplated a super tax. In his major Budget of 1907 Asquith had introduced the important new principle of taxing unearned income at a higher rate than earned, while at the same time he reduced income tax for the middle classes and food taxes for the workers. Hence (as Bruce Murray has argued) the path had already been prepared for Lloyd George's famous 'People's Budget' of 1909; and, given the need to find extra money to pay for the Dreadnoughts and old age pensions, together with the general direction of Liberal social thought over the previous decade, the new Chancellor's proposals were neither singular nor unexpected. Many of them had already been put forward by the New Liberals, and the general thrust of Lloyd George's financial package fitted in with their redistributionist principle of using the Budget as a tool of social policy. Lloyd George recognized this. 'This is a War Budget', he told the House of Commons. 'It is for raising money to wage implacable warfare against poverty and squalidness.' (Murray 1980: 172)

Though Morley lamented the end of Gladstonian retrenchment and was again perturbed by the likely political effects of the Budget in estranging 'the sober, sensible middle class', there was much in Lloyd George's immediate tax changes to please the 'old' as well as the New Liberals. The extra duties on drink and tobacco obviously appealed to the middle-class Nonconformists; the increase in death duties and the introduction of the super tax continued, apparently, the work of the Gladstonian Radical, Sir William Harcourt; while the rise in income tax (owing to the differentiation between earned and unearned income) hardly affected the ordinary middle-class salary earner. The Budget was clearly directed against the wealthy.

Even more significant from the point of view of Victorian Radicalism were the projected land value taxes: a 20 per cent capital gains tax on the unearned increment of land values; a capital levy on unused land and mining royalties; and a tax payable when leases expired. Ostensibly, this was Lloyd George's programme for providing future long-term sources of revenue, and before the plan could really operate a land valuation scheme had to be carried through. The taxes were not, therefore, expected to raise very much in the current financial year 1909–10; and indeed their total yield until their final demise in 1920 only amounted to about half a million pounds compared with £2 millions in administering this new 'Domesday Survey'. What then was the real point of the taxes?

Their purpose was political and social rather than fiscal. They singled out one particular group of the rich, the landowners – the major recipients of unearned income – for special punitive treatment, the aspect of the Budget that particularly incensed the House of Lords. But the leading landowners were in fact still the richest men in the country and formed a fairly closed caste (Rubinstein 1981); they also remained the Radicals' chief *bête noire*. What Lloyd George was doing therefore in 1909 was launching a new, virulent attack on 'the land monopoly' – a re-evocation on a wider scale of the Welsh rural Radicalism of his early political years. He deliberately appealed to the deep instinctive strain of anti-landlordism and anti-privilege within the 'progressive movement' in order to whip up support for the Budget and the coming struggle with the House of Lords, and undermine further the case for tariff reform. 'I do not agree with you', he told Harold Spender, 'that we ought never to have introduced the land clauses. . . . The Party had lost heart . . . and we wanted something to rouse the fighting spirit of our own forces. This the land proposals have undoubtedly succeeded in doing.' (Emy 1971: 43) Lloyd George was thus using in a way the residual spirit of Victorian Radicalism which still remained strong within the Liberal Party and its supporters. The formal demand for 'free trade in land and the taxation of land values' went back to the Newcastle Programme of 1891; and that itself rested upon the social experience and debate of the 1880s, and ultimately (as Avner Offer argues) upon a radical 'mythology' which went back to Cobden and beyond. As Offer writes of the proposed land taxes in 1909: 'The scheme was designed to provoke; but it grew out of a long tradition of resentment and out of a peculiar vision of British society. . . . The plan appealed to the instincts of British Radicalism in its extremist mood, and threw down the gauntlet to the opposition.' (Offer 1981: 327)

It was Lloyd George's rhetoric in the Budget Crisis then, that formed the background to the general elections of 1910. For the Liberal leadership those elections were to be concentrated on the central issue of ending the absolute veto of the House of Lords; a slogan which Asquith believed, rightly, would unite all the traditional anti-Unionist forces in the country. Hence in his remarkable speech on 10 December at the Albert Hall, he argued powerfully that it was the Upper House that was the major barrier to the realization of the hopes of the Nonconformists, over education, for example, and the Welsh and Irish over disestablishment and Home Rule; while the peers' opposition to 'democracy' was an affront to the working classes. Asquith's appeal to the faithful was largely successful. The 'ending or mending' of the House of Lords had been another item in the Newcastle Programme, reinforced by the Lords' rejection of the Second Home Rule Bill in 1893 and, more recently, their destruction of important Bills on education, licensing and land during Campbell-Bannerman's ministry.

Much of the Liberal rhetoric in 1910 had indeed a Gladstonian ring about it – even a touch of the Midlothian campaign. 'The Liberal Party', wrote Edwin Montagu, 'is once more in its old and almost traditional position. . . . Land is against it, Property is against it, Beer is against it.' (Blewett 1972: 330) Something of a Gladstonian crusade therefore developed during the election against the House of Lords, due particularly to the fervour of many Nonconformists, though for some of them 'class' issues were already eating away at older allegiances. The United Kingdom Alliance was also active. 'The House of Lords', wrote the *Baptist Times*, 'is the champion and bulwark of sectarianism in the schools . . . and of the Drink Trade. Unless that power of veto is destroyed, no reforms in these directions are possible.' 'At last', proclaimed John Clifford, the militant Nonconformist leader, 'it seems possible to have a hand-to-hand fight with all the tyrannies and despotisms at once . . . 1910 will open with Armageddon.' (Blewett 1972: 344–5) It did not end quite in that way. In the elections of that year, the Liberals lost about 100 seats: but the anti-Unionist alliance of Liberals, Irish and Labour held up, and led eventually to the ending of the Lords' absolute veto by the Parliament Act of 1911. Another Victorian Radical goal had been achieved.

'The fall of the House of Lords was not merely a political event', wrote H. J. Massingham, now editor of the Radical *Nation*, in 1912, 'it was the beginning of a new economic order.' (Gilbert 1978) By that time Lloyd George's mind was turning once again to schemes for continuing the attack on the landed interest. He felt more and more that the existing system of land ownership was not only pernicious in itself, but an impediment to the effective development of British agriculture and the welfare of the rural community. Nor was this just a rural problem. Owing to the peculiarities of the English rating system, the ground landlord was largely spared the payment of rates on unoccupied or agricultural land and was therefore reluctant to release land on to the housing market. Hence Lloyd George believed that landlordism was a major contributor to the housing problem in the great cities and thus to overcrowding among the working classes with all its attendant social evils. One solution to this latter problem, he came to accept, and in this he was strongly supported by the New Liberals, was site-value taxation to be levied on the ground landlord. This would not only be more equitable than the present system (in which rates were paid largely by the leaseholder) it would also stimulate the release of more land on to the urban market; and in addition, it would help to relieve the increasingly heavy rate burden on the ordinary householder which was a direct result of the ever-increasing expenditure of the local authorities. These were the problems that the Chancellor hoped to tackle through his land campaign of 1913–14 and the Budget of 1914. But once again his motives were as much political as fiscal and altruistic. For the Parliamentary Liberal Party, exhausted and depressed after the long-drawn-out struggles of 1909–11, needed something to revive its enthusiasm, especially as it was now faced by a successful counter-attack by the Unionist Party at by-elections. 'For Liberalism', Lloyd George had always believed, 'stagnation is death.' (Wilson 1970: 70)

In 1913, therefore, on his own initiative, Lloyd George set up a Land Commission led by a group of left-wing Liberals under the chairmanship of Seebohm Rowntree to investigate the conditions of rural life. On the basis of its reports and his own generous but inchoate ideas, he launched his land programme in the autumn of 1913. Through a system of state encouragement and supervision, especially of rent, Lloyd George envisaged a rural revolution which would raise labourers' wages, encourage smallholdings, deal with tenant rights, land taxation, etc. The heart of the programme still remained, however, the political attack on the landlord class – the rest was window-dressing (Gilbert 1978). As he told C. P. Scott, the Radical editor of the *Manchester Guardian*, describing to him his 'Two Year Plan' for the land: 'At present three dominant objects of landlord class were first Power, then Amenity, last profitable use of the land in the public interest. The order must be reversed.' (Wilson 1970: 69)

But the campaign suffered from a multitude of weaknesses. It was long on rhetoric, short on practical objectives. Though he had the support of Asquith, important members of the Cabinet and the Parliamentary Party were unimpressed or hostile; and the Chancellor's personal standing within the party (partly through incidents such as his 'coalition' proposals of 1910, and the later Marconi scandal) was no longer as high as it had been during the heady days of the People's Budget. Moreover, the schemes had no obvious immediate appeal to the industrial working class: as Chamberlain had discovered in the 1880s – where was the 'urban cow'? In the end, some of the proposals in the land programme which could be applied to urban areas were dealt with in the 1914 Budget. That Budget proposed further substantial increases in direct taxation on the rich, partly to provide grants-in-aid for the local authorities; and these items went through. But Lloyd George's plan for the reconstruction of local finance and taxation, based on site-value rating, collapsed, owing to bitter opposition from a group of wealthy Liberal MPs, and constitutional and political complications. This section of the Budget was therefore withdrawn. 'You can imagine the blow this has been to Lloyd George', wrote a close colleague, Walter Runciman, 'and the dreadful muddle we are now in. Banks and local authorities and electioneering Radicals are all enraged; our programme and legislation are horribly upset.' (Offer 1981: 398)

Lloyd George's venture into the Serbonian bog of the English land system during these years, represents almost the last attempt by a New Liberal to come to terms with the tenurial part of the Victorian Radical heritage; and it ended in failure. Apart from its own internal weaknesses, 'The Victorian Radical programme was strangled in the anti-Radical backlash of 1919–22. It fell to Lloyd George to preside over the programme's demise.' (Offer 1918: 403) It fell to Lloyd George too to make the final attempt to interest the British people in the subject, through his famous Green Paper of 1925, *The Land and the Nation*. It flashed briefly across the political sky and fell harmlessly to earth; then darkness fell on 'the land question'.

Though opposition to Lords and landlords was a cause which could unite both Old Radicals and New Liberals, there were other questions which were peculiarly the concern of radical Nonconformity, education and disestablishment especially. The Nonconformist militants had contributed much to the Liberal victory of 1906 as a result of the moral fervour they injected into the campaign through their opposition to the Unionist Education and Licensing Acts, as well as their abhorrence of 'Chinese slavery'. 'We have been put into power by the Nonconformists', observed Campbell-Bannerman. The new House of Commons seemed to reflect this. More Nonconformists than ever before sat on the Liberal benches, 180 MPs out of 400, amounting (in Halévy's view) to a political revolution; and the same proportion was maintained after the general elections of 1910 (Halévy 1961: 64). 'There is no getting away from the fact', observed Edwin Montagu to Asquith, 'that ours is a Nonconformist Party with Nonconformist susceptibilities and Nonconformist prejudices.' (Koss 1975: 76) Yet Nonconformity got little for its pains. Though Birrell's Education Bill of 1906 attempted to accede to some Nonconformist demands over religious teaching in schools, no attempt was made to dismantle the administrative structure of Balfour's great Act; and in any case the Bill was thrown out by the Lords. The Education Bills of Birrell's successor, McKenna, in 1907–8, collapsed in a welter of inter-denominational bickering and confusion, 'amid universal indifference' (Halévy 1961: 73). Nothing further was done by the Liberal government for the Nonconformists over education, or indeed the liquor question after the Lords' destruction of the Licensing Bill of 1908. Hence the indignant cries of 'betrayal' that rent the air during these years.

Yet even apart from the prickly problem of the Lords' opposition to Liberal legislation, the end result was perhaps not unexpected. The position of English Nonconformity was in fact much weaker than it appeared. In terms of religious and social influence, as Halévy stresses, the movement was in decline (Halévy 1961: 76–7). Many of the 'Nonconformists' on the Liberal benches were only nominal adherents of any Dissenting sect, and the issues of rate-aid to church schools or compensation to publicans seemed petty and irrelevant to the mass of the Edwardian public – including many Nonconformists, especially as social issues became more intrusive. Politically too, the relationship between Nonconformity and the Liberal Party remained as ambiguous as it had been in the days of Gladstone. Though there were many Nonconformists on the Liberal back benches, there were few in the government; and though the Liberal leaders were not unmoved by their debt to Nonconformity and the pull of traditional Radical issues, they had their own problems and priorities to worry about, as even Lloyd George (one of the leaders of the militant campaign against the 1902 Education Act) soon showed. Besides, as the gulf between Unionism and Liberalism widened in Edwardian England, militant middle-class Nonconformists found that they were bound hard and fast to the Liberal Party; politically they had, as yet, nowhere else to go.

In some respects the particular position of the Welsh Nonconformists was not unlike that of their English brethren. But it was difficult for a Liberal government to ignore their long-standing demand for disestablishment of the Church of Wales, as membership of that Church became more and more confined to a privileged minority. In the later nineteenth century that demand had been part and parcel of a developing Welsh nationalism, and was linked also with the economic and social structure of the Principality. Welsh disestablishment had also had the consistent support of the NLF since the later 1880s. Moreover, in a shifting political world Wales remained a bedrock of Liberalism. The Liberal Party had been swallowing up the Welsh parliamentary seats since 1880, and in 1906 all thirty-four seats were won by the Liberals or their Labour allies! Yet the political problems of carrying through disestablishment and disendowment were formidable, even apart from the inevitable opposition of the

House of Lords. When he became Prime Minister in 1905, despite his pre-election commitment to the cause of Welsh disestablishment, Campbell-Bannerman procrastinated, merely giving the Welsh the sop of a Royal Commission on the position of the Churches.

Nor was the cause much advanced after 1908. The support of Asquith and Lloyd George for the principle of Welsh disestablishment was firm and unequivocal; but it was thoroughly practical and unsentimental. Old debts were to be paid; but only when the timing was right. Asquith steered a Second Welsh Disestablishment Bill through the House of Commons in 1909 (as he had done the First in 1894), but this was purely a paper exercise. Nothing could really be done, the two ministers believed, until the Lords' veto had been destroyed. It was a view that in the end the Welsh reluctantly accepted as a result of the friendly persuasion of their erstwhile champion, Lloyd George. The cause of disestablishment was in any case losing its potency. As the Anglican bishop of St Davids acutely observed: 'Though Disestablishment is still a Radical political cry in Wales, there is nothing like the real solidarity of conviction . . . that there was twenty or thirty years ago. Free Trade, Labour and Land, the Navy and the House of Lords are the real living issues. . . .' (Bell 1969: 246)

It was not until April 1912 then that a Third Welsh Disestablishment Bill was introduced by the government, and the arguments in its favour were grounded firmly on practical considerations: the three-to-one majority of non-Anglicans to Anglicans in the Principality (revealed by the Royal Commissions's figures) and the manifest existence of a Welsh majority in its favour. The Bill easily passed through the Commons; but owing to the opposition of the House of Lords it took a further two years (by the terms of the Parliament Act) for the measure to become law, in August 1914. Even then, the question of disendowment had to wait until 1920 before it was finally settled. The cause of Welsh disestablishment was thus finally successful: but it came perhaps too late for much rejoicing. 'The culminating achievement of Welsh nonconformist radicalism was . . . carried out in an atmosphere of profound anticlimax, in an empty Commons and with the minds of all on the international crisis.' (Morgan 1963: 271)

The last and most taxing domestic problem that Victorian Liberalism bequeathed to its successors after 1900 was Irish Home Rule. Whatever its status during the last phase of Gladstone's leadership, it was now a question that divided rather than united the party. For the Liberal Imperialists (and to some extent the New Liberals) Irish Home Rule had become an unpopular distraction, diverting Liberal energies away from more urgent plans for imperial and social reconstruction. To old-fashioned Radicals, however, it remained a fundamental article of faith – the hallmark of Liberalism, as it had been in 1886. 'You will find me very slack about One Man One Vote, Land Values and Welsh Church', Morley told Rosebery in 1905. 'The only thing about which my ardent soul is still ready to *blaze* is Irish Home Rule!!!' (Jalland 1980: 25) In the centre of this spectrum of opinion were the party leaders, Campbell-Bannerman and Herbert Gladstone. Though committed Home Rulers, they saw their primary responsibility as the reorganization and reunification of the Liberal Party; and they were well aware of the lessons of 1895 and the unpopularity in England of the Home Rule issue. As a result, Gladstone favoured a policy of 'disengagement' towards Ireland, an attitude which was facilitated by the Irish Nationalists playing for independence in 1900 and breaking their old alliance with the Liberal Party (McCready 1962–63). And as the decline of the Unionist government became more evident in the early years of the new century, the desire for Liberal unity to prepare for the coming election became paramount. All sections of the party, therefore (even John Morley) accepted C-B's formula, adopted in the nick of time early in 1905, of a 'step by step' approach to the Irish question. Irish reform – yes; but (in Herbert Gladstone's phrase) 'no pledge either as to method or time' over Home Rule (McCready 1962–63).

This more flexible (or opportunist) policy did not mean the abandonment of this traditional Liberal commitment: even moderate Liberal Imperialists like Asquith and Grey (the author of the 'step by step' phrase) shied away from Rosebery's policy of expunging Home Rule completely from the Liberal slate. 'Home Rule', said Lord Crewe, a leading Liberal peer, in 1905, 'has never ceased to be the policy of the Liberal Party since 1886 though there have been differences of opinion as to methods.' (Jalland 1980: 26) The Irish issue, it is true, was played down in the electoral campaign of 1906. But once the Irish Nationalists had shown by their violent reaction against Bryce's Irish Council Bill later that year that they would have nothing to do with half-measures, the Liberal government advanced rather than retreated in its support for the Irish claim, though its slow and clumsy steps exacerbated rather than diminished the inevitable opposition (O'Day 1979). Birrell, the new Irish Secretary, told Redmond, the Irish Nationalist leader, a year before the elections of 1910 had drastically cut down the Liberal majority, that Home Rule was 'the live policy of the Party without limitation or restriction' (Jalland 1980: 26). Patricia Jalland argues, therefore, that it was *not* Liberal dependence upon Irish votes in the House of Commons that led to the introduction of the Third Home Rule Bill in 1912 (since if Irish Nationalist votes were excluded, the Liberals still possessed a majority over the Unionist Party); rather it was 'the logical consequences of a long-standing commitment' (Jalland 1980: 27). Only an overwhelming belief by the Liberal Party that, for the sake of honour and conviction, it *must* attempt to secure Home Rule for Ireland, can explain why over the next two years it was prepared to endure the storms and passions of another and greater Home Rule Crisis.

If the long arm of Gladstone reached out from the grave to impose the *principle* of Home Rule upon the Edwardian Liberal Party, the *form* of the new Home Rule Bill was also his. Once again, as in 1886 and 1893, Ulster was to be included in a new self-governing Ireland. This was due not only to the pull of the past; self-deception and complacency also operated. There was little real discussion of the Ulster problem among Liberals, whether in Cabinet, the House of Commons or even in the columns of the Liberal press; and many, like Morley, convinced themselves that Unionist opposition in Ireland was 'artificial'. Even when the Ulster Unionists (tacitly supported by the English Unionist Party) were prepared to push their opposition to the new Bill to the point of armed revolt, Asquith remained unable or unwilling to give a real lead to his party. Nevertheless, despite the bitter opposition of the Unionists, and restiveness among some Liberal back-benchers, the Home Rule Bill was pushed through the House of Commons in May 1912. Yet the two-year waiting period, between the introduction of the Bill and the moment when in 1914 – the Lords having exhausted their powers of rejection under the new Parliament Act – it became law, saw mounting menace in Ireland: the formation of private armies north and south of the border, the growing grip on the province of the Ulster Unionist Council, and the Curragh Mutiny.

It was the Curragh Mutiny, Asquith believed, that destroyed any prospect for the Liberals of coercing Ulster; the only alternative available was some sort of accommodation with the Unionists. In March 1913, therefore, the government agreed to offer the opposition an Amending Bill which would have postponed the application of Home Rule to Ulster for six years. This was dismissed by Carson, the Irish Unionist leader, as 'a stay of execution'. Curiously, in this new crisis for the Liberal Party, it was the 'old' Radicals who were now in favour of compromise. Morley, worried about the use of force and the legitimate rights of minorities, asserted that 'for his own part he would give up Home Rule rather than witness its inception with bloodshed' (David 1977: 152). The New Liberals, on the other hand, though no less averse to the use of force, were much more vehement in their anti-Unionism. 'Better far to my mind', wrote L. T. Hobhouse to C. P. Scott, 'to lose Home Rule than to accept a compromise based on the dictation of Carson with the backing of the army and society.' (Wilson 1970: 84) This was a viewpoint which was accepted by many moderate Liberals when Asquith agreed to the Buckingham Palace Conference held in July 1914 to make one final attempt to agree on a solution with the opposition leaders. This was, almost inevitably, a failure, and with its collapse and Britain's entry into the First World War about a week later, the problem of Ireland's future was shelved for the duration.

The juxtaposition of the two great crises in the summer of 1914 seemed morally appropriate, since both raised the searching question, for Radicals especially, of the legitimate use of force. The Liberal Party 'bore the burden of Gladstonian Liberalism in Irish and Foreign policy' (Jalland 1980: 264). Over Ireland, Gladstonian principles had clearly failed. How were they applied to the wider problems of 'the international anarchy' that prevailed in the world in the earlier part of the twentieth century?

The principles adopted by the critics of British foreign policy during this period, were largely an updated version of the stock-in-trade of the Victorian Radicals: peace, non-intervention and disarmament; opposition to the balance of power and foreign entanglements; distrust of 'secret diplomacy' and the élitism of the Foreign Office; denunciations of the 'hidden hand' of imperialists, financiers and armaments manufacturers. As far as the armed forces were concerned, Radicals had no great interest in Haldane's reorganization of Britain's minuscule army so long as 'insubstantial and reactionary ideas about universal military service' (in the *Nation*'s words) were not considered (Morris 1972: 85). The navy was the problem. Technical advances – particularly the launching of the 'Dreadnoughts' – and the naval challenge from Germany, meant demands even by Liberal governments for increased naval expenditure. One hundred and thirty-six MPs had supported a motion in favour of a reduction in the naval estimates in 1907; but two years later at the time of the 'naval scare', Asquith's government was able to get the support of the House of Commons for a programme of eight new Dreadnoughts – four now and four later – as a result of its (inaccurate) revelation of Germany's naval construction programme. Less than 100 'reductionists' voted against. In fact, though there were still divisions within the Cabinet, Radical opposition to England's naval programme declined during the years down to the outbreak of the First World War; only twenty-eight reductionists voted against the naval estimates in 1913. This was partly because even Radicals were influenced by the traditional view of the 'defensive' role of the British navy, and found it difficult to justify Germany's naval policy in similar terms, especially after her refusal to discuss disarmament at the Hague Peace Conferences.

What concerned Radicals more, were the implications of the *ententes* with France and Russia and their relationship to the balance of power (Weinroth 1970). They were not unsympathetic to the *entente* with France formed in 1904 by Lansdowne, the Unionist Foreign Secretary, and strongly supported by his Liberal successor, Sir Edward Grey. They respected Grey, and support for France was very much in the Radical tradition. 'Every Englishman rejoices, and particularly every Gladstonian Englishman', wrote J. L. Hammond in his journal *The Speaker*, of the 1904 *entente* (Taylor 1969: 101). But they were insistent that the *entente* should not become a definite alliance directed against Germany, and were worried (rightly as it turned out) about the possible existence of secret commitments to France. France was at least a liberal state; the same could not be said of Russia with whom another *entente* was concluded in 1907. This agreement was greeted with bitter hostility by most Radicals, particularly the publicists of the New Liberal movement, men like Gooch, Brailsford, Nevinson, Scott and Hobhouse, and the leaders of the Labour Party. The people of Britain, wrote Brailsford, had no wish to be entangled with a power which 'hanged its Socialists, imprisoned its Deputies, flogged its noblest citizens, oppressed its Jews' (Hinsley 1977: 84). But Grey's moderate but firm defence of the agreement convinced the House of Commons, and only fifty-nine MPs voted against the new 'Holy Alliance', as Nevinson termed it.

After the 'naval scare' of 1909 the problem of Britain's relations with Germany still remained. Germany, argued the Radicals, should be treated in a conciliatory spirit. At a time when Russia was extending her power in Persia and France advancing in North Africa, Noel Buxton, writing to Grey in 1911 on behalf of the Radical Liberal Foreign Affairs Group, protested against 'a policy of "hemming Germany in" from a share in the colonial world' (Hinsley 1977: 14). As a result of Radical and other pressures Grey was prepared to consider some sort of gesture towards Germany. But this was halted by the Agadir Crisis of July 1911, when Germany made a second bid (following the First Moroccan Crisis of 1905) to break the Anglo-French *entente* or obtain colonial compensation in Africa. From one point of view, Agadir seemed to justify French and British suspicions of German policy; hence Lloyd George's desertion of the Radical camp and his famous rebuke to Germany at the Mansion House Speech on 21 July. Is Britain 'to be treated where her interests were vitally affected as if she were of no account in the Cabinet of Nations' (Halévy 1961: 427). From the Radical point of view, however, Agadir also revealed how closely Great Britain was now linked with France. This was a view which was given much justification by the curious meeting of the Committee of Imperial Defence on 23 August 1912 (from which the 'neutralist' Morley was deliberately excluded) to discuss British strategy in the event of war. Lord Loreburn, another 'neutralist' member of the government, discussed the incident indignantly with C. P. Scott, who commented: 'He agreed with me that the root of the recent mischief was the perversion of the friendly understanding with France into an alliance.' (Wilson 1970: 56)

The demand for a more sympathetic approach towards Germany therefore persisted. A leading figure here was the 'old' Radical, Sir John Brunner who, having become President of the NLF in 1911, was determined to use that somnolent body as a mouthpiece for his own views on foreign policy. In 1912 he circulated a personal letter to the chairmen of the Liberal Associations arguing in favour of an *entente* with Germany; but, though he was strongly supported by the Radical Press, the letter had little dramatic effect within the NLF. It was in fact mainly important as a neat summary of the Radical case against the whole trend of British foreign policy since 1902, in terms that would have received the wholehearted approval of John Bright. Secret diplomacy; 'dangerous entanglements'; hostility to Germany; British naval rights; the misleading of Parliament; the destruction of British prosperity through the financial burdens of rearmament – all were attacked. 'It is the plain duty of the Liberal party, the inheritor of Gladstone's teachings, to express itself now in language which the Prime Minister and his colleagues cannot mistake.' (Koss 1970: 293–5) Yet, unhappily perhaps, the world had moved on since Gladstone's day. As Zara Steiner comments, the Radicals believed 'their inherited Gladstonian principles could be made to work in the world at large and refused to recognize the extent to which the base which underlay the long and exceptional Victorian peace had been eroded' (Steiner 1977: 147).

After 1911 the Radical case against the government began to falter. The year of Agadir was also the year of the Lords' Crisis and a projected national railway strike, with other domestic problems looming upon the horizon. This was a difficult time, therefore, for Radicals to rock the Liberal boat or to expect deep public concern with their criticisms of the government's foreign policy. Grey partially disarmed his critics by his speech in the House of Commons in November 1911 defending his policies as a contribution to peace, and he drove his point home by releasing the unpublished secret articles of the Anglo-French *entente*. Besides, the attitude of the Radicals was purely refractory and negative; and by 1914 Grey's policies seemed to be working. His diplomacy (in collaboration with Germany) had helped to prevent a European conflagration during the Balkan Wars of 1912–13; the Haldane mission to Berlin in 1912, though unsuccessful in producing any fundamental change in German policy, was a salutary gesture; and in 1914 a number of minor colonial problems were sorted out by the two governments. Hence, 'it now appears that it was not the Foreign Secretary who accepted their case but the radicals who accepted his. . . . In the end they accepted the balance of power principle because peace was preserved.' (Steiner 1977: 145–6)

As far as Anglo-German relations were concerned, it was therefore into a relatively blue sky that the Sarajevo Crisis burst in the summer of 1914; followed, inexorably, by the outbreak of war on the Continent, the German ultimatum to Belgium, and Britain's declaration of war on Germany on the night of 4 August. A small hardcore of Radicals and socialists in Parliament and the country opposed the government's decision. Three ministers resigned: John Burns, C. P. Trevelyan, and John Morley, the most distinguished representative of traditional Radicalism. Morley's decision to resign was conditioned as much perhaps by the past as the present – he was only too conscious of the historical precedents from the previous century that lay behind his action. He resented the subtle ways in which the diplomatic and military links between Britain and France had been tightened; and, as he told Asquith, 'to swear ourselves to France is to bind ourselves to Russia' – the symbol of illiberalism (Morley 1928: 31). In the August crisis he preferred neutrality to 'armed intervention' against Germany, and, unlike his old friend and colleague, James Bryce, he remained unmoved by the emotional appeal of 'little Belgium'. Morley had after all been a great admirer of Bismarck and the new Germany in his controversies with his Positivist friend, Frederic Harrison, over the *Kulturkampf* of the 1870s; just as for his part Harrison had been a leading denunciator of 'Bismarckism', and was now a rabid Germanophobe and jingoist.

'Liberalism as we have known it', Morley declared in 1914 shortly after his resignation from office, 'is dead beyond resurrection.' (Hamer 1968: 369) For once his vision of the future was a sound one. Whatever the state of British politics and society after the war, and whatever the fate of the Liberal Party itself, the impulse of Victorian Radicalism, with which Morley had been identified for so long, was now clearly exhausted.

BIBLIOGRAPHY

ABBREVIATIONS

E.H.R.	*English Historical Review*
Ec.H.R.	*Economic History Review*
F.R.	*Fortnightly Review*
H.J.	*The Historical Journal*
I.H.S.	*Irish Historical Studies*
J.Ecc.H.	*Journal of Ecclesiastical History*
J.M.H.	*Journal of Modern History*
N.C.	*Nineteenth Century*
P. and P.	*Past and Present*
Qu.R.	*Quarterly Review*
T.R.H.S.	*Transactions of the Royal Historical Society*

UNPUBLISHED SOURCES

John Bright Papers, the British Library, Add. Mss. 43383–84.
Joseph Chamberlain Papers, University of Birmingham Library.
Richard Cobden Papers, the British Library, Add. Mss. 43650.
Sir Charles Dilke Papers, the British Library, Add. Mss. 43885, 43898.
T. H. S. Escott Papers, the British Library, Add. Mss. 58798.
Gladstone Papers, the British Library, Add. Mss. 44270.
Frederic Harrison Papers, British Library of Economics and Political Science.
George Howell Papers, Bishopsgate Institute, London.
Records of the Liberation Society, Greater London Record Office, County Hall.

PUBLISHED WORKS, ETC.

(*Place of publication is London unless stated otherwise*)

Adams, E. D., 1925. *Great Britain and the American Civil War*, 2 vols.

Adams, Francis, 1882. *History of the Elementary School Contest in England.*

Anderson, Olive, 1967. *A Liberal State at War.*

Anderson, Olive, 1974a. 'The Administrative Reform Association 1855–67', in *Pressure from Without in Early Victorian England*, Patricia Hollis (ed.).

Anderson, Olive, 1974b. 'Gladstone's abolition of compulsory church rate: a minor political myth and its historiographical career', *J.Ecc.H.*, **25**, 1974.

Annan, Noel, 1951. *Leslie Stephen.*

Annan, Noel, 1955. 'The intellectual aristocracy', in *Studies in Social History*, J. H. Plumb (ed.).

Arnold, Matthew, 1869. *Culture and Anarchy.*

Arnold, Matthew, 1886. 'The nadir of Liberalism', *N.C.*, **19**, 1886.

Arnold, Matthew, 1887. 'The zenith of Conservatism', *N.C.*, **21**, 1887.

Atherley-Jones, L. A., 1889. 'The New Liberalism', *N.C.*, **26**, 1889.

Aydelotte, William O., 1967. 'The country gentlemen and the repeal of the Corn Laws', *E.H.R.*, **82**, 1967.

Bagehot, Walter, 1876. 'The Conservative vein in Mr Bright', *The Economist*, 29 April 1876.

Bahlman, Dudley W. R. (ed.), 1972. *The Diary of Sir Edward Walter Hamilton, 1880–85*, 2 vols, OUP.

Barker, Michael, 1975. *Gladstone and Radicalism*, Brighton.

Bebbington, D. W., 1982. *The Nonconformist Conscience. Chapel and Politics, 1870–1914.*

Bell, P. M. H., 1969. *Disestablishment in Ireland and Wales.*

Best, Geoffrey, 1971. *Mid-Victorian Britain.*

Binfield, Clyde, 1977. *So Down to Prayers. Studies in English Nonconformity, 1780–1920.*

Blewett, Neal, 1972. *The Peers, the Parties and the People.*

Boyd, C. W., 1914. *Mr. Chamberlain's Speeches*, vol. 1.

Boyson, Rhodes, 1970. *The Ashworth Cotton Enterprise*, OUP.

Brewster, David, 1867. *The Radical Party.*

Briggs, Asa, 1950–52. 'The background of the parliamentary reform movement in three English cities (1830–2)', *Cambridge Historical Journal*, **10**, 1950–52.

Briggs, Asa, 1952. *History of Birmingham*, vol. 2, OUP.

Briggs, Asa, 1956. 'Middle-Class consciousness in English politics, 1780–1846', *P. and P.*, **9**, 1956.

Briggs, Asa, 1959. *Age of Improvement.*

Briggs, Asa, 1960. 'The language of "class" in early nineteenth century England', in *Essays in Labour History*, Asa Briggs and John Saville (eds).

Briggs, Asa, 1965. 'John Bright and the creed of reform', in *Victorian People*, Pelican.

Briggs, Asa, 1968. *Victorian Cities*, Pelican.

Bright, John and Rogers, James E. Thorold, 1870. *Speeches on Questions of Public Policy by Richard Cobden MP*, 2 vols.

Broadbent, Anthony, 1977. 'The New Radicals and the making of programme politics', unpublished Ph.D. thesis, University of London.

Brock, Michael, 1973. *The Great Reform Act*.

Brock, Peter, 1953. 'Polish democrats and English Radicals 1832–1862', *J.M.H.*, **25**, 1953.

Brodrick, George, 1878. 'Liberals and Whigs', *F.R.*, **23**, 1878.

Brodrick, George, 1883. 'The progress of democracy in England', *N.C.*, **14**, 1883.

Brodrick, George, 1900. *Memories and Impressions*.

Brown, B. H., 1943. *The Tariff Reform Movement in Great Britain 1881–1895*, Columbia UP.

Brown, Lucy, 1965. 'The Chartists and the Anti-Corn Law League', in *Chartist Studies*, Asa Briggs (ed.).

Buckle, G. E., 1916. *Life of Benjamin Disraeli, Earl of Beaconsfield*, vol. IV.

Bulwer-Lytton, Edward, 1833. *England and the English*, 2 vols.

Burns, J. H., 1969. 'J. S. Mill and democracy 1829–61', in *Mill. A Collection of Critical Essays*, J. B. Schneewind (ed.).

Cannon, John, 1973. *Parliamentary Reform 1640–1832*, CUP.

Chadwick, Owen, 1966. *The Victorian Church*, vol. 1.

Chamberlain, Joseph, 1873. 'The Liberal Party and its leaders', *F.R.*, **14**, 1873.

Chamberlain, Joseph, 1874. 'The next page of the Liberal Programme', *F.R.*, **16**, 1874.

Chamberlain, Joseph, 1877. 'A new political organisation', *F.R.*, **22**, 1877.

Chamberlain, Joseph, 1883. 'Labourers' and artisans' dwellings', *F.R.*, **34**, 1883.

Chamberlain, Joseph, 1885. *The Radical Programme*.

Chamberlain, Joseph, 1953. *A Political Memoir 1880–92*, C. H. D. Howard (ed.).

Chamberlain, M. E., 1974. *The Scramble for Africa*.

Chambers, J. D. and Mingay, G. A., 1966. *The Agricultural Revolution*.

Churchill, Randolph S., 1969. *Winston S. Churchill*, vol. 2, *Companion* Part 2, 1907–1911.

Clapham, Sir John H., 1945–46. 'Corn Laws repeal, free trade and history', *Trans. Manchester Statistical Society*, 1945–46.

Clark, G. Kitson, 1950. *The English Inheritance*.

Clark, G. Kitson, 1951a. 'The electorate and the repeal of the Corn Laws', *T.R.H.S.*, **1**, 1951.

Clark, G. Kitson, 1951b. 'The repeal of the Corn Laws and the politics of the forties', *Ec.H.R.*, **4**, 1951.

Clark, G. Kitson, 1953. 'Hunger and politics in 1842', *J.M.H.*, xxv, 1953.

Clark, G. Kitson, 1965. *The Making of Victorian England*, University Paperbacks.

Clarke, P. F., 1972. 'Electoral sociology of modern Britain', *History*, **57**, 1972.

Clarke, P. F., 1978. *Liberals and Social Democrats*, CUP.

Clegg, H. A., Fox Alan and Thompson, A. F., 1964. *A History of British*

Trade Unionism since 1889, vol. 1, OUP.

Cobden, Richard, 1867. *The Political Writings of Richard Cobden*, 2 vols.

Collini, Stefan, 1979. *Liberalism and Sociology*, CUP.

Cooke, A. B. and Vincent, John (eds), 1971. *Lord Carlingford's Journal. Reflections of a Cabinet Minister 1885*, OUP.

Cooke, A. B. and Vincent, John, 1974. *The Governing Passion. Cabinet Government and Party Politics in Britain 1885–86*, Brighton.

Cornford, J. P., 1963–64. 'The transformation of Conservatism in the late nineteenth century', *Victorian Studies*, **7**, 1963–64.

Cosgrove, P., 1981. *The Rule of Law. Albert Venn Dicey, Victorian Jurist*.

Cowherd, Raymond G., 1956. *The Politics of English Dissent*, New York UP.

Cowling, Maurice, 1967. *1867. Disraeli, Gladstone and Revolution*, CUP.

Cox, Homersham, 1868. *A History of the Reform Bills of 1866 and 1867*.

Curtis, L. P., Jnr, 1968. *Anglo-Saxons and Celts*, Univ. of Bridgeport, Connecticut.

Dale, A. W. W., 1898. *Life of R. W. Dale*.

Dale, R. W., 1873. *The Elementary Education Act (1870) Amendment Bill and the Political Policy of Nonconformists*, Birmingham.

David, Edward (ed.), 1977. *Inside Asquith's Cabinet. From the Diaries of Charles Hobhouse*.

Davis, R. W., 1966. 'The strategy of "Dissent" in the Repeal campaign, 1820–1828', *J.M.H.*, **38**, 1966.

Dicey, A. V., 1886. *England's Case against Home Rule*.

Dunckley, Henry, 1880. 'Mr. Gladstone', *F.R.*, **27**, 1880.

Ellison, Mary, 1972. *Support for Secession. Lancashire and the American Civil War*, Chicago UP.

Emy, H. V., 1971. 'The land campaigns: Lloyd George as a social reformer, 1909–14', in *Lloyd George. Twelve Essays*, A. J. P. Taylor (ed.).

Emy, H. V., 1973. *Liberals, Radicals and Social Politics, 1892–1914*, CUP.

Escott, T. H. S., 1883. 'The future of the Radical Party', *F.R.*, **34**, 1883.

Escott, T. H. S., 1884. 'Mr Chamberlain', *F.R.*, **36**, 1884.

Everett, E. M., 1939. *The Party of Humanity*, N. Carolina UP.

Fairlie, S., 1965. 'The nineteenth-century Corn Laws reconsidered', *Ec.H.R.*, XVIII, 1965.

Fowler, Edith Henrietta, 1912. *The Life of Henry Hartley Fowler, 1st Viscount Wolverhampton*.

Fowler, W. S., 1961. *A Study in Radicalism and Dissent. The Life and Times of Henry Joseph Wilson 1833–1914*.

Fraser, Derek, 1974. 'Edward Baines', in *Pressure from Without in Early Victorian England*, Patricia Hollis (ed.).

Fraser, Derek, 1976. *Urban Politics in Victorian England*, Leicester UP.

Fraser, Derek, 1978. 'The middle class in nineteenth century politics: a comment', in *The Middle Class in Politics*, John Garrard *et al* (eds).

Fraser, Peter, 1966. *Joseph Chamberlain*.

Freeden, Michael, 1978. *The New Liberalism*, OUP.

Gardiner, A. G., 1923. *The Life of Sir William Harcourt*, 2 vols.

Garrard, John, 1978. 'The middle classes and nineteenth century national and local politics', in *The Middle Class in Politics*, John Garrard *et al.* (eds).

Garrard, John, Jarry, David, Goldsmith, Michael and Oldfield, Adrian (eds), 1978. *The Middle Class in Politics*.

Garvin, J. L., 1932–34. *Life of Joseph Chamberlain*, vols 1–3.

Gash, Norman, 1953. *Politics in the Age of Peel*.

Gash, Norman, 1965. *Reaction and Reconstruction in English Politics 1832–1852*, OUP.

Gilbert, Alan, D., 1976. *Religion and Society in Industrial England*.

Gilbert, Bentley B., 1966. *The Evolution of National Insurance in Great Britain. The Origins of the Welfare State*.

Gilbert, Bentley B., 1978. 'David Lloyd George: the reform of British land-holding and the Budget of 1914', *H.J.*, **21**, 1978.

Gillespie, F. E., 1927. *Labor and Politics in England 1850–1867*, Duke UP.

Gladstone, W. E., 1877. 'The county franchise', *N.C.*, **2**, 1877.

Glaser, John F., 1957–58. 'English Nonconformity and the decline of Liberalism', *American Historical Review*, **63**, 1957–58.

Glaser, John F., 1960–61. 'Parnell's fall and the Nonconformist conscience', *I.H.S.*, xii, 1960–61.

Glicksberg, Charles I., 1942. 'Henry Adams reports on a trade union meeting', *New England Quarterly*, Dec. 1942.

Griffiths, P. C., 1976. 'The caucus and the Liberal Party in 1886', *History*, **61**, 1976.

Guedella, Philip (ed.), 1933. *The Queen and Mr. Gladstone*, 2 vols.

Guttsman, W. L. (ed.), 1967. *A Plea for Democracy. The 1867 Essays on Reform and Questions for a Reformed Parliament*.

Gwynn, S. and Tuckwell, G. M., 1918. *Life of Sir Charles Dilke*, 2 vols.

Halévy, Elie, 1961. *The Rule of Democracy 1905–14*.

Hamburger, Joseph, 1965. *Intellectuals in Politics. John Stuart Mill and the Philosophic Radicals*, Yale UP.

Hamburger, Joseph, 1977. *James Mill and the Art of Revolution*, Greenwood Press.

Hamer, D. A., 1968. *John Morley*, OUP.

Hamer, D. A., 1971. *Introduction to The Radical Programme*, Brighton.

Hamer, D. A., 1972. *Liberal Politics in the Age of Gladstone and Rosebery*, OUP.

Hamer, D. A., 1977. *The Politics of Electoral Pressure*, Brighton.

Hammond, J. L., 1964. *Gladstone and the Irish Nation*.

Hanham, H. J., 1959. *Elections and Party Management*.

Hansards Parliamentary Debates, 3rd Series.

Harris, Jose, 1972. *Unemployment and Politics. A Study in English Social Policy 1886–1914*, OUP.

Harrison, Brian, 1971. *Drink and the Victorians*.

Harrison, Frederic, 1911. *Autobiographic Memoirs*, 2 vols.

Harrison, Royden, 1965. *Before the Socialists*.

Harvie, Christopher, 1976a. *The Lights of Liberalism*.

Harvie, Christopher, 1976b. 'Ideology and Home Rule: James Bryce, A. V. Dicey and Ireland, 1880–1887', *E.H.R.*, **xci**, 1976.

Hay, J. R., 1975. *The Origins of the Liberal Welfare Reforms 1906–1914*.

Hennock, E. P., 1973. *Fit and Proper Persons. Ideal and Reality in Nineteenth Century Urban Government*.

Herrick, Francis H., 1945. 'The origins of the National Liberal Federation', *J.M.H.*, **17**, 1945.

Heyck, T. W., 1974. *The Dimensions of British Radicalism. The Case of Ireland 1874–95*, Illinois UP.

Hinsley, F. H. (ed.), 1977. *British Foreign Policy under Sir Edward Grey*, CUP.

Hirst, F. W., 1927. *Early Life and Letters of John Morley*, 2 vols.

Hobsbawm, Eric, 1969. *Industry and Empire*.

Hodder, Edwin, 1887. *The Life of Samuel Morley*.

Holland, Bernard, 1911. *The Life of Spencer Compton, 8th Duke of Devonshire*, 2 vols.

Hollis, Patricia and Harrison, Brian, 1967. 'Chartism, Liberalism and the life of Robert Lowery', *E.H.R.*, **82**, 1967.

Hollis, Patricia, 1974. *Pressure from Without in Early Victorian England*.

Holyoake, George Jacob, 1892. *Sixty Years of an Agitator's Life*, 2 vols.

Hooper, A. F., 1978. 'Mid-Victorian Radicalism. Community and class in Birmingham, 1850–1880', unpublished Ph.D. thesis, University of London.

Howard, C. H. D., 1947. 'The Parnell manifesto of 21 November, 1885, and the schools question', *E.H.R.*, **62**, 1947.

Howard, C. H. D., 1950. 'Joseph Chamberlain and the "Unauthorised Programme"' *E.H.R.*, **65**, 1950.

Howard, C. H. D., 1952–53. 'Joseph Chamberlain, Parnell and the Irish "central board" scheme, 1884–5', *I.H.S.*, **8**, 1952–53.

Hurst, Michael, 1972. 'Liberal versus Liberal. The general election of 1874 in Bradford and Sheffield', *H.J.*, **15**, 1972.

Hurst, Michael, 1973–74. 'Joseph Chamberlain and late-Victorian Liberalism', *Durham University Journal*, 1973–74.

Ingham, S. M., 1964. 'The disestablishment movement in England 1868–74', *Journal of Religious History*, **2**, 1964.

Inglis, K. S., 1960. 'Patterns of religious worship in 1851', *J.Ecc.H.*, II, 1960.

Inglis, K. S., 1963. *Churches and the Working Classes in Victorian England*.

Jalland, Patricia, 1980. *The Liberals and Ireland. The Ulster Question in British Politics to 1914*, Brighton.

Jay, Richard, 1981. *Joseph Chamberlain*, OUP.

Jephson, Henry, 1892. *The Platform*, 2 vols.

Jones, E. R., 1885. *Life and Speeches of Joseph Cowen M.P.*.

Jones, I. G., 1961. 'The Liberation Society and Welsh politics, 1844 to 1868', *Welsh History Review*, 1961.

Judd, Denis, 1977. *Radical Joe. A Life of Joseph Chamberlain*.

Kellas, James G., 1964. 'The Liberal Party and the Scottish Church disestablishment crisis', *E.H.R.*, **79**, 1964.

Kellas, James G., 1965. 'The Liberal Party in Scotland 1876–1895', *Scottish Historical Review*, **44**, 1965.

Kemp, Betty, 1961–62. 'Reflections on the repeal of the Corn Laws', *Victorian Studies*, **5**, 1961–62.

Kent, Christopher, 1978. *Brains and Numbers: Elitism, Comtism and Democracy in Mid-Victorian England*, Toronto UP.

Koss, Stephen, 1970. *Sir John Brunner*, CUP.

Koss, Stephen, 1973. *The Pro-Boers*, Chicago UP.

Koss, Stephen, 1975. *Nonconformity in Modern British Politics*.

Leech, H. J. (ed.), 1895. *Public Letters of John Bright*.

Levanthal, F. M., 1971. *Respectable Radical. George Howell and Victorian Working-Class Politics*.

Lloyd, Trevor, 1968. *The General Election of 1880*, OUP.

Lowe, Robert, 1867. 'Review of *Essays in Reform*', *Qu.R.*, **123**, 1867.

Lucy, H. W. (ed.), 1885. *Joseph Chamberlain's Speeches*.

Lynd, Helen Merrell, 1968. *England in the 1880s*, Cass.

Maccoby, Simon, 1935. *English Radicalism 1832–1853*.

Maccoby, Simon, 1938. *English Radicalism 1853–1886*.

Maccoby, Simon, 1953. *English Radicalism 1886–1914*.

Maccoby, Simon, 1955. *English Radicalism 1786–1832*.

Maccoby, Simon (ed.) 1961. *The English Radical Tradition*.

McCord, Norman, 1958. *The Anti-Corn Law League*.

McCord, Norman, 1967. 'Cobden and Bright in politics 1846–1857', in *Ideas and Institutions of Victorian England*, Robert Robson (ed.).

McCready, H. W., 1962–63. 'Home Rule and the Liberal party, 1899–1906', *I.H.S.*, **13**, 1962–63.

McGill, Barry, 1962. 'Francis Schnadhorst and Liberal Party organization', *J.M.H.*, **34**, 1962.

Machin, G. I. T., 1967. 'The Maynooth grant, the Dissenters and disestablishment, 1845–1847', *E.H.R.*, **82**, 1967.

Machin, G. I. T., 1974. 'Gladstone and Nonconformity in the 1860s: the formation of an alliance', *H.J.*, xvii, 1974.

Machin, G. I. T., 1977. *Politics and the Churches in Great Britain 1832 to 1868*, OUP.

Macintyre, Angus, 1965. *The Liberator. Daniel O'Connell and the Irish Party 1830–1847*.

Mackintosh, William H., 1972. *Disestablishment and Liberation*.

Maehl, W. H., 1963. 'Gladstone, the Liberals and the election of 1874', *Bulletin of the Institute of Historical Research*, **36**, 1963.

Marriot, W. T., 1882. 'The Birmingham Caucus', *N.C.*, II, 1882.

Martin, David, 1974. 'Land reform', in Patricia Hollis (ed.), *Pressure from Without in Early Victorian England*.

Martin, Kingsley, 1963. *The Triumph of Lord Palmerston*.

Marx, Karl and Engels, Friedrich, 1962. *On Britain*, Moscow.

Matthew, H. C. G., 1973. *The Liberal Imperialists*, OUP.

Mayor, Stephen, 1967. *The Churches and the Labour Movement*.

Miall, Arthur, 1884. *Life of Edward Miall*.

Mill, James, 1820. *On Government*.

Mill, J. S., 1839. 'A letter to the Earl of Durham on reform in Parliament', *London and Westminster Review*, xxxii, 1839.

Mill, J. S., 1859. *Dissertations and Discussions*, vol. 1.

Mill, J. S., 1862. 'The contest in America' *Fraser's Magazine*. 1862.

Mill, J. S., 1910. *Utilitarianism, On Liberty, On Representative Government*, Everyman.

Mill, J. S., 1924. *Autobiography* (1873), H. J. Laski (ed.), OUP.

Mill, J. S., 1975. 'The subjection of women' (1869), in *Three Essays*, R. Wollheim (ed.), OUP.

Mill, J. S., 1977, 'Thoughts on parliamentary reform' (1859), in *Essays on Politics and Society*, J. M. Robson (ed.), Toronto UP.

Mineka, Francis E. (ed.), 1963. *The Earlier Letters of John Stuart Mill, 1812–1848*, 2 vols, Toronto UP.

Mineka, Francis E. and Lindley, Dwight N., 1972. *Later Letters of John Stuart Mill 1849–1873*, 4 vols, Toronto UP.

Moore, D. C., 1965. 'The Corn Laws and high farming', *Ec.H.R.*, **18**, 1965.

Morgan, Kenneth O., 1963. *Wales in British Politics 1868–1922*, Wales UP.

Morgan, Kenneth O., 1971. *The Age of Lloyd George*.

Morley, John, 1867. 'Young England and the political future', *F.R.*, **1**, 1867.

Morley, John, 1873. *The Struggle for National Education*.

Morley, John, 1875. 'The Liberal eclipse', *F.R.*, **17**, 1875.

Morley, John, 1903. *The Life of Richard Cobden*, 1903 edn.

Morley, John, 1905. *Life of Gladstone*, 2 vols.

Morley, John, 1918. *Recollections*, 2 vols.

Morley, John, Viscount, 1928. *Memorandum on Resignation August 1914*.

Morris, A. J. Anthony, 1972. *Radicalism against War 1906–1914*.

Morris, A. J. A., 1974. *Edwardian Radicalism 1900–1914*.

Murray, Bruce K., 1980. *The People's Budget 1909/10: Lloyd George and Liberal Politics*, OUP.

National Liberal Federation, 1877. *Proceedings attending the Formation of the National Federation of Liberal Associations held in Birmingham, Thursday May 31, 1877*, Birmingham.

N(ational) L(iberal) F(ederation), 1878–1900. *Annual Conference Reports*.

O'Day, Alan, 1979. 'Irish Home Rule and Liberalism' in *The Edwardian Age: Conflict and Stability 1900–1914*, Alan O'Day (ed.).

Offer, Avner, 1981. *Property and Politics 1870–1914*, CUP.

Ostrogorski, M., 1964. *Democracy and the Organization of Political Parties*, vol. 1 (1902). Edited and abridged by Seymour Martin Lipset.

Packe, Michael St J., 1954. *The Life of John Stuart Mill*.

Park, J. H., 1920. *The English Reform Bill of 1867*, New York.

Parkin, Frank, 1968. *Middle-Class Radicalism*, Manchester UP.

Patterson, A. Temple, 1975. *Radical Leicester*, Leicester UP.

Pattison, Mark, 1885. *Memoirs*.

Pelling, Henry, 1956. *America and the British Left*.

Pelling, Henry, 1965. *The Origins of the Labour Party 1880–1900*, 2nd edn, OUP.

Pelling, Henry, 1967. *Social Geography of British Elections*.

Perkin, Harold, 1969. *The Origins of Modern English Society 1780–1880*.

Perkin, H. J., 1973. 'Land reform and class conflict in Victorian Britain', in *The Victorians and Social Protest*, J. Butt and I. F. Clarke (ed.).

Porter, Bernard, 1968. *Critics of Empire*.

Prentice, Archibald, 1968. *History of the Anti-Corn Law League*, 2 vols (1853), W. H. Chaloner (ed.).

Prest, J. M., 1977. *Politics in the Age of Cobden*.

Ramm, Agatha (ed.), 1952. *The Political Correspondence of Mr. Gladstone and Lord Granville, 1868–1876*, 2 vols.

Ramm, Agatha (ed.), 1962. *The Political Correspondence of Mr. Gladstone and Lord Granville 1876–1886*, 2 vols, OUP.

Read, Donald, 1967. *Cobden and Bright. A Victorian Political Partnership*

Reader, W. J., 1966. *Professional Men*.

Reid, T. Wemyss, 1888. *Life of W. E. Forster*, 2 vols.

Roach, John, 1957. 'Liberalism and the Victorian intelligentsia', *Cambridge Historical Journal*, **13**, 1957.

Robbins, Keith, 1978. 'John Bright and the middle class in Politics', in *The Middle Class in Politics*, John Garrard et al, (eds).

Robbins, Keith, 1979. *John Bright*.

Robinson, Ronald and Gallagher, John, 1961. *Africa and the Victorians*.

Rogers, J. E. T., 1883. *Speeches on Public Policy of John Bright M.P.*

Rogers, J. Guiness, 1884. 'Chatter versus work in Parliament', *N.C.*, **16**, 1884.

Rogers, J. Guiness, 1903. *An Autobiography*.

Royle, Edward, 1974. *Victorian Infidels*, Manchester UP.

Royle, Edward, 1980a. *Chartism*.

Royle, Edward, 1980b. *Radicals, Secularists and Republicans. Popular Freethought in Britain, 1866–1915*, Manchester UP.

Rubinstein, W. D., 1977a. 'The Victorian middle classes: wealth, occupation, and geography', *Ec.H.R.*, **30**, 1977.

Rubinstein, W. D., 1977b. 'Wealth, elites and the class structure of modern Britain', *P. and P.*, **74–77**, 1977.

Rubinstein, W. D., 1981. *Men of Property*.

Russell, A. K., 1973. *Liberal Landslide. The General Election of 1906*.

Russell, Bertrand and Patricia (eds), 1937. *The Amberley Papers*, 2 vols.

Ryan, Alan, 1974. *J. S. Mill*.

Salter, F. R., 1953. 'Political Nonconformity in the eighteenth-thirties', *T.R.H.S.*, **3**, 1953.

Savage, D. C., 1961. 'Scottish politics, 1885–6', *Scottish Historical Review*, 1961.

Saville, John (ed.), 1952. *Ernest Jones. Chartist*.

Schreuder, D. M., 1969. *Gladstone and Kruger*.

Sellers, Ian, 1977. *Nineteenth-Century Nonconformity*.

Seymour, Charles, 1915. *Electoral Reform in England and Wales*, Yale UP.

Shannon, Richard, 1963. *Gladstone and the Bulgarian Agitation 1876*.

Shannon, Richard, 1974. 'David Urquhart and the foreign affairs committees', in *Pressure from without in Early Victorian England*, Patricia Hollis (ed.).

Sidgwick, A. S. and E. M., 1906. *Henry Sidgwick. A Memoir*.

Simon, Alan, 1970. 'Joseph Chamberlain and the Unauthorized Programme', unpublished D. Phil. thesis, University of Oxford.

Simon, Alan, 1975. 'Church disestablishment as a factor in the general election of 1885', *H.J.*, xviii, 1975.

Smith, F. B., 1966. *The Making of the Second Reform Bill*, CUP.

Smith, G. B., 1881. *The Life and Speeches of John Bright M.P.*, 2 vols.

Smith, Goldwin, 1886. 'The moral of the late crisis', *N.C.*, **20**, 1886.

Stansky, Peter, 1964. *Ambitions and Struggles. The Struggle for the Leadership of the Liberal Party in the 1890s*, OUP.

Steele, E. D., 1970–71. 'Gladstone and Ireland', *I.H.S.*, 1970–71.

Steiner, Zara A., 1977. *Britain and the Origins of the First World War*.

Stephen, Leslie, 1875. 'Order and progress', *F.R.*, **17**, 1875.

Taylor, A. J. P., 1969. *The Trouble Makers. Dissent over Foreign Policy 1792–1939*, Panther.

Taylor, A. J. P., 1976. *Essays in English History*.

Tholfsen, T. R., 1953–54. 'The artisan and the culture of early Victorian Birmingham', *Birmingham Historical Journal*, **4**, 1953–54.

Tholfsen, T. R., 1959. 'The origins of the Birmingham caucus', *H.J.*, **2**, 1959.

Tholfsen, T. R., 1961. 'The transition to democracy in Victorian England', *International Review of Social History*, **6**, 1961.

Thomas, William, 1974. 'The Philosophical Radicals', in *Pressure from without in Early Victorian England*, Patricia Hollis (ed.).

Thomas, William, 1979. *The Philosophic Radicals*, OUP.

Thompson, David M., 1972. *Nonconformity in the Nineteenth Century*.

Thompson, David M., 1974. 'The Liberation Society, 1844–1868', in *Pressure from without in Early Victorian England*, Patricia Hollis (ed.).

Thompson, F. M. L., 1959. 'Whigs and Liberals in the West Riding, 1830–60', *E.H.R.*, **74**, 1959.

Thompson, F. M. L., 1965. 'Land and politics in the 19th century', *T.R.H.S.*, **15**, 1965.

Thompson, Paul, 1964. 'Liberals, Radicals and Labour in London 1880–1900', *P. and P.*, **27**, 1964.

Thompson, Paul, 1967. *Socialists, Liberals and Labour. The struggle for London 1885–1914*.

Thornton, A. P., 1959. *The Imperial Idea and its Enemies*.

Thorold, A. L., 1913. *The Life of Henry Labouchere*.

Trevelyan, G. M., 1913. *Life of John Bright*.

Trevelyan, G. M., 1932. *Sir George Otto Trevelyan*.

Trollope, Anthony, 1980. *An Autobiography* (1883), OUP.

Tuckwell, W., 1905. *Reminiscences of a Radical Parson*.

Vincent, John, 1966. *The Formation of the Liberal Party*.

Vincent, John, 1977. 'Gladstone and Ireland', *Proceedings of the British Academy*, 1977.

Wade, John, 1833. *History of the Middle and Working Classes*.

Wallace, Elizabeth, 1957. *Goldwin Smith: Victorian Liberal*, Toronto UP.

Wallas, Graham, 1898. *The Life of Francis Place*.

Walling, R. A. J. (ed.), 1930. *The Diaries of John Bright*.

Walpole, Spencer, 1889. *Life of Lord John Russell*, 2 vols.

Ward, W. R., 1972. *Religion and Society in England 1790–1850*.

Watson, R. Spence, 1907. *The National Liberal Federation*.

Webb, Beatrice, 1938. *My Apprenticeship*, 2 vols, Pelican.

Webb, Sidney and Beatrice, 1920. *The History of Trade Unionism*.

Weinroth, Howard S., 1970. 'The British Radicals and the balance of power, 1902–1914', *H.J.*, **13**, 1970.

Williams, G. L., 1976. *John Stuart Mill: Essays on Politics and Society*.

Wilson, Alexander, 1974. 'The suffrage movement', in *Pressure from Without in Early Victorian England*, Patricia Hollis (ed.).

Wilson, Edward, 1866. 'Principles of representation', *F.R.*, **4**, 1866.

Wilson, Trevor (ed.), 1970. *The Political Diaries of C. P. Scott 1911–1928*.

Wright, D. G., 1970. *Democracy and Reform 1815–85*.

Yarmie, Andrew H., 1975. 'The captains of industry in mid-Victorian Britain', unpublished Ph.D. thesis, University of London.

Zimmer, Louis B., 1976. 'John Stuart Mill and democracy 1866–7', *The Mill News Letter*, Summer 1976.

INDEX

165